Casanova
and
Enlightenment

Casanova and Enlightenment

His Study of Life and Other Writers

David John Thompson

PEN & SWORD
HISTORY
AN IMPRINT OF PEN & SWORD BOOKS LTD.
YORKSHIRE – PHILADELPHIA

First published in Great Britain in 2024 by
PEN AND SWORD HISTORY
An imprint of
Pen & Sword Books Ltd
Yorkshire – Philadelphia

ISBN 978 1 39905 583 3

A CIP catalogue record for this book is available from the British Library.

Typeset in Times New Roman 11/14 by
SJmagic DESIGN SERVICES, India.
Printed and bound in the UK by CPI Group (UK) Ltd.

Pen & Sword Books Limited incorporates the imprints of Atlas, Archaeology, Aviation, Discovery, Family History, Fiction, History, Maritime, Military, After the Battle, Military Classics, Politics, Select, Transport, True Crime, Air World, Frontline Publishing, Leo Cooper, Remember When, Seaforth Publishing, The Praetorian Press, Wharncliffe Local History, Wharncliffe Transport, Wharncliffe True Crime and White Owl.

For a complete list of Pen & Sword titles please contact
PEN & SWORD BOOKS LIMITED
George House, Units 12 & 13, Beevor Street, Off Pontefract Road,
Barnsley, South Yorkshire, S71 1HN, England
E-mail: enquiries@pen-and-sword.co.uk
Website: www.pen-and-sword.co.uk

or

PEN AND SWORD BOOKS
1950 Lawrence Rd, Havertown, PA 19083, USA
E-mail: uspen-and-sword@casematepublishers.com
Website: www.penandswordbooks.com

MIX
Paper | Supporting responsible forestry
FSC www.fsc.org
FSC® C013604

Contents

Acknowledgements

Special thanks to the inspiration, encouragement, advice and help from Ian Kelly, Lisetta Lovett and Chris Booth, and, of course, to Kev, Jan, Vincenza and Richard. But most of all to chance.

Introduction

> 'We talk, and we become good friends. It was the illustrious Abate Winckelmann, who twelve years later was assassinated in Trieste.'
>
> Giacomo Casanova, *History of My Life*

In *Casanova's Life and Times: Living in the Eighteenth Century* the focus was on the wider social context of Casanova's day-to-day life and, in particular, his relationship with women. To have a rounder understanding of the man we need to turn our attention to his life as an Enlightenment man of letters. Casanova's engagement with the intellectual and cultural concerns of the day were an important part of who he was, and in this, as with so many other aspects of his life, he was shaped by the age in which he lived.

What constitutes the Enlightenment is a matter of debate but typically its beginning is dated from the mid- to late seventeenth century, ending with the start of the French Revolution in 1789. Broadly speaking, the Enlightenment was a movement that was influential in the creation of a mental outlook commonly described as Western. This outlook is marked by a range of generally accepted values. Inalienable and universal individual rights are acknowledged to be of primary importance. There is an understanding that reality is grounded in what is material, observable and measurable as opposed to what can be deduced from, or asserted by, authority, custom and tradition. Physical well-being is prioritised over spiritual well-being – it would not be acceptable to kill a person to save their soul. It is recognised that all have an equal claim to happiness, and that a person's happiness should not be compromised by appeals to supernatural deities. Democracy is believed to be a superior system of government. Toleration, freedom of expression, universal education and equality before the law regardless of identity or status, are all typically regarded as essential to a civilised society. While certain groups or individuals may question these values and the extent to which they should be regarded as norms, they are part of the fabric of European institutions and laws, and for most Europeans are uncontroversial.

In essence, the Enlightenment was a movement of emancipation from the strictures of the past. 'People became more reflective about their feelings, their social positions, their rights and duties, the state of religion, and all that touched them near or far,' writes Louis Dupré. 'They also became more critical than any previous generation, and this self-consciously critical mentality induced them to question tradition.'[1] The movement confronted established beliefs and practices. It pushed the Church, state, and social and cultural institutions to reassess the nature of society and their functions within it. The Enlightenment may have suffered at times from a misplaced confidence in the power of reason but its impact was nonetheless transformative.

The reference to Winckelmann at the opening of the introduction alludes to another related dimension of this intellectual and cultural landscape: antiquity. It was during a visit by Casanova to Rome in 1760 that he befriended Johann Joachim Winckelmann. The Brandenburg-born scholar was an art historian and archaeologist. He was to become famous for his work *The History of Art in Antiquity* (1764) and his influence upon the development of Neoclassicism. This was an important artistic movement that was inspired by ideas of form and beauty derived from ancient Greece and Rome. Yet while Neoclassicism may have risen to prominence from the middle of the eighteenth century onwards, interest in classical aesthetics did not materialise from out of nowhere. Fascination with the ancients was well established. Familiarity with Latin and Greek, of ancient history, pagan schools of philosophy, and the works of writers such as Homer, Horace, Virgil and Cicero, had long been commonplace among the well-educated. If contemporaries wanted to make comparisons between the achievements of the Europe of their own day and the past, it was to ancient Rome they looked, not so much the Middle Ages. Voltaire records: 'The members of the English Parliament like to compare themselves, as far as they can, to the ancient Romans.'[2]

The importance of classical civilisation to the development of the Enlightenment can hardly be exaggerated, to the extent that Peter Gay describes Enlightenment thinkers as 'modern pagans'.[3] The Greeks and Romans were not only a source of ideas but offered approaches to intellectual inquiry and governance untainted by Christianity. These Enlightenment pagans admired the ancients' polytheism. A polytheistic society did not insist that there was only one right way to think and live. It was eclectic and tolerant.

Recognising the achievements of the ancients was to issue a challenge to the Christian narrative. It questioned the assumption that the rise of Christianity inaugurated a righteous and blessed age. Instead, the secular was elevated above the sacred, philosophy and science above theology and religion, and history above myth. Supporters of the Enlightenment wanted a society characterised by freedom of thought, moral relativism and experience-based knowledge rather than authority, moral absolutes, revelation and totalising metaphysics. From their perspective, explains Gay, 'classicism was a bridge thrown across the swamp of the Christian millennium.'[4] Along with those already mentioned, a pantheon of revered ancients was pressed into service. Epicurus, Hadrian, Herodotus, Juvenal, Lucan, Lucretius, Marcus Aurelius, Plutarch, Seneca, Socrates, Tacitus, Thucydides, Trajan, Zeno all provided inspiration and material with which to pursue the goal of a more rational, just and permissive world. Plato and Aristotle were less favoured, implicated as they were in Christian theology, although Plato was an important influence upon Jean-Jacques Rousseau (1712–1778).

The ancients exercised their appeal in other ways. One of the written forms that was particularly popular with Enlightenment thinkers was that of the dialogue. It was a flexible genre that allowed its author to explore and dramatize philosophical ideas. During an age in which the publication of unwanted opinion could have severe repercussions, the dialogue had the additional benefit of distancing the writer from whatever content was delivered by this or that particular character. Scottish philosopher, David Hume, wrote his *Dialogues Concerning Natural Religion* (1779), a devastating critique of natural religion – the deistic belief that God is to be understood through their divinity in nature by means of reasoning and the senses rather than revelation. The masterpiece *Rameau's Nephew* by Denis Diderot (1713–1784), published posthumously in 1805, is a dialogue based upon a satire by Horace. Gotthold Lessing, Montesquieu, Adam Smith, Voltaire and Christoph Wieland were a few among many who exploited the genre. The dialogue depicted a style of open and personal exchange, often set within a congenial social space. Famously, one of Plato's own dialogues, known as the *Symposium* (c 385–370 BCE), portrays Socrates and others holding forth on the theme of love following upon a meal. In the case of Hume's *Dialogues*, it was a library, and in Diderot's *Rameau's Nephew* it was a café.

There were exceptions, such as Rousseau, but on the whole the modern pagans were like-minded people who tended to form loosely aligned, cosmopolitan groups. Echoes of Plato's *Symposium* are apparent not only in the dialogues of these scholars and *philosophes* but in their daily lives. They were urbanites whose shared classical education make it unsurprising to find them regularly in each other's company in an age that prized sociability. The salon of the wealthy *philosophe* Baron d'Holbach attracted a host of intellectuals. Likewise, Voltaire held court during his self-imposed exile in Geneva, initially at Les Délices and then later at Ferney. In Scotland, David Hume, Adam Ferguson, Adam Smith and other distinguished figures would regularly meet to chew the fat. Typically, these champions of the Enlightenment were cultivated generalists, people of letters who, while perhaps gifted in some particular area, were nonetheless able to switch easily from rôle to rôle in their quest to educate and promote change. No one epitomised this more than Voltaire. He could present himself as a poet, playwright, philosopher, historian, scientist, scientific populariser, encyclopaedist and journalist.

The overlapping cultural frameworks of antiquity, Christianity, Renaissance humanism, and the Enlightenment, particularly the French Enlightenment, moulded Casanova's thought and writing. His works abound with classical references while his philosophical concerns echoed the likes of Voltaire, Diderot and Rousseau. Accordingly, much of this book will be structured around a selection of writers and thinkers who were of particular importance both to Casanova and to the Enlightenment, stretching back to the pre-Christian era.

Chapter 1
Enlightenment Roots

'The next day at nine o'clock, I saw the language teacher. He was a respectable-looking man, polite, modest, speaking little and well, reserved in his answers, and with an old-fashioned education. He began by making me laugh when he told me that a Christian could only accept the Copernican system as a scholarly hypothesis. I answered him that it could only be the system of God since it was that of nature, and that the holy scripture was not the book from which Christians could learn physics.'

Giacomo Casanova, *History of My Life*

The moral mind

Imagine that you are talking to a neighbour and discover that they regularly punished their child after being informed by a teacher that their child is left-handed. Up until that moment you only knew them to be a well-respected member of the community. They were sociable, honest, educated, devout, had a good occupation and had appeared to be a loving parent. They explain to you that they are training their child to be right-handed because they are concerned that otherwise their child will go to hell. You might conclude that this person was suffering from some sort of delusion and you would likely report them to social services. Yet this calculation, sacrificing earthly pleasures and well-being in the hope of attaining paradise in the afterlife, was unexceptional for members of Abrahamic religious traditions (Jewish, Christian and Muslim) and rooted in their most fundamental conceptions of reality. For generations such societies were in thrall to a supernatural cosmos that supervised and judged each moment of their lives. Yet to a citizen of the modern Western world, even to those who are members of one these traditions, many of those attitudes and behaviours now appear baffling.

But consider the following. In Europe from the end of the fifteenth century until the middle of the eighteenth, it is estimated that some 200,000 people were tortured, burnt or hanged as witches. Pain was lauded as a purgative. Punishments of the most gruesome kinds were meted out in rituals of purification and redemption. Fire was particularly valued. It is in the nature of fire to move up towards the heavens and so it occupied a position in the order of the cosmos that was closer to God. Running alongside those Abrahamic traditions, and frequently merging with them, were numerous other supernatural beliefs. We have faeries stealing babies and replacing them with half-wit changelings. We have the royal touch whereby because of their divinity monarchs had the power to heal disease (as did the right hand of an executed prisoner – note, not the left hand). We have horseshoes to ward off evil and the breaking of mirrors that brought bad luck (because the image reflected was a person's soul and breaking the mirror disconnected the soul from the body). The souls of the dead migrated or transformed into birds and beasts. In seas, lakes and rivers we find mermaids, mermen and water-guardians along with cursed monsters of the likes of Grendel sheltering in the murky depths. Dwelling in the woods and forests we have spectral hounds, phantom huntsmen, mysterious warriors and pest maidens. To live in pre-modern Europe was to share a parallel dimension populated by more angels, spirits, elves and the dark forces of evil than you could shake a stick at, and in the mountains, the occasional giant. The signs were all around you, if you knew where to look and how to read them. For thousands of years the existence of the supernatural was an almost tangible reality of daily life that had to be navigated and assuaged.

For Christian societies of the Middle Ages, the universe had an intrinsic moral quality. It had been created by a divine entity whose essence was perfection, including moral perfection. The more anything resembled that perfection, then the more God-like and morally good it could claim to be. And to the medieval mind, reasoning by analogy, such as using allegory and metaphor, was as legitimate an avenue to demonstrating truth as science is today. Like the parables of the Bible, they were means by which God was communicating to man. Christ sat on the right-hand side of God. On the Day of Judgement, when people would be held accountable for their earthly behaviour, those destined for heaven were also to be placed on the right-hand side of God, and those destined for hell on the left. The right was, therefore, understood to be morally superior to the left. 'Up', being closer to God, was morally superior to 'down'. The Earth, at the centre of the universe, was at the furthest extent from God, and those who inhabited it were inferior to celestial beings that existed between the Earth and God, such as the planets and the angels. In his *Divine Comedy* (1321), Dante Alighieri depicts hell to be at the centre of the Earth, the furthest point from the Almighty. Numbers, too, could be morally better or worse. For St Augustine (354–430 CE), 6 is the most perfect number as it is equal to the sum of its positive divisors: 1+2+3 = 6. This is why God created the universe in 6 days. It was a consequence of God's perfection. Christian allegorical interpretation of scripture was established in the third century by the theologian Origen of Alexandria (185-253 CE), following upon the practice of the Jewish thinker Philo of Alexandria (b 25 BCE). It became a means by which Christians were able to develop a more consistent and comprehensible moral understanding of the Bible. Allegorising had been a device employed by the ancients in their readings of Homer and Greco-Roman myths as a way of handling apparent ethical contradictions.

The pre-Enlightenment mind perceived the material and the non-material as having an all-pervasive, moral unity. Much scholarly effort was expended in the construction of hierarchies of perfectness, attempting to place all things in their proper relationship to God and to each other. Accordingly, social inequality was an inevitable consequence of a hierarchically structured universe. Wherever you were on that sliding scale, it was a fact you were expected to accept. To attempt to rise above your place was to succumb to the sin of pride and to transgress against the natural God-given order.

From the High Middle Ages, thinkers such St Thomas Aquinas (1225–1274) and his followers had demonstrated that it was possible to reconcile Christian theology and Greek Neoplatonism to create a coherent intellectual framework with which to make sense of the universe, including the mysteries and truths of Christianity. Neoplatonism was derived from a reworking and development of the ideas of Plato, notably by the philosopher Plotinus (204/5–270 CE). One of the features of this conceptual frame was the Aristotelian system of causality, an essential tool in the investigation of the nature of the world. Aristotle was one of a number of scholars to tackle the issue of causes, with their ultimate aim being to understand why things came to be. This system was also known as the doctrine of the four causes:

- The material cause: 'that out of which', e.g., the bronze of a statue.
- The formal cause: 'the form', 'the account of what-it-is-to-be', e.g., the shape of a statue.

- The efficient cause: 'the primary source of the change or rest', e.g., the artisan, the art of bronze-casting the statue, the man who gives advice, the father of the child.
- The final cause: 'the end, that for the sake of which a thing is done', e.g., health is the end of walking, losing weight, purging, drugs, and surgical tools.[1]

Part of the value of this four-part system of causality was that it allowed Christian theologians to demarcate different existences and forms, and thereby produce a scale of perfections otherwise known as a Great Chain of Being. This chain was a hierarchical continuum that stretched from the heavens to the Earth. At the top was the immutable perfection of an immaterial God, who was followed by angels – an immaterial intelligence but imperfect; and then man – possessing free will, reasoning and a soul but a material body. These three categories shared spiritual qualities such as love and reason. The three levels below were comprised of animals – material beings that possessed a soul but lacked reason and free will; plants – which possessed a soul and could grow but lacked the ability to choose; down to stones – which were entirely material and without a soul.

A distinction was also made between 'essence' and 'existence' which was the basis for all things. 'Essence', as derived from Plato, was a thing's potentiality, its nature, a fixed and timeless possibility of existence. Without an essence, an object could not have any identity or form (hence the formal cause). 'Existence' was the material substantiation of that essence. This did not mean all objects of a particular essence were identical in every detail but rather that they were of a characteristic type, such as a horse, a man or a table. The only being whose existence was its essence, its pure actuality, was God. It was also God that determined the final cause, or the purpose, of all things. The study of final causes was known as the science of teleology. Without a final cause, without a divinely ordained purpose, nothing would exist. Without purpose, there could not be an efficient cause. The efficient cause necessary to actualise a form, that is, to bring an object into existence, would have no goal, no reason to be. As the understanding of the purpose of things gave an insight into understanding God's intentions, the science of teleology became one of the great projects of pre-Enlightenment scholars.

Running parallel with this blending of Christian theology and Greek philosophy, was the development of an intellectual method that was to absorb much of the energy of Europe's educated elite for over 600 years, remaining influential well into the eighteenth century. It was called

'Aristotelian scholasticism', or just 'scholasticism'. Its practitioners were the scholastics, or schoolmen, most notably Peter Abelard (1079–1142) and Thomas Aquinas. Prior to scholasticism was monastic learning, which took place, as its name suggests, in monasteries. Monastic study was centred on the Bible and texts authored by the Church Fathers – theologians such as St Augustine. The aim was to understand, clarify and comment on these religious texts, but in an uncritical and meditative way. It was not part of the purpose to contest the claims or ideas contained in those texts. By contrast, scholasticism evolved in schools and universities which existed in more disputatious, urbanised environments, and consequently came to operate quite differently from monastic learning.

Central to scholasticism was the *disputatio*, a method of assessing knowledge and resolving contradictions. Works studied included those written by natural authorities as well as by the supernatural authorities favoured in monastic study and included pagan thinkers such as Aristotle and Cicero. In the Middle Ages, texts which had stood the test of time were particularly revered. Scholastics would find apparent discrepancies and engage in vigorous debate in their quest to resolve them. A master would typically choose the Bible or some other ancient text, for example Aristotle's *Physics* or Cicero's *On Duties*, which would serve as the starting point for a subject of investigation. Apparent contradictions within or between texts would be used to generate two opposing arguments. The aim was to reconcile these arguments and demonstrate how the texts were in agreement. The correctness of these ancient authorities was deemed to be settled and unquestionable. Direct experience of nature was not used as the basis for systematic investigation (science as we know it today) but as a source of illustration. It is not hard to see how the scholastic method could help to facilitate the integration of elements of Greek philosophy into Christian doctrine, especially Neoplatonism.

From the mid-fourteenth century the theological shackles of Christianity began to loosen with the advent of the Italian Renaissance and the humanist movement. Humanists were largely secular people of letters rather than clerics. They were overwhelmingly men but not exclusively so, exceptions being women such as Cassandra Fedele (1465–1558) and Laura Cereta (1469–1499). An important early figure in the movement was the poet Francesco Petrarch (1304–1374) who, along with other scholars, prompted a revival of interest in the literature of classical civilisation. Significantly, humanists scoured Italy and Europe unearthing copies of ancient manuscripts, usually found languishing in private collections or monastic libraries like

Monte Cassino and St Gall, forgotten and neglected. Alongside Petrarch, famous book hunters included the Florentines Giovanni Boccaccio (1313–1375), Niccolò Niccoli (1364–1437) and Poggio Bracciolini (1380–1459), the latter unearthing Lucretius's immensely important *On the Nature of Things* (c 60 BCE). Translations and the invention of printing in the early fifteenth century were to bring these discoveries, and the literature of classical civilisation more generally, before a wider audience. In 1453 the fall of Constantinople fuelled this humanist endeavour further, provoking as it did an influx westward of other important ancient manuscripts, and with them academic expertise on ancient Greece.

Humanists were concerned less with man's relationship to God, which, after all, had been the intellectual preoccupation of Christendom for a long time now, and more with man's relationship to man. Scholars could exploit historical sources that were not only recovered from obscurity but shorn of centuries of Christian interpretation, and so be able to re-examine the past for themselves. This reframing of attention, focusing upon human society, invested man with greater significance relative to the sinful, degraded and passive state that they occupied in the cosmic scheme of the scholastics. From this humanist perspective, individual agency became more salient. At the level of society, human behaviour could be distanced from the divine comedy in a similar way that today we might divorce the laws of physics from the workings of history or politics; ultimately the two will be causally connected, albeit in barely fathomable ways, but for practical purposes we can deal with them as separate domains of knowledge.

This shift of perspective enabled the flourishing of a more critical mentality, one that could be applied equally to the actions of the Church, court, priests, aristocrats and commoners. The myths, ideological premises and analogical reasoning that infused Christian assumptions could be treated more sceptically. The reliability of the Bible as a source of literal truths with regards to history and science were questioned. The astronomer and mathematician Nicolaus Copernicus (1473–1543) was casting doubt on the belief that the Sun revolved around the Earth while the statesman and political philosopher Niccolò Machiavelli (1469–1527) discarded orthodox Christian virtues in his political treatise *The Prince* (published posthumously in 1532), a work that was condemned for having been inspired by the Devil and which was banned by the pope. Added to discoveries about antiquity were discoveries abroad, beyond the familiar world of the Mediterranean and Europe. Travellers' reports of the existence of strikingly different kinds of societies provoked speculation over the extent to which moral norms were relativistic or universal, such as by the French philosopher Michel de Montaigne (1533–1592).

At the end of the sixteenth century and the beginning of the seventeenth, thinkers emerged such as Francis Bacon, Galileo Galilei, Johannes Kepler, René Descartes and John Locke. Their ideas began more radically to undermine the scholastic conception of reality and its methods of facilitating knowledge – with their 'great abuse of words', their 'endless train of syllogisms' and their love of maxims and axioms.[2,3,4] Nature was found to obey mechanical laws, not the will of God, casting doubt on the role of free will. Truth claims not grounded in empirical evidence were treated with suspicion. And as the authority of government could no longer be so easily underwritten by divine prescription so questions revolving around the consent of the governed acquired greater potency. But unlike many of their Enlightenment descendants, humanists looked to reconcile their faith with the new scholarship, not dismantle religious and political orthodoxies in a quest for social change or the establishment of a more secular morality. Whatever their intentions, however, the gap between man and God which the humanists had opened up was only to widen further.

As Renaissance humanism gave way to the Enlightenment no aspect of society was exempt from scrutiny: government, the law, religion, ethics, rights, the arts, freedom, happiness, the boundaries of knowledge. The clashing of ideas ignited intense human dramas. Those who disputed the legitimacy of established authority were staking their reputations, livelihoods and indeed, their lives. Voltaire on different occasions was imprisoned in the Bastille, exiled to England and banished from Paris. Writers would resort to subterfuges to try and protect themselves. They would use pseudonyms, often in the name of a real person but who was now dead. Some, such as Hume, would have friends publish their works posthumously. Others would spread false information about the authorship of a text. To avoid the attentions of the censor, copies of texts would be hand-written rather than printed. In France, texts would be printed abroad and smuggled back. One way of releasing dangerous arguments into print was to publish a text which on the surface attacked those arguments (usually quite ineffectively), endorsing a more traditional and respected position. The author would be able to clarify at length the ideas he wanted to raise while at the same time protect himself from censure. This was a strategy used by Julien Offray de La Mettrie, the notorious author of *Man a Machine* (1747), and, as it happens, Casanova himself.[5] The tragic case of the Barre affair in Abbeville, near Amiens, illustrates what was being risked. François-Jean Lefebvre de la

Barre was a poor aristocrat who was only 20 years old and with no family. In 1766 he was tortured, beheaded and burned on a pyre with Voltaire's *Philosophical Dictionary* (1764) nailed to his torso. De la Barre's crime? Blasphemy. He had failed to remove his hat when a religious procession passed by. He had vandalised a crucifix. He had sung impious songs. And he had possessed 'foul and abominable' books.

Casanova's Europe, dominated for over 1,000 years by Christianity, was at the nexus of the old supernatural traditions and the emerging Western traditions that are dominant today. The Enlightenment was at the centre of the transition from the one to the other. Understanding the explosive nature of the challenge laid down to the established order helps us also to understand some of the preoccupations of Casanova himself in his struggle to make sense of the world, the universe and his own nature. It was a struggle that was being replicated in the lives of large numbers of more literate and educated citizens.

Government

It was inevitable that the ideas of Enlightenment thinkers would have a political impact. The philosophies and theologies that underpinned people's perception of the universe had direct judicial and institutional consequences about how society should be governed. Up to the 1500s the nation state did not exist. Pre-Enlightenment Europe was a place where the legitimacy of any particular ruler or mode of governance was a source of ideological dispute. From where did a ruler (or ruling body) derive their right to govern? What was the nature of the relationship between ruler and ruled? How constrained was a ruler's authority? To what extent was a ruler themselves subject to the law and judicial institutions?

Key resources that informed the debate around what constituted legitimate government included the Bible, ancient scholars and custom. The Bible described a world that was ruled by kings or emperors, in which subjects must obey even wicked rulers. As all power came from God then such obedience was a religious duty. To rebel against your king was to be disobedient to God (and so face damnation). The power of kings was only limited when their demands came into conflict with those of God. Later Christian theologians such as William of Ockham in the fourteenth century, did argue that on rare occasions a ruler could be rightfully overthrown, for example when they became a despot.

Ancient pagan authorities such as Aristotle similarly allowed that in some circumstances rebellion might be justified. For him, the members of a political community, which did not include all its residents (it excluded women and slaves), formed a partnership that sought their common good, was stable and based upon law rather than the individual desires of a particular ruler. Kingship, for Aristotle, could produce the best form of government but risked the danger of tyranny. The least harmful government would be one that would allow citizens to hold its leaders accountable. In the Carolingian Empire, most notably under Charlemagne in the eighth century, a ruler was a religious figure who had a duty not only to enforce the law but to obey it. Laws were established partly by royal decree but also according to custom, which implied that rulership was to some extent based upon the consent of the governed.

From the twelfth century, distinctions were made between different kinds of law and rights. Natural rights would be like individual human rights today in that they transcended the law of specific communities. For this reason, natural rights acquired particular significance during the Enlightenment as a means of overcoming the breakdown of the authority of the Catholic Church. With the old certainties under question, there was a desire to set down universal values based on reason, and that extended beyond an historically contingent state or religion. As part of the attempt to do so, thinkers made use of the concept of natural law – 'law' in this case to be considered akin to a law of nature, in contrast to an institutional law legislated by the state, known as positive law. In a fundamental sense natural law recognised the equality of all its members, rooted as it was in the moral, religious and biological nature of the human race. It was part of the order of a divinely ordained universe. Self-preservation would be an essential moral right (not least because it was the basis for exercising all other rights). That a man should have authority over a woman could be underpinned by the primacy of Adam over Eve. The authority of a parent over their child (even into adulthood) could be grounded in biology. Natural rights could be overridden but there would have to be good reason. As well as natural law, there was territorial law, which was more expedient and mutable, and the divine law of God, which was eternal and immutable.

Central to any form of government was the need for a system of institutions and laws to regulate property use and ownership, which in turn raised questions about the status of property. The Bible sanctioned individual property rights (including slavery) but also rights to hold property in common (as illustrated by monastic communalism, itself linked to biblically derived beliefs regarding voluntary celibacy and the fellowship of Christ and his disciples). Property was a gift from God that should be treated, to some extent at least, as a common good. It was generally held that there should be a limit to the extent to which anyone should own property purely for their own use. In effect, the rich man was a steward and had a duty to manage his property in a way that benefited society as a whole. Ownership of property was not regarded as an absolute right that allowed an individual to use or restrict its use as they saw fit. It was generally held to be legitimate, on the basis of natural law, for an individual to make use of the property of another in the case of dire need.

The boundaries of rights and legitimate authority were keenly patrolled and subject to interpretation. One area of controversy was papal fullness of power. This was the claim that the pope had whatever power was possessed by any other authority in the Church. It was a claim disputed by those who argued that bishops obtained their authority directly from God and were not mere agents of the pope. Another controversy was sparked in the thirteenth and fourteenth centuries by theologians such as Giles of Rome. They asserted the right of popes to intervene in secular affairs on the basis that the universe was structured as a single hierarchy and that all earthly authority flowed via the pope from God. This was challenged by advocates in favour of secular authority. Marsilius of Padua, drawing upon Aristotle, argued that power was ultimately derived from the people and that a people could only have one ruler with whom that power was entrusted. He pointed out that as Christ forbade the clergy from being involved in secular affairs then a ruler could not be a member of the clergy. Marsilius went so far as to maintain that the Church was subordinate to secular government.

Overlapping with the early stirrings of the Enlightenment, we see the development in the seventeenth century of the political theory of the divine right of kings and the growth of absolutist states, archetypically the France of Louis XIV. Theologians such as Jacques-Benigne Bossuet argued that monarchs received their authority directly from God. In this way, involving as it did the exchange of local autonomy for political stability, absolutism was able to resolve to some extent the generations of religious strife that had followed upon the Protestant Reformation. While religion was being tied more closely to concepts of monarchy and power, society as a whole was becoming less dominated by the Church. Growing affluence through trade as well as the expansion of professional groups, partly because of the development of more centralising nation states, was creating an increasingly secular environment. One sign of this was the loosening of the grip of the clergy and religious institutions upon scholarship, and the shaping of a new intellectual climate. From this space emerged three seventeenth-century philosophers who were instrumental in laying the foundations of Enlightenment political thought.

The first was Thomas Hobbes (1588–1679). He studied at Oxford but not the scholasticism of medieval Christianity that dominated European universities. Hobbes decided to go his own way and spent his time examining the classical authors of antiquity. After Oxford, he became a tutor to the son of William Cavendish, Baron of Hardwick, which allowed him to pursue his philosophical interests, unimpeded by religious orthodoxy and dogma to a degree that would have been unthinkable had he taught at a university or been a member of the clergy.

Hobbes argued that humans could only know material things and could only know them through their senses. What's more, these material things obeyed fixed mechanical laws. There could be no such thing as free will as all events required a prior cause and so, in this sense, were determined. This was a direct challenge to key doctrines of the Christian faith. His rejection of claims to any understanding of immaterial things was also a challenge to Descartes. He responded to Descartes' '*Cogito ego sum*' ('I think therefore I am') with 'I think, therefore matter is capable of thought.' Consistent with these ideas was his rejection of moral absolutism. He replaced free will with a causal mechanism based upon pleasure and pain, and it was this mechanism which drove the behaviour of living organisms. Morality thus became an aspect of human behaviour which was contingent upon people's social and physical environment, not the immutable creation of a divine being: the good is that which we perceive to promote our well-being; the bad is that which we perceive to promote our suffering. Part of the power of Hobbes's system of thought lay in its coherence, and although scholars of the time rejected his conclusions, they recognised the strength of his arguments and were forced to confront and debate them.

For Hobbes, the authority to govern was derived not from God but from man, by means of an implicit social contract. In his great work *Leviathan* (1651), he contemplated what life would be like in a state of nature, without government or laws or arbitration. Unusually for his time, he included women in his analysis and maintained that women could be sovereigns. He pointed out that in a society where men and women pursued what was conducive to their own individual well-being without fear of certain punishment, they would do so even if that involved harming their fellow man. The consequence would be a 'war of all against all'. Having both witnessed the English Civil War (1642–1652) and read Thucydides' *History of the Peloponnesian War* (late 5th century BCE), Hobbes was under no illusion as to the horror of such a state of nature. He concluded that to live in peace men and women not only had to relinquish to a supreme authority their freedom to act but that this authority should have absolute power and required total political obedience. According to some readings of Hobbes, consistent with his argument in favour of absolute governmental authority, subjects had no right to rebel under any circumstances. Others maintain that he did allow subjects the right to resist on the grounds of self-preservation. Hobbes's materialist metaphysics set up a challenge to Platonic essentialism that was to be one of the central intellectual contests of the eighteenth century.

Another key seventeenth-century thinker was the Englishman John Locke (1632–1704). He was an empiricist who believed that our mind was a blank slate and that all our knowledge and ideas were acquired through experience of the world. This was a theory of mind which rejected the established Christian doctrine that man was possessed of an innate understanding of goodness. He was also a theist who believed that man understood good and evil by interacting with the environment that God constructed. However, being based upon evidence of the external world, our knowledge could only ever be probable as there was always the possibility of discovering new evidence that would change our ideas.

Locke's influential political ideas were expounded in his *Two Treatises of Government* (1689) and *Letters Concerning Toleration* (1689–1692). Concerned that Hobbes could be used to justify tyranny, he drew on the older tradition of natural law to assert that people possessed certain fundamental rights as individuals. Such rights were universal and independent of membership of any political community. They thereby acted as a moral constraint upon government action. These included rights to life, liberty and property. For Locke, the political state evolved out of natural law, upon which he based his own conception of a social contract, motivated by human sociability. He maintained that these rights were distinct from divine law but consistent with it. Unlike Hobbes's social contract, Locke's model allowed subjects to resist and replace a government that failed to promote the public good and failed to protect people's rights. This increasingly tied legitimate governance to the explicit consent of the governed. For his part, Locke held in favour of majority rule, the separation of executive and legislative powers, was opposed to churches having coercive power over their members and was against the state having the right to compel an individual to follow any particular religious doctrine. Unsurprisingly, Locke found a particularly receptive audience among the revolutionaries of America and France.

Our third philosopher is Spinoza. His key political texts included *A Theologico-Political Treatise* (1670) and *A Political Treatise* (1677). Spinoza was a rationalist who anchored knowledge in reason and logic rather than Locke's probabilistic experience. He favoured religious toleration, was opposed to superstition and opposed to Descartes' mind-body dualism. Like Hobbes and Locke, Spinoza saw government as a necessary evil to prevent anarchy. He did not specify any particular kind of government as being optimal although he did suggest that democracy was most conducive to individual freedom (while being the most unstable form of government). He challenged Locke's contention that individuals possessed natural rights. For Spinoza, where men existed outside of any governing authority, moral concepts such as 'good' and 'bad' were meaningless. Individuals would simply do what they had the power and capacity to do if they judged that a greater compensating benefit would accrue to them, whatever the truth or falsity of that judgement. In a state of nature, might was right. When individuals accepted a governing authority, they were not transferring their moral rights to the state but their use of power (again, because they judged that they would obtain a greater compensating benefit). A consequence of this purely power relationship was that individuals were under an obligation to respect any government only as long as they did not have the power to disobey it. Likewise, a sovereign's actions were only restrained relative to the power at their disposal and by what they perceived to be beneficial to themselves. There was no moral or constitutional limit.

As we move into the Enlightenment proper, these ideas become developed and refined. In 1748, Montesquieu (1689–1755) published his influential *The Spirit of the Laws*. He was critical of moral and religious absolutes and emphasised the importance of different cultural modes in determining social practice – an area he had explored in an earlier work called *The Persian Letters* published in 1721. He argued that the best form of government was one elected by the people and in which the powers were divided into three parts (the executive, the legislative and the judicial). Each part would act as a check upon the power of the others and in so doing diminished any threat to individual freedom. It was this system of a separation of powers which was to be adopted as the basis for the US constitution through the agency of James Madison, who was also one of the principal advocates of the separation of church and state. Montesquieu outlined the dangers for democracy of factionalism and the need for such political communities to value public good above private interest. Scottish philosopher Adam Smith, with his publication of *The Wealth of Nations* (1776), applied the Lockean principal of limited government to the economic sphere, favouring free trade and minimal state interference in the marketplace.

In the writings of Hobbes, Locke and Spinoza we can see an exploration of concepts which have evolved to form the foundations of modern western democracies. There is the use of a social contract model with which to consider the relationship between the individual and the state (and with it, the implication that the authority of the state relies upon the consent of the governed). There is the contention that individuals have inalienable rights, including, as citizens, the right to rebel. There is the idea that man is subject to fundamental psychological drives, such as pleasure, pain and a desire for self-preservation. Morality is treated as something which is relative, at least to a degree, and religious toleration a moral good. The notion that a political community should be constructed by trying to discern divine intent is cast into doubt. There is the argument that religion's place is subordinate to the state, while the primary purpose of the state itself should be to restrain people's destructive impulses, and thereby ensure security for themselves and their possessions. To this final idea can be traced the roots of libertarian traditions, realised most powerfully in the political and economic culture of the US. This was in contrast to the more interventionist philosophies of utopian thinkers such as Plato who asserted that the purpose of government, at least in part, was to improve man's essential character.

Casanova was born less than two generations after the Glorious Revolution, which in England had put to bed any claims that the sovereign had a divine right to unrestricted rule. Sovereigns were, instead, bound by the 'ancient rights and liberties' of their subjects. But on the continent absolutism prevailed, and further afield America was a patchwork of colonies governed by Europe. By the time of his death Casanova had witnessed two more revolutions, those of France and America, and the collapse, at least in the west, of this old political order.

Religion

By the eighteenth century, Christianity had been the overwhelmingly dominant religious tradition in Europe for over fifty generations. This was a huge span of time during which it had become entrenched into every aspect of society and a part of every individual's mental landscape. To get some perspective on how massive a length of time that is let us consider a period of just ten generations into the past from 2020, taking a generation to be twenty years. In 1820, George III was succeeded by George IV and the British empire would continue to expand for almost another century. The nation states of Germany and Italy did not exist. The first successful surgical procedure performed with anaesthesia had yet to take place. Charles Darwin's *On the Origin of Species*, John Stuart Mill's *On Liberty* and Karl Marx's *Capital* had yet to be published. In 1831 only 4,500 adult males out of a population of 8 million could vote in the UK and life expectancy from birth in the same year was 40. Yet, for five times those ten generations, the colossal religious, intellectual, political and cultural force that was Christianity endured.

Stretching back over a millennium prior to the rise of Christianity, the cultures of the Mediterranean that were to culminate in the glories of ancient Greece were dominated by polytheistic religious traditions centred upon Zeus and Mount Olympus. They were traditions which were to be adopted pretty much wholesale by the Romans. Meanwhile Judaism, the progenitor of Christianity, originated in the Middle East sometime around the thirteenth century BCE. It was not until the fourth century CE, under Emperor Theodosius I, that the monotheism of Christianity, in the version of the Nicene Creed (the basis of the Catholic Church), was adopted as the state religion of the Roman Empire, building upon Emperor Constantine's edict of toleration in 313.

As it spread throughout Europe, and as its own ideas and theology evolved, Christianity drew upon these older cultural and intellectual pagan traditions. The gods of earlier religions became absorbed into the Christian celestial hierarchy, morphing into angels and acquiring the role of servants to the single supreme God. Spring and midwinter pagan festivals were similarly appropriated to do service in the Christian schema. The ideas of pagan philosophers such as Plato and Aristotle were used to add intellectual ballast to Christian theology. Paralleling the organisational model of the Roman Empire, united under the rule of an Emperor, the Catholic Church was similarly to acquire a single ruling authority in the figure of the pope along with many other of the structural and bureaucratic features of the Empire (including Latin).

As the Roman Empire in the west disintegrated in the fifth century, the papacy acquired increased political as well as religious significance. With the donation of territory in the eighth century from the Frankish King Pepin

III (751–768), which was to become the basis of the Papal States, it acquired secular power in its own right. Conflicts in the eleventh century between the Greek church in the east and the Latin church in the west, partly over papal authority, led to an east–west split and the establishment of the Eastern Orthodox church. By the fifteenth century, the Roman Catholic Church was a long-settled religious and secular power at the heart of Western Europe.

There were two major threats to this religio-political monolith. One was external: the Ottoman Empire. The other was internal: the Protestant Reformation. The external threat from the Ottomans was to continue as a serious menace until the end of the seventeenth century. It then receded following the 1683 Battle of Vienna and the failure of Sultan Mehmet IV (1648–1687) to capture what was the seat of power of the Holy Roman Empire and the Habsburg Monarchy.

More significant in terms of the Enlightenment and challenging the status of the Catholic Church within Europe, was the internal threat of Protestantism. The primary cause of the Reformation was widespread concern regarding corruption, malpractice and the teaching of false doctrine within the Catholic Church, such as the selling of indulgences which would exempt buyers from punishment for their sins. 'As soon as the gold in the casket rings,' according to the notorious indulgence seller Joahnn Tetzel, 'the rescued soul to heaven springs.' Calls for ecclesiastic reforms and a return to biblical values had been voiced in the late fourteenth and early fifteenth century by figures such as John Wycliffe and Jan Hus. But it was not until the attacks upon the Church in the sixteenth century by Martin Luther was the Protestant Reformation proper set in motion. For over a century Europe was to be mired in violent religious conflict. These religious wars were not to be resolved until the peace treaties of Westphalia in 1648, in the teeth of opposition from Pope Innocent X. Westphalia recognised three separate Christian traditions within the Holy Roman Empire (Roman Catholicism, Lutheranism and Calvinism). It was also to lead to the emergence of sovereign nation-states as the dominant political model in Europe. Both elements undermined the strength of the Catholic Church.

So, what was the relationship between Protestantism and the Enlightenment? To what extent did it contribute to the conditions that allowed Enlightenment ideas to take root? Crucially, the Reformation, vitalised by Gutenberg's printing press, made room for new thinking. For a thousand years the Catholic Church had been the supreme moral authority of Latin Christendom, interpreting and pronouncing upon the will of God. Underpinned by courts, universities and churches, manned by an army of lawyers, theologians and priests, its comprehensive network of dioceses and parishes ensured that the doctrines of the Church found their way into every corner of its domain, and were enforced. There were few aspects of a person's life or understanding of the world that were not in some way mediated by its teachings and operations: What constituted sin? How should a sin be punished? Did animals possess souls? How was the universe created? Why did fire travel heavenwards? When could you, or could you not, eat meat? And all of this was reinforced through decorative art, music, festivals and sacred rituals, brim full with messages and symbolism, ever-present ingredients of the daily rhythms and routines of life. This ubiquity is what Protestantism dismantled. Its theology undermined the doctrinal positions of Catholicism, most notably its claim to be the mediating institution between man and God, while the establishment of Protestant states limited the Church's territorial reach.

Central to the Reformation was its understanding of the relationship between man, God and salvation. For Martin Luther, man was irredeemably corrupted. This belief subverted and restricted the role of the Catholic Church as much of its operation was based upon directing men and women to paradise and diverting them from the torments of hell. It did this by divining the intentions of the Almighty, enabling it to identify what was sinful, what was virtuous and how to cleanse the spirit. If no amount of worldly intervention was going to make a ha'penny worth of difference to your salvation then one of the central functions of the Catholic Church was now redundant. Salvation, for Luther, was to be obtained through faith alone. You could not reason your way to heaven. The gap between man and God was too great. But God had gifted individuals a soul, and through their soul they had direct access to their Creator. There was no middleman or -woman. The relationship between any individual and God became a deeply personal affair, and an individual's actions rested on the dictates of their own conscience (although the tension between individual conscience and external authority was never to be easily resolved).

The private and the religious spheres were consequently to be separated from the public and the secular. How this shift of perspective played out in the everyday world can be seen in economics. As with every other aspect of human affairs, economic activity had been perceived to have spiritual ramifications, notably in contract and property law. If a contract was deemed not to be just and equitable then it could not be enforced. But in the new Protestant world there was no such constraint. Individual accrual of wealth was not a moral concern in a spiritual sense. The earthly realm and the heavenly realm were separate kingdoms. Brian McCall observes: 'Moral and legal rules are merely necessary to make the earthly kingdom run smoothly. That divests those rules of their gravity and nobility. Honouring those norms does not result in eternal consequences but merely political, economic, and social efficiency in the earthly kingdom.'[6] From the Protestant perspective, the wealthier someone became, the better. They could then use their wealth to help those in need. It was a matter of individual conscience to decide, not the Church or state. The Enlightenment was thus a beneficiary of both the increased scepticism of authority (intellectual and institutional) and of the increased freedom from political and religious restraint that Protestantism precipitated. It is of no surprise that some of the most radical and influential ideas out of which the Enlightenment grew were authored by thinkers who were least under the jurisdiction of the Catholic Church: Bacon, Hobbes, Newton and Locke were all English; Spinoza was Dutch; and even Descartes, who was French, spent much of his working life in the Dutch Republic and Sweden for fear of the attentions of the papal authorities. The fates of those scholars who were under the jurisdiction of the Catholic Church and were deemed not to toe the line, such as Giordano Bruno (who was burned at the stake) and Galileo (who died after eight years under house arrest having been found guilty of heresy), serve to reinforce the point.

The principle of freedom of individual conscience and the questioning of authority that characterised the Reformation challenge to the Catholic Church was to become a more generalised feature of the Enlightenment itself. How could any claim to knowledge or truth be justified, not merely the claims of the Catholic Church? It was for good reason that '*Nullius in verba*' ('Take nobody's word for it') was the motto of the Royal Society. Authority and tradition were no longer adequate.

With the breakdown of a single supreme religious authority how did thinkers begin to address issues of religious truth? As we have seen, Luther rejected the power of human reason as an adequate tool to comprehend God. This chimed in well with other currents of intellectual scepticism, both contemporary and ancient. During the sixteenth century there had been a revival of the classical scepticism that had originally been formulated in ancient Greece almost two millennia earlier by philosophers such as Pyrrho and his adherent Timon. Such scepticism doubted the possibility of ever obtaining certain truth. If a person were to make a truth claim a sceptic would ask, 'What is your criterion for truth?' and if a criterion was supplied then they would ask 'What is your criterion of truth for your criterion of truth?' and so on. For scholars such as Luther a person could only know

God through faith. The doctrine that knowledge of God depended upon faith or revelation was to become known as 'fideism' from the Latin for 'faith' (*fidem*). Throughout the period of the Enlightenment fideism was to be an influential current of thought and a powerful corrective to any claims that religious knowledge could be based upon reason or empirical evidence.

Among the most powerful champions of fideism was Blaise Pascal (1623–1662) a brilliant mathematician and scientist who abandoned his academic career to devote himself to religion. Pascal was a Jansenist. He argued that man was intellectually flawed, hopelessly in thrall to his passions and emotions, bound by contradictions and insufficiently equipped without God's intervention to comprehend the perfect being that was the Creator. Pascal notes in his influential work *Thoughts*: 'The heart has its reasons of which reason does not know.'[7]

Of a very different ilk was Pierre Bayle (1647–1706), a Calvinist who advocated the primacy of faith over reason and whose 1697 *Historical and Critical Dictionary* (a work in excess of 6,000,000 words, 95 per cent of which comprised the footnotes) was the most widely owned book in private libraries in France in the eighteenth century, described by the online Stanford Enyclopedia of Philosophy as 'a hodge-podge encyclopedia of intellectual curiosities, serious argument on a variety of topics, salacious stories, exacting textual scholarship, and much more'. Belying its rather sedate title, Bayle's dictionary was profoundly subversive, and was to be an important influence on the *Encyclopedia* of Jean le Rond d'Alembert (1717–1783) and Denis Diderot. Using the form of a dictionary, Bayle was able to defend himself from charges of blasphemy or heresy by claiming that he was simply relating the words of others (notably, those of classical scholars), although this did not prevent the work from being proscribed by the French authorities. He used the dictionary as a way of dismantling doctrines, ideas and claims to knowledge, thereby demonstrating the futility of using reason to search for truth. He cited the case of King David in a discussion on ethics. He pointed out that based on any human measure of goodness David was immoral, and yet he was beloved of God. From this it was clear that man was incapable of fathoming the mysteries of God through reason alone and must rely upon faith and conscience.

The ideas of empirical philosophers, such as Locke's sensationalism, further drove a coach and horses through established Christian doctrines and many of its related social norms. Claims to knowledge and authority that were not based upon empirical evidence or logical deduction, such as biblical events, miracles, witchcraft, the structure of the cosmos and so on, were undermined. For Locke, man did not possess innate ideas and all information about the world was in the first instance harvested by our senses, which could then be combined and reflected upon to generate more complex knowledge and understanding.

Perhaps the greatest Enlightenment sceptic of them all was David Hume. Writing in the aftermath of the phenomenal achievements of Newton, at a time when there was growing optimism as to what the power of human reason could achieve, Hume's scepticism demonstrated the limitations of what could be known. He argued that human behaviour was governed by passion, not reason, and that causality could never be proved with certainty. In his *Dialogues Concerning Natural Religion* (1779) Hume demolishes claims that the existence of an omnipotent and beneficent God can be supported by evidence from the natural world. He pointed out that God's flawless perfection, infinite goodness, immutability and eternal being were directly contradicted by what we could see around us.

Deism dominated the religious convictions of many Enlightenment thinkers and those among the educated public. Central to deism was a rejection of particular providence – the idea that God directly intervenes in the affairs of man, in contradiction to the laws of nature. This has been labelled negative deism and was characterised by attacks on the veracity of the scriptures and biblical prophecy. It is critical of the immorality of the Judeo-Christian God, and the power, privilege and abuses of the priestly caste. Positive deism, on the other hand, asserted that man could know God according to his creation. God's relationship with man was through nature and the laws of nature which it was possible for human reason to understand. Positive deism affirmed divine goodness and asserted that God's purpose for man was for man to achieve happiness. Already Descartes had attempted to provide proofs of God's existence by means of logical deduction, but it was natural philosophy, or science as it came to be known, and the work of Newton which caught the imagination.

One particularly important variation of deism was reflected in the ideas of Rousseau. In works such as *Emile* (1762) he celebrated what was natural, primitive and sincere in man and execrated the artificiality and decadence of civilization. A difficulty for many with regards to deism was its coldness. The God of the deists was very abstract and impersonal. Rousseau challenged this. His deism was intensely emotional, prefiguring Romanticism in discovering the presence and spirit of God in beauty and nature. Although not part of the intellectual mainstream in France, Rousseau's ideas proved to be enormously popular, and his writings generated a large and devoted following.

A third current of thought that addressed religion was atheism. Atheists themselves were few in number but the idea exercised the passions of many. Chapter 1 of Pascal's *Thoughts* was titled 'Against the indifference of atheists'. Those who were prepared to champion atheism tended to be figures of the mid-eighteenth-century French Enlightenment, *philosophes* such as d'Holbach whose *System of Nature* (1770) unashamedly put forward the case for a godless universe. He argued that morality arose because of the mechanisms of the material world. For d'Holbach belief in God and religion was an error which 'has in all times overwhelmed mankind', perpetrated by 'tyrants and priests'.[8]

It was perhaps in France where the culmination of forces unleashed by Protestantism, the collapse of the supremacy of Catholicism in Europe, and the struggle for intellectual, religious, political and moral legitimacy that characterised the Enlightenment reached its most dramatic conclusion. Not for nothing was the Church designated as the First Estate – the Second being the nobility and the Third all the rest – inherent as it was to the absolute authority of the crown. And it was the Catholic Church more than any other institution in France that was subject to unrelenting attack by those who were inspired by the values and ideas of Enlightenment thought. There were many causes of the French Revolution but the undermining of the legitimacy of the Catholic Church was undoubtedly one of them. By the end, so weakened had this legitimacy become that the Jacobins were able to implement a campaign of dechristianisation, temporarily sweeping away Catholicism and instituting their own state religion.

During the eighteenth century, religion remained an important political and social force but the pre-eminence of religious institutions and religious concerns in the life of society diminished. Across parts of Europe a process of secularisation was underway. This was a consequence of more than the Enlightenment, as significant as that may have been. As we have seen, as early as the fourteenth century, humanism had begun to switch the attention of scholarly inquiry away from the heavens to matters more temporal, and from the seventeenth century there was the growth of the state and the consolidation of monarchical power. Then running in parallel with the Enlightenment, and helping to facilitate it, was the development of the public sphere. Private citizens began to organise among themselves, constructing associations and institutions accessible to the general population but outside the immediate control and authority of either the Church or the state.

Natural philosophy

Derived from Aristotle, the notion of natural philosophy evolved as a form of analytical enquiry that was distinct from mathematics and metaphysics. From the Renaissance and into the Enlightenment natural philosophy came to encompass a wide array of subjects including ones that today we might label as anthropology, astronomy, biology, chemistry, economics, medicine, physics and psychology. Natural history, by contrast, concerned studies of nature that were descriptive. In the fourteenth century the word 'science' was originally synonymous with 'knowledge', and only from the eighteenth century did science begin to acquire the specialist usage that we employ today.

Crucial to the scientific revolution, particularly physics, was astronomy. Mankind has always speculated about the nature of the cosmos, both from an ontological perspective, being the source of numerous religions and creation myths, and from a practical perspective in terms of the measurement of time and navigation. For over 1,500 years the belief that the Earth was the centre of the universe (geocentrism) was the settled view of Christianity. It was not until the nineteenth century that the Catholic Church dropped entirely its resistance towards the belief that the Earth orbits the Sun (heliocentrism). That man should see himself as the centre of the universe was not, as is popularly believed, testament to his arrogance and pride but, as we have seen, quite the reverse. The heavenly bodies themselves were assumed to be immutable and everlasting, qualities that constituted part of God's perfection. This significance entailed that astronomy was a field of study held in particularly high regard, and one of enormous importance to religion. To question the order of the cosmos was to stray into sensitive territory.

Heliocentrism was proposed as early as the third century BCE by the Greek Aristarchus, but it was Ptolemy's geocentric model which gained favour, partly because of its accuracy in calculating the positions of the planets and its usefulness to travellers. But from the fifteenth century onwards the ancient Ptolemaic model was undermined by the growing influence of the neo-Pythagorean quantitative conception of the universe as opposed to a qualitative conception, and by the work of scholars such as Copernicus, Kepler and Galileo. The qualitative conception viewed the universe in terms of divine qualities and perfections, such as love, wisdom, immutability and so forth. The quantitative conception discerned the hand of God in ratios, proportions and geometrical harmonies. For such scholars, the book of nature, not the book of scripture, was the way to reveal God's work and the perfection of his design. This was illustrated most dramatically through Kepler's heliocentric laws of planetary motion, which Kepler achieved by analysing Tycho Brahe's observations of the movements of Mars - Brahe's undertaking being one of the most laborious in scientific and arithmetical history.

For a while, the geocentric and heliocentric theories coexisted without much controversy. Problems arose at the beginning of the seventeenth century when Galileo defended the heliocentric theory against scripture, notably that the Earth was set in place by God and could not be moved – as understood by references in the Psalms and Chronicles. Unwisely, Galileo asserted that heliocentrism did not contradict the Bible and, moreover, he disputed that the Bible was an authority on science. He was accused of reinterpreting the Bible, and the case was set before the Inquisition who found against heliocentrism in 1616. In 1633, following upon further controversy, Galileo was placed under house arrest until his death in 1642. Beyond the specific dispute of heliocentrism itself, Galileo also fundamentally challenged the idea of qualitative perfections. He distinguished subjective secondary qualities, which were dependent upon human perceptions (and included most Aristotelian qualities), from objective primary qualities, such as dimension, shape and number. Galileo's observations of the planets were a case in point. Using a telescope of his own making he revealed that the heavenly bodies were far from the perfect, immutable spheres as had previously been understood, but objects that were subject to erosion and change. For Galileo, God's creation could only be known through empirical observation and inductive reasoning using the tools of mathematics, not deductive reasoning based upon authority.

Ironically, one of the most influential figures in the development of science was someone who contributed little of note to scientific knowledge itself. Francis Bacon (1561–1626) was born to a well-connected family. His father, Sir Nicholas Bacon, was a Tudor politician and the Lord Keeper of the Great Seal. Francis Bacon grew up in a period when the printing press had stimulated a growth in education that extended beyond the confines and institutions of religion. He was consequently one of an increasing number of educated men who began to concern themselves with the operations of the natural as well as the supernatural world. To get to grips with the natural world Bacon decided it was necessary to jettison the dominant scholastic deductive tradition, which for him comprised little more than sophistry and rhetorical tricks – a concern for words rather than genuine enquiry – and adopt a new approach to learning.

The approach to learning Bacon promoted was nothing less than the scientific method as we understand it today. Outlining his vision in *The Great Instauration* (1620), the second part of which was his key text *The New Organon*, Bacon argued that it was man's Christian duty to reduce human suffering and increase well-being. 'I would address one general admonition to all,' he declares, 'that they consider what are the true ends of knowledge, and that they seek it not either for pleasure of the mind, or for contention, or for superiority to others, or for profit, or power, or any of these inferior things, but for the benefit and use of life, and that they perfect and govern it in charity.'[9] The notion that an empirical understanding of the world would enhance mankind's temporal well-being was one that could be traced back to Epicurus and was to become a central theme of the Enlightenment, evidenced most notably in the *Encyclopedia*.

For Bacon, the key to acquiring such knowledge was to study nature directly rather than through the filter of human and scriptural authority, and to make use of experiment and inductive reasoning, building generalisations upon evidence derived from systematic observations of particular instances. Sources of error and individual human bias would be combatted by divorcing religious speculation from the study of nature, and through careful testing. Unlike the *disputatio* of scholasticism, scientific endeavour would be cooperative. Knowledge would be acquired surely and cumulatively. Progress would not be dependent upon the genius of particular individuals but communities. As we shall see, the establishment of such secular 'learned societies' along the lines proposed by Bacon was to play a major role in the development of science from the second half of the seventeenth century.

Bacon may have questioned the utility of scholasticism but he did not challenge its philosophical underpinnings or its theological claims. The same could not be said of René Descartes (1596–1650), a philosopher, mathematician and scientist who, along with his followers, represented a profound intellectual assault upon scholasticism. Once again, as with Bacon, we find that it is earthly well-being that is prioritised. In Descartes' *Discourse on Method* (1637) he writes how the mastery of nature 'would not only be desirable in bringing about the invention of an infinity of devices to enable us to enjoy the fruits of agriculture and all the wealth of the earth without labour, but even more so in conserving health, the principle good and the basis of all other goods in this life.'[10]

Descartes wrote at a time when the question of how to determine truth had acquired particular urgency. Firstly, the Protestant Reformation was establishing alternative authorities with their own alternative claims to truth to those of Rome. And secondly, a revival of ancient Greek scepticism was casting doubt on the very possibility of obtaining certain knowledge about anything. Descartes' response was to out-sceptic the sceptics, and in so doing proposed solutions that radically opposed those of the scholastics. He rejected as inadequate the attempt to establish knowledge on the basis of human or supernatural authority. His ambition was to build knowledge on much stronger foundations, and to do so he employed a method dubbed 'hyperbolic doubt', famously illustrated with *cogito ergo sum* ('I think, therefore I am'). It may be possible to doubt everything else, but it was not possible to doubt the existence of a thinking mind. This was a criterion for certain knowledge. Reason, the thinking mind, was thus elevated above authority and faith. Although knowledge acquired by the senses failed the test of hyperbolic doubt, Descartes was able reinstate the value of sensory perception after he proved the existence of God (the proofs for which, unsurprisingly, have always been contested). God, being benevolent, was not a deceiver, and if he furnished mankind with senses and data to be sensed then there had to be an external world. The senses must therefore offer a potential source of knowledge. Deductive reasoning may provide the most reliable basis for knowledge, but inductive experimentation was an important means of verification.

Descartes distinguished between material and immaterial existence. On the one hand, material existence was best understood objectively as extension in space (which was also the view of Galileo), not subjectively through the senses. On the other hand, immaterial existence – such as thought, mind or soul – did not occupy space. He concluded that the physical world operated through matter communicating force to matter, and that only matter could affect matter. God, he maintained, set matter in motion, and God's fixed, immutable will entailed that matter operated according to equally fixed, immutable laws. Material existence, such as the body, worked like a machine, and the purpose of science was to understand its mechanisms. As far as the mind was concerned, or the ghost in the machine, Descartes held to a rationalist theory of innate ideas whereby knowledge of reality was ultimately derived from ideas with which the mind was already stocked (ideas such as height, width and depth), not the senses, which only conveyed a shadowy version of reality. This dualistic system, which posited the existence of separate material and immaterial entities, was faced with reconciling how a material substance, such as the body, that obeyed only mechanical, physical laws, could interact with an immaterial substance such as the mind. It is a problem, the mind-body problem, which has haunted philosophers to the present day.

Where did Descartes leave the ideas of the scholastics? Well, gone was the Aristotelean division of substance into matter and form. Gone was the concept of final ends and divine purpose as an explanation for the character of things. Gone was human and scriptural authority over the book of nature. So radical were these ideas that Descartes was accused of deism (and even atheism). The Christian world was a world of the supernatural, of miracles and divine intervention. The Christian God was hands on. The God of Descartes was a disappointingly abstract and distant being.

While on the continent Descartes' rationalist philosophy was demolishing the basis of scholasticism, in England a more Baconian and scientific culture was taking root, albeit one that did utilise the mathematics of Descartes. Although scholasticism continued to dominate European universities and was to remain active until the end of the eighteenth century, within the public sphere other institutions of learning developed, notably, in 1660, the Royal Society (or, to give it its full title, the Royal Society of London for Improving Natural Knowledge). Increasing numbers of people were actively engaged in exploring the natural world and took on board the vision of natural philosophy as promoted by Francis Bacon in his *New Organon* and his unfinished *New Atlantis*. They began conducting their own experiments and meeting together to discuss them. The foundation and activity of the Royal Society, particularly the publication of its journal *Philosophical Transactions*, greatly increased awareness of, and participation in, this new field of scholarly endeavour. The Society's motto, '*Nullius in verba*', was clearly a snub to the principles of scholasticism. 'It is an expression of the determination of Fellows to withstand the domination of authority and to verify all statements by an appeal to facts determined by experiment,' declares the Royal Society website. Early contributors included such luminaries as Christopher Wren, Edmond Halley, Robert Boyle, John Wilkins and, of course, Isaac Newton whose *Opticks* was published in the *Transactions* in 1704.

By the time the Royal Society had published Newton's *Opticks*, Newton was already famous. The crowning glory of the scientific revolution of the seventeenth century had been the publication in 1687, in Latin, of his three-volume *Mathematical Principles of Natural Philosophy* (*Philosophiæ Naturalis Principia Mathematica*), overseen by Edmond Halley of the Royal Society. The *Principia* outlined the three essential laws of mechanics which would become the foundation of modern physics. The first, the principal of inertia, repudiated the belief that ongoing motion had to be sustained by an external source – that is, God – while his discovery of gravity was initially opposed by Cartesians – followers of Descartes – who rejected the idea of spooky effects at a distance. Newton had shown that gravity existed, and that its operation accounted for events in nature, such as Kepler's laws of planetary motion, but he was not going to attempt to explain why or how gravity operated. He was not going to pretend to know more than that which the evidence allowed. Along with the discovery of calculus and his investigations into the nature of light, Newton had transformed man's understanding of the universe. His accomplishment astonished the educated world, his reputation as the greatest genius who had ever lived being immortalised in Alexander Pope's epitaph: 'Nature and nature's laws lay hid in night;/ God said "Let Newton be" and all was light.'

Based upon observation of nature, experiment, mathematics and inductive reasoning, Newton's achievements were a massive vindication of the new ideas that were transforming the intellectual landscape both of Europe and North America.

Chapter 2

Horace: 65–8 BCE

> 'Horace, whom I know by heart, is my guide [in studying humanity], and I find him everywhere.'
>
> Giacomo Casanova, *History of My Life*

Popularity

Quintus Horatius Flaccus was Casanova's favourite Latin poet, ranking alongside the Renaissance poet Ludovico Ariosto in the Venetian's literary affections. Casanova's memoirs contain dozens of references to him, such as the one above. Horace had been a significant cultural figure for centuries before the Enlightenment and was to continue to be so after it. His writing was appreciated not only for its craftsmanship, originality and beauty but for moral guidance, on what constituted a good life, and observations on social conduct. Particularly influential was his treatise *The Art of Poetry* (19 BCE), itself a poem in the form of a letter on poets, poetry and poetry writing. From his work we also learn much about everyday Roman life as well as his own, all against the backdrop of momentous political change as the Roman Republic transitioned under Augustus into the Roman Empire.

Horace was particularly esteemed in the late seventeenth and the eighteenth century and was an educational staple of Europe's elite. This meant that Casanova could expect his readers and, in company, his listeners, to have some familiarity with him. He records a number of times how not just he himself but others made references to Horace in conversation. On one social occasion he attended in Warsaw, which included King Stanislas of Poland (1764–1795) and several guests, the conversation turned to Horace, 'each quoting one or two of his maxims, expressing his opinion on the deep philosophy of the great poet of reason'.[1] Literary and intellectual European luminaries of the likes of Alexander Pope, Pietro Metastasio, Nicolas Boileau, Voltaire, Diderot, Fredrich von Hagedorn, Christophe Wieland along with a host of less-gifted writers found inspiration in Horace, often interacting directly with his work as translators or imitators. From 1660 to 1790 there were 120 English translations, more than those of Virgil and Homer put together.[2]

As well as the various editions and translations of his poems themselves, 'in the first half of the eighteenth century,' notes David Money with regards to the English market, 'there were well over 100 imitations of individual Horatian poems, quite apart from complete editions.'[3] It is worth pointing out that to imitate or borrow from the work of another writer was a literary practice without the stigma that might be attached to it today. Ideas, structures, subjects, phrases lifted in their entirety from the translations of others were all fair game. In fact, imitations might in some ways be understood as a loose form of creative translation that allowed writers considerable freedom in the way they worked their chosen material, for instance by integrating concerns relevant to contemporary society. An example would be the satires and epistles of Alexander Pope with titles such as *The Seventh Epistle of the First Book of Horace. Imitated in the Manner of Dr. Swift*. Part of the pleasure for the reader was to be able to identify how the imitator was playing with the original, rather like someone today recognising a director's references in their own work to other films and filmmakers.

Given his long-venerated reputation and celebrated imitators, and the rapid expansion of printed texts in lockstep with increasing literacy, it is unsurprising that Horatian moral and aesthetic sensibility reached beyond the highly educated few. This sensibility was characterised by a spirit of good-humoured moderation that shunned ideological extremism and subjects that were overtly political. Horace himself projected an affable, humane persona, someone who was self-deprecating and put great store on friendship. In deliberate contrast to the aggressiveness of other Roman satirists such as Lucilius, his satire was comic and gentle. Before we think of criticising others Horace exhorts us to recognise that we all have our faults: 'no one is born without vices.'[4] He contemplates how a person can take pleasure from life without being consumed by their passions be they for food, drink, sex, wealth or glory. His message was that you can enjoy yourself, even be indulgent now and then, as long as you do not overdo things and you do not neglect your duties: 'I feel no shame at having indulged myself in pleasures; the shame would come from not having cut them short.'[5]

The appeal of Horace was understandable. The late seventeenth century was emerging from generations of conflict fuelled by religious intolerance, in echoes of the bloody turmoil that had beset ancient Rome prior to the establishment of Augustus as its uncontested ruler – turmoil that Horace had witnessed up-close on the battlefield. There was a desire to find ways of transcending the inflammatory loyalties of religion, lineage and state that had seemed so often to have been the cause of terrible suffering. This same motivation encouraged the spread throughout Europe of masonic lodges and the increasing philosophical and social importance that was attached to the concept of sociability, epitomised in France by the salon and in Britain by the coffee house. It was a quality that was believed to distinguish civilised society from barbarism. According to Jean-Jacques Rousseau, without 'the sentiments of sociability … it is impossible to be a good citizen or a faithful subject.'[6] With the development of the public sphere, the domestic and economic concerns of commoners and the social dilemmas they faced in their everyday lives began to take centre stage, accompanied by the growth of institutions like libraries, learned academies, the theatre, concert halls, spas, leisure gardens and, as mentioned, coffee houses and a burgeoning print culture. And along with the public sphere emerged public opinion, an acknowledged moral and political force. 'He who judges of manners,' declares Rousseau, 'judges of honour; and he who judges of honour takes his law from opinion.'[7]

One phenomenon which both testified to this shift and accelerated it was the moral weekly with its focus on manners, good taste and the private domain. It was a remarkably popular genre both in Britain and on the continent, modelled on the London journals *The Tatler* (1709–1711) and its successor *The Spectator* (1711–12) which drew on Horace along with other classical authors for their inspiration. James Melton notes how *The Spectator* adopted 'a moderate and gentle tone that sought to instruct its readers with humour and wit.'[8] One of the founders and main contributors of these two periodicals was Joseph Addison, a leading thinker on the notion of polite sociability and a translator of Horace. Just as the satire cultivated by Horace was much softer than his predecessors so did Addison look to distance himself from the satirical viciousness that characterised the Restoration era of the late seventeenth century. In an extract from *The Spectator* that could have been penned by Horace himself he writes: 'True happiness is of a retired nature, and an enemy to pomp and noise;

it arises, in the first place, from the enjoyment of one's self, and in the next, from the friendship and conversation of a few select companions.'[9] These types of respectable periodical helped to expand the space for the development of a more secular, less religiously doctrinaire morality.

But Horace did more than provide enchanting poetry and disarming reasonableness. In that seemingly unobjectionable passage on true happiness cited above lay hidden a challenge to the foundational beliefs of Christianity. Horace was a portal to an age prior to the cultural domination of Christianity. It was a source of highly wrought philosophical ideas that were to be utilised by Enlightenment thinkers in their critique of Christian metaphysics and the beliefs that stemmed from it. Addison's reflections on the good life arose from principles derived from the Greek philosophical school that offered the sharpest rebuttal of Christian theology: Epicureanism. It is a thread which is woven throughout much of this book.

Life

Horace was born 8 December 65 BCE in Venusia, in what is now the region of Basilicata in southern Italy. This was a gruesome period in the history of Rome. From 133 BCE internal tensions between the plebian class and the ruling elites within the city-state of Rome itself triggered a century of political instability and civil wars that ended the Republic. Rome had become a victim of its own success. Presiding over an empire that encompassed much of Europe, North Africa and parts of Asia, wealth flowed into the hands of a few powerful men at its centre, men who used those resources to sustain what became essentially personal armies. Internal political rivalries consequently escalated in scale to unprecedented levels of violence and destruction. The central protagonists of these wars during Horace's lifetime included Pompey, Marcus Crassus, Julius Caesar, Mark Antony and Octavian, the latter being the adopted son of Julius Caesar and who renamed himself Augustus (27 BCE–14 CE). This century of turbulence ended with Octavian's victory over Mark Antony and Cleopatra at the naval Battle of Actium in 31 BCE. Horace was 33 and had previously fought on the losing side against Octavian at the Battle of Philippi in 42 BCE at the age of 22. It was an event which, if we are to believe him, led to him becoming a poet.

One striking feature of Roman society which shaped his literary career was its adoption of Greek culture, or Hellenization, a process that took place over several centuries. 'Captive Greece took captive her fierce conqueror, and introduced her arts into rude Latium,' Horace writes in an epistle addressed to Augustus.[10] Some exposure to Greek civilisation had taken place prior to the second and third centuries BCE but from that period onwards the influx of highly educated Greek slaves taken as prisoners of war introduced Roman elites more directly and personally to Hellenistic philosophical and artistic sophistication. They were highly esteemed and became entrusted with important responsibilities within their masters' households, including as tutors. The history of Latin literature itself can be traced back to one such third-century Greek, Livius Andronicus, who translated Greek works into Latin, including Homer's *Odyssey*, and composed Greek-style Latin works. Greek literary genres and forms of verse were adopted in their entirety as models by Roman writers. As Rome grew in importance many other Greeks made their way to the city of their own volition. High-ranking Romans learned Greek, and over time Roman education came to resemble that of the Greeks. Greek sculpture, art and architecture became popular, obtained as the spoils of war, or copied. Not all Romans were happy with this makeover. Men like Cato the Elder saw the Greeks as effete and attempts to emulate them a threat to traditional Roman martial virtues such as seriousness, discipline and a sense of public duty. But by the time of Horace much Greek culture had become fully assimilated. Virgil's epic, *The Aeneid*, that describes the founding of Rome and integrates into this myth contemporary figures such as Augustus, drew directly from Homer and the Trojan epics *The Odyssey* and *The Iliad*.

Roman society was profoundly hierarchical with rights closely bound to different grades and divisions of rank. Your wealth, gender and occupation, whether your ancestors were of the patrician or plebian class, whether you were a citizen, freedman or slave, all affected your social status and how you would be treated by the law. A plebian could be as wealthy as they liked but they could not become a patrician although, later in the Republican era, they could be appointed as a senator, the highest social rank, followed by the knight (or equite, of the equestrian class). Horace was born a free citizen of Rome but was sensitive to the fact that he carried the stigma of being the child of an ex-slave, in the same way that over one and a half thousand years later Casanova similarly carried the stigma of being the son of actors.

Horace's father was a freedman who had possibly been enslaved during the Social War of 91 to 88 BCE when Italian Allies of Rome had demanded Roman citizenship. He was an auctioneer, an important and profitable occupation which included acting as a financial agent between the seller and the buyer. It was to his father that Horace credited his sound moral upbringing and decent character, as the poet makes clear in an epistle to his patron Maecenas, an effective way of establishing the narrator's ethical, self-effacing persona: 'And yet if my disposition be culpable for a few faults, and those small ones, otherwise perfect (as if you should condemn moles scattered over a beautiful skin), if no one can justly lay to my charge avarice nor sordidness nor impure haunts; if (to speak in my own praise) I live undefiled and innocent and dear to my friends, my father was the cause of all this.'[11] Horace's father was evidently very successful. He became a property owner and was able to provide his son with the sort of education usually reserved for the offspring of senators and knights.

From a young age it was obvious that Horace was a rare talent. Ambitious for his son's success and social advancement, Horace's father accompanied him to Rome where he oversaw his studies. Horace's teacher was the renowned Orbilius of Beneventum, a fierce disciplinarian. Horace continued his education at Athens where he studied philosophy, enrolling at 19 at the prestigious Academy founded by Plato. All that said, there is a question mark over whether Horace's family status was as humble as he makes out or whether it was an exaggeration to emphasize the beneficence of Maecenas and his willingness to become his patron.

Horace's fortunes now changed dramatically. Following the assassination of Julius Caesar, Horace found himself embroiled in the civil war of the Liberators (43–42 BCE). Brutus and Cassius arrived in Athens to recruit officers from among Roman aristocrats to the faction that supported Caesar's murder, known as the Liberators. They conferred on Horace the rank of military tribune, a position usually awarded only to men of the senatorial or equestrian class. Horace was now a member of the officer corps in command of a Roman legion, and an equite with all the privileges that came along with it. The decisive confrontation between the two sides occurred in late October at Philippi, in Macedonia, north-eastern Greece, the Second Triumvirate led by Mark Antony and Octavian. Two battles took place involving as many as 200,000 men, the Triumvirs enjoying a numerical advantage of perhaps 20,000. The first battle was inconclusive despite the defeat and resulting suicide of Cassius, but in the second the forces of the Second Triumvirate triumphed, Brutus going the way of Cassius. Horace recalls his 'precipitate flight, having shamefully enough left my shield when valour was broken and the most daring smote the squalid earth with their faces.'[12]

In the immediate aftermath he managed to escape the usual fate reserved for those on the losing side, which was either execution or enslavement.

A little later, either because of a pardon he may have obtained directly or the general amnesty that Octavian granted to his defeated enemies, Horace was given the opportunity to rehabilitate himself and become reconciled to the new political reality. But there was an economic cost. The family farm at Venusia was among land confiscated to keep promises made by Octavian to resettle his army veterans. Horace now returned to Rome, and the consensus seems to be that he purchased the position of treasury clerk.

At this time there was an immense gulf between the poor and the rich. The latter enjoyed lives of tremendous indulgence with sumptuous country villas and town residences, enhancing their reputations with the masses by funding lavish spectacles and public amenities. But conditions were abysmal for the poor. It was a huge city by ancient standards, somewhere in the region of half a million or more, but with an absence of the kind of planning, regulation, policing or municipal services you might expect of a modern urban space. Dwellings were often cramped and poorly built. If they did not collapse of their own accord, there was a fair chance they would burn down. Many buildings were constructed from wood, and as people cooked indoors then fires were the inevitable result. It was also a dangerous place, plagued as it was by gangs. Partly this was due to Roman culture. The exercise of private violence within local communities, either by oneself, one's allies or hired agents, was regarded as sometimes necessary, and even a duty, to maintain individual safety. But during the late Republic such private violence was employed not just for public order but for political ends, and matters got out of hand. They were not brought back under some degree of control until the rule of Augustus when the problem at least became depoliticised.

If it is true that Horace was able to purchase an administrative post it indicates that he was not entirely broke. But even if we take with a pinch of salt his claim that following Philippi 'poverty urged me on to the composition of verses,' it was nonetheless through his success as a writer that he was able to restore his fortunes, facilitating as it did his introduction to Maecenas, his future patron and Augustus's most trusted adviser alongside Agrippa.[13]

A central institution of ancient Rome was clientship. This was a network of clients with at its centre a man of status and wealth, typically an aristocrat. It was a mutually beneficial arrangement, and although it was non-contractual it did include a legal dimension; patrons and clients, for example, could not testify against each other in court. Clients could access help and support when they were in need, while the patron accumulated a bevy of loyal allies upon whom he could call when it was useful for him, perhaps politically. The more clients a patron attracted, and the more significant those clients, the more conspicuous his importance. A patron might also be a client of another man. The most destitute Romans were excluded from this arrangement as they were unlikely ever to be able to repay their debt. Clientship could set up sensitive personal dynamics that had to be navigated with care. It is a dilemma which Horace explores at length in his poetry. If a client was not to incur contempt all round, they should be respectful to their patron, restrained in any requests for favours, and not reduce themselves to being a shallow flatterer. They needed to strike a balance between asserting their freedom and acknowledging their dependence, between being frank and being offensive.

With his growing reputation as one of Rome's finest poets, along with his close friend Virgil who had introduced him to Maecenas, Horace settled into a rather comfortable existence, dividing his time between the city and his farm in the country, a gift from his patron. But as an ex-rebel he still had to be careful. He avoids being philosophically dogmatic, and skirts politically sensitive issues. His writings are characterised by an endorsement of the rule of Augustus, and modesty and playfulness, as here: 'When you have a mind to laugh,' he writes at the end of an epistle addressed to Albius Tibullus, 'you shall see me fat and sleek with good keeping, a hog of Epicurus' herd.'[14]

Horace's caution was nowhere more evident than when the emperor made overtures of friendship, looking to entice him away from Maecenas, highlighting even more acutely the tension between dependence and freedom, especially artistic freedom. As well as being open to accusations of becoming an imperial hack, close connections with Augustus were bound to entail some degree of risk – anyone tied to the imperial court would become an object of political significance. Given what was to happen to Ovid years later, banished in 8 CE to a miserable existence on the Black Sea, his hesitancy seems justified. Augustus may have been irritated by Horace's prudence but the poet managed to turn down the offer of a post to write the emperor's personal letters without doing too much harm to their relationship. Augustus made some light-hearted jibes at Horace's expense but also commissioned him to write his masterpiece the *Song of the Ages*. This was a lyric poem to be publicly performed as part of a celebratory festival. Under pressure from Augustus, the emperor became an increasing presence in Horace's work, but Horace refers to Augustus in a way that allows the poet to maintain his honesty. 'Horace's solutions to imperial suggestion,' Michèle Lowrie explains, 'demonstrate artistic integrity, partly by distancing techniques such as folding Augustus as a topic into poetic issues, displacing him from centre stage, and introducing an intervening voice or *laudandus* [that which is to be praised], but always by the originality of the treatment.'[15]

The willingness of Maecenas and Augustus to receive Horace back into Roman society and then elevate him to its highest circles was likely a matter of politics as much as friendship. The Roman Republic was in a dire state following generations of civil war. The page needed to be turned. One strategy was to bring on board former enemies who were prepared to endorse the new regime. Another was a programme of social and religious reforms to improve moral conduct and revive traditional Roman values. Another was investment in infrastructure such as roads and buildings. And culture, too, was to play its part. Writers such as Virgil, Ovid, Livy and, of course, Horace, ushered in a Golden Age of Latin literature that was to rival the accomplishments of the Greeks.

Works

Horace's poetry can be divided into four main categories, *Epodes*, *Satires*, *Epistles* and *Odes*, and two important individual works already mentioned, the *Art of Poetry*, and the *Song of the Ages*. Unusually for ancient authors, it seems that all his work has survived, partly because its moral themes appealed to a Christian culture, and partly because the elegance of his Latin made it a valuable stylistic and teaching resource.

He began writing his *Epodes* upon his return to Italy in 42 BCE until their completion in 30 BCE, the period bookended by the battles of Philippi and Actium that were to establish the beginning of the imperial Roman age. The *Epodes* are the earliest of Horace's works, overlapping with his *Satires*, and thematically are remarkably diverse, ranging from wine drinking to love to civil war to poetry to social climbing. One of the poet's claims to fame lay in his unsurpassed skill at adapting Greek metrical forms and genres to Latin. In the case of his *Epodes*, he took as his model the iambic meter – a short, or unstressed, syllable followed by a long, or stressed, syllable – devised by the seventh-century Greek poet Archilochus. It was meter which the Greek used for satire and the epode, the latter being a lyric form also attributed to Archilochus. Interestingly both men were soldiers, and both write about a time when they discarded their shields in their haste to flee 'when the fighting got hot.'[16]

While Archilochus made use of the epode to launch venomous attacks on personal enemies, Horace was on the whole more restrained. Some individuals, real or fictional, he treats as figures representative of wider social problems and anxieties, like witchcraft. Other attacks are entirely playful, for example when he rounds on Maecenas for feeding him too much garlic at a dinner party. Elsewhere he takes aim at society in general, such as the atavistic tendency of Romans to degenerate into fighting among themselves. The epodes are on occasion sexually explicit and coarse and, for modern readers, disturbingly misogynistic. In epode eight he is pitiless in his description of how physically repulsive he finds an unnamed old woman 'grown rank with lengthened age' who makes sexual advances towards him.[17] Here is an extended curse he directs against Maevius, a rival poet (possibly fictional), at the opening of his tenth epode:

> The vessel that carries the loathsome Maevius makes her departure under an unlucky omen. Be mindful, O south wind, that you buffet it about with horrible billows. May the gloomy east, turning up the sea, disperse its cables and broken oars. Let the north arise as mighty as when he rives the quivering oaks on the lofty mountains; nor let a friendly star appear through the murky night in which the baleful Orion sets: nor let him be conveyed in a calmer sea than was the Grecian band of conquerors when Pallas turned her rage from burned Troy to the ship of impious Ajax.[18]

Horace's *Satires* occupy two books. Book 1 was completed around 34 BCE, making his name as a gifted poet, and Book 2 in 30 BCE. His poetical forebear in this case is Lucilius (d 103 BCE) regarded as the originator of Roman satire. Lucilius established the generic convention of using hexameters that Horace followed. A hexameter was the meter of Homer's epics. It was a line comprising six feet and usually dactylic – one stressed, or long, syllable followed by two unstressed, or short, syllables. Only disconnected fragments of Lucilius's writings have survived although they can give a flavour of his work: 'Just as little children believe that all the statues of brass are alive and human beings, just so these men believe all these fables to be true, and think there is a heart inside these brazen statues;'[19] 'Albinus, in grief, confines himself to his house, because he has divorced his daughter;'[20] 'When he sees me, he wheedles and coaxes, scratches his head, and picks out the vermin.'[21]

Satire was a literary form which was home grown. Its social and political criticism was anchored in traditional Roman virtues such as duty, loyalty, courage, plain living and plain speaking, in contrast to the sophistication, deceptiveness and self-indulgence Romans associated with the Greeks. In its rejection of what was ostentatious or phony it happily embraced the down-to-earth realities of life, including the bodily and the vulgar. The use of hexameter as the vehicle for such unseemly content deliberately subverted epic poetry, the genre above all which embodied what was lofty and noble. As with the *Epodes* and Archilochus, likewise with the *Satires* and Lucilius, Horace adopts a less aggressive pose. He declares that his aim is to give good advice, not to scourge. Unlike Lucilius, the objects of his censure tend not to be Roman aristocrats but people of middling or lower status, and character types: misers, adulterers, spendthrifts, social climbers, witches, glory hunters.

In the process of expounding his good advice Horace interweaves the story of himself and his own life. Slowly we get to know him. We are introduced to friends and associates. Bit by bit a portrait emerges of a man who is flawed but amiable. We learn about his humble origins, his education, how much he respected and was close to his father, how he had been a tribune entangled in the political misfortunes of Rome. We see him wrong-footed and disgruntled but willing to poke fun at himself. We are even given some insight into his sex life. He is clearly an intelligent man, and funny.

This biographical realism is underpinned by his style. The poetry is so deftly crafted it sounds utterly natural, and Horace, tongue firmly in cheek, denies that he is writing poetry at all but rather conversational prose. He incorporates personal anecdotes, trivia, jokes, homely animal fables, snatches of dialogue, speaks to the reader directly, reveals his own moral dilemmas, and counts his blessings. References to food and drink and socialising add to a sense of convivial ordinariness. He confronts moral failings but is not bullying or vicious. His approach is informal, catching flies with honey. Here he describes being accosted by a social climber while out walking in Rome – the man wants Horace to introduce him to Maecenas:

> Meanwhile he kept prating on anything that came uppermost, praised the streets, the city and, when I made him no answer, he said, 'You want terribly to get away. I perceived it long ago but you effect nothing. I shall still stick close to you. I shall follow you hence. Where are you at present bound for?'

> 'There is no need for your being carried so much about. I want to see a person who is unknown to you. He lives a great way off across the Tiber, just by Caesar's gardens.' 'I have nothing to do and I am not lazy, I will attend you thither.' I hang down my ears like an ass of surly disposition, when a heavier load than ordinary is put upon his back. He begins again …[22]

But, of course, do we accept this man as the true Horace or is he, at least in part, an invention, a persona moulded by Horace the poet to best convey the milder kind of social criticism he advocated? Arguments have been made for both sides but this is academic as far as we are concerned. The eighteenth century took him at face value: Horace the poet and Horace the protagonist of the *Satires* were one and the same.

The *Epistles* pick up where Book 2 of the *Satires* leaves off. In Book 2 of the *Satires* Horace seems to modulate away from the satire of Book 1 to create a more introspective and philosophical space, one which it could be argued was hardly satirical at all were it not for its exploration of ethics, and the *Epistles* follow suit – Book 1 in 20 or 19 BCE and Book 2 in 14 BCE. These are poems and poem essays in the guise of letters addressed to specific individuals although the two collections are quite different. Book 1 of the *Epistles* comprises twenty hexameter poems of varying length and Book 2 only two (or three if we include the *Art of Poetry*), the first addressed to Augustus, the second to a man called Florus. Epistolic poetry was not unique to Horace in the ancient world, but composing two books in that form was certainly unusual.

From the outset of Book 1 the focus on moral philosophy is made clear to his supposed correspondent, Maecenas. In 23 BCE he had published his third book of *Odes* and wants to move on from writing lyric poems. He is older and has changed. He feels that it would be more fitting if he spent time considering what it is to live a good life. He was, after all, a more established and respected figure, accepted by Augustus as well as Maecenas. He reassures his patron that he does not feel bound to any particular school of philosophy. He is open minded: sometimes the rather austere ideas of the Stoics appeal to him, at other times the pleasure-seeking of the Cyrenaics.

The personal and private nature of letter-writing helps to reproduce the biographical realism of the *Satires*. The paradox at the heart of this powerful and convincing illusion, of course, is that the spontaneity that Horace evokes is meticulously planned. He takes pains to create a sense of letter-writing authenticity by asking for news, proffering advice, referring to previous interactions, embarking on unnecessary detours, tailoring his comments and register to fit his correspondent, and so forth. In epistle 15 from Book 1 he is planning to spend winter by the sea and is pumping his friend Vala for information, peppering his letter with all kinds of questions, asides, observations and snatches of dialogue:

> Write to me … what sort of a winter it is at Velia, what the air at Salernum, what kind of inhabitants the country consists of, and how the road is (for Antonious Musa pronounces Baie to be of no service to me yet makes me obnoxious to the place when I am bathed in cold water even in the midst of the frost by his prescription. In truth, the village murmurs at their myrtle groves being deserted, and the sulphurous waters, said to expel lingering disorders from the nerves, despised …).[23]

The private world that he reveals to us becomes populated by more friends and associates, for the most part relatively minor figures given the elite company he kept: poets, businessmen, attendants, advocates, would-be philosophers. By engaging with them in various ways Horace, implicitly and explicitly, can investigate ideas, concerns and attitudes about life. He invites an advocate friend to a dinner party, urging him to set aside business worries for one evening in order to dine and socialise with friends.[24] The message is clear; we should strive to achieve a balance between pleasure and duty. Elsewhere he makes the case that equanimity is the foundation for happiness: 'To admire nothing is almost the one and only thing, Numicious, which can make and keep a man happy.'[25] In a letter to his city-loving friend Fuscus, he praises the advantages and moral virtues of the country over those of the city.[26] The audience is positioned as an eavesdropper privy to honestly held beliefs expressed in good faith. Horace is not a fanatical preacher with all the answers but an entirely relatable human being in search of wisdom, which makes his opinions all the more seductive.

The fourth category, the *Odes*, were inspired by Greek lyric poets such as Pindar (c 518–c 437 BCE) and Alcaeus (c 625/620–580 BCE) and comprise 103 short poems, the first three books published in 23 BCE and a fourth ten years later. A diverse range of subjects include travel, the seasons, love, friendship, wine, morality, adultery, Homer, numerous references to pagan deities, and praise of Augustus. His ambition was to be the greatest lyric poet in Latin, and laid claim to be the first to successfully import Greek lyric meters, which he applies to contemporary Rome. Like the *Epistles*, most of the *Odes* are addressed to someone (or more than one person) with whom the poet directly engages. The beginning of an ode to a group of drinking buddies demonstrates how skilfully he could carve out a believable personal and social space: 'To quarrel over your cups, which were made for joy, is downright Thracian. Away with the barbarous custom and protect modest Bacchus from bloody frays. How immensely disagreeable to wine and candles is the sabre of the Medes! O my companions, repress your wicked vociferations, and rest quietly on bended elbow.'[27] The setting he chooses enables him to riff on a traditional Hellenistic custom, a symposium, or drinking party, one that usually followed a meal such as a banquet. Into the drama he adds an underlying message, the superior civilised norms of Romans compared to those of rival cultures, in this case that of the Thracians in the east.

Philosophy

Philosophy is a recurring theme throughout Horace's works and underpins many of his ethical observations. This is not surprising. He had studied philosophy in Athens, it was part of the common interests and discourse of educated Romans, and it was closely tied to religion. He may claim not to be beholden to any particular school but his poetry has a distinct Epicurean leaning, and certainly there is evidence that other ancient authors believed that he had been a follower of Epicurus, at least at some point. This happened to be a time when interest in the ideas of Epicurus had been energised in Rome by the work of Lucretius (c 99–c 55 BCE) and the presence of a particularly important scholar, Philodemus of Garda (c 110–c 30 BCE), who was also a Greek poet and literary critic. The significance of Lucretius lay in his masterpiece the didactic poem *On the Nature of Things* to which Horace alludes in his own work. At over 7,000 lines long it is the most important description of Epicurean physics to have survived antiquity. For the purpose of this chapter, we will be focusing on the philosophy's moral implications and will go into more detail on its materialist foundations when we discuss Pierre Gassendi (Chapter 4). Philodemus lived and worked in the vicinity of Rome, possibly at a villa in Herculaneum which contained a large library of Epicurean texts to which he contributed his own writings. His followers included Virgil and a number of other poets in the circles of Maecenas and Horace.

Epicurus (c 341–c 271 BCE) established his philosophical school in Athens around 306 BCE. It was known as The Garden as the school was set up in the garden of a house that Epicurus owned. At heart, Epicureanism was an ethical programme. Its aim was to reduce human suffering, and it was as much concerned with practical lifestyle choices as with abstract theorising. Indeed, the two were intimately connected. The object was to maximise pleasure over the longer term, recognising that short-term gratification of one's desires might lead to greater physical and mental suffering further down the line. If the sum outcome of any behaviour was pleasurable to the individual, then, for Epicurus, it was morally good. If the outcome was greater suffering, then it was bad. What was moral became curiously retrospective, ambiguous and egocentric. Under this formulation it would be justifiable to cheat if any material or psychological harms were ultimately outweighed by the rewards.

The greatest pleasure was the absence of pain, and the ideal state of mind was tranquillity, best acquired through the application of a hedonic calculus that weighed up the likely pros and cons of one's actions. Over two millennia later this ethical dimension of Epicureanism was to have a significant influence on the development of utilitarianism through Enlightenment philosophers such as Claude Adrien Helvétius (1715–1771) and Jeremy Bentham (1748–1832). For Epicurus and his followers, the outcome was a preference for a life of simplicity and frugality although this was not pursued in any fanatical way as was sometimes the case with other philosophical and religious cults such as the Cynics. Epicurean principles as interpreted by Philodemus did not preclude the possession of great wealth, a position that was no doubt reassuring to Philodemus's prospering Roman benefactors. Epicurus himself argued that it was possible to live well on little and was acknowledged even by his opponents to be a man of impeccable virtue.

Epicureanism remained an evangelising tradition with active followers for several centuries, and certainly into the second century CE – Philodemus had travelled to Italy to spread its ideas. A measure of its success in Rome is the extent to which it aroused strong opposition on the part of Stoics such as Cicero (106–43 BCE). Despite its longevity most of the writings of its founder and adherents have been lost, partly a result of the antipathy of Christianity. Epicurus himself is believed to have written around 300 books almost all of which have disappeared. It was a philosophy that aspired to investigate every aspect of knowledge and human experience on the foundational premise that reality was a wholly material phenomenon, a monist system in contrast to the material and non-material dualism of other pagan schools like those of Plato and Aristotle. It is hardly surprising that Christians were hostile. It is worth pointing out that Epicureans were not atheists, despite being pilloried as such, but believed in gods that were material, self-sufficient beings, and who were entirely passive and divorced from human affairs. Epicurean study of epistemology, perception, memory, atomism, meteorology, cosmology, theology, language and free will, in addition to psychological well-being and the ethics intrinsic to living a good life, give an indication of its range of interest.

The key tenet underpinning Epicurean ethics was that pleasure was a moral good in and of itself, a belief derived from its atomist theory of creation from which all things, including sentient beings, were constructed. It was also the primary good against which any other had to be measured. But to optimise pleasure, which should be an individual's ultimate moral goal, reason was required. It would not be justifiable to avoid the discomfort of surgery if it were likely to improve your health. A similar calculation should inform all your decision-making. You may covet another man's wife, be politically ambitious or attracted by the appeal of big-city living but achieving those desires might incur heavy costs that you would be wise to consider in advance.

These are the very sorts of scenarios we find depicted by Horace. Here he describes the fate of adulterers: 'it is worth your while to hear how they are hampered on all sides and that their pleasure, which happens to them but seldom, is interrupted with a great deal of pain, and often in the midst of very great dangers. One has thrown himself headlong from the top of a house, another has been whipped almost to death, a third, in his flight, has fallen into a merciless gang of thieves, another has paid a fine.'[28] Instead, he suggests, if you do need to have sex just take that which is readily available and uncomplicated: 'When your passions are inflamed and a common gratification is at hand [i.e. a female servant or a slave boy], would you rather be consumed with desire than possess it? I would not: for I love such pleasures as are of easiest attainment.'[29] A clear illustration of Epicurean hedonic calculus.

A major form of suffering addressed by Epicureanism, and already highlighted by Horace above, is mental anguish, often the result of uncontrolled desire. Philodemus devised a careful taxonomy of different kinds of desire. Some were required for life and happiness while others were not required and should not be actively pursued, such as the desire for wealth or luxuries. If you are gifted wealth by a friend, perhaps, let us say, in gratitude for your sage moral and philosophical counsel, then that was acceptable because you had not been actively seeking such an outcome and it involved no unhappy toil on your part. But the more powerful a desire had its hold over someone the greater the likelihood of damaging behaviours and psychological disturbance. The lover can become obsessive or consumed by jealousy. The miser can become paranoid that someone might steal his money. Other causes of deep-seated anxiety included fear of gods, the supernatural or death. These were harms based upon unnecessary beliefs akin to the harms based upon unnecessary desires.

To foster well-being, Epicureanism encouraged a philosophical therapy that involved attending to your emotions to abandon those that were negative and enjoy those that were positive. It advocated moderation, prudence, friendship, retreat from public life, the cultivation of intellectual pleasures and, of course, the use of reason both to optimise the beneficial outcomes of one's actions and to combat debilitating assumptions about the nature of reality. All these virtues were expounded by Horace. Friendship and socialising appear regularly in his poetry. He informs us that he was in a position to become a senator but chose not to, keeping his distance from the centre of Roman politics in the same way that he was cautious about getting too close to Augustus. He favours the simpler life of the country over that of the city and devotes himself to philosophy. Now it should be pointed out that these prescriptions were not all unique to Epicureanism. The Stoics equally valued friendship, and Aristotle promoted moderation; courage, for example, was the sweet spot between cowardice and recklessness. But there were clear differences. Retreat from public life was a distinctly unRoman sentiment and a source of sharp disagreement with the Stoics. Also, the instrumental quality of Epicurean virtues, notably friendship, clashed with those traditions that considered virtues as ends in themselves, not simply means.

Horace refers to a range of other philosophical schools, the most prominent in his writing being Stoicism. It was founded by Zeno (c 334–c 262 BCE), around 310 BCE and was active into the third century CE, making it contemporaneous with Epicureanism. Its most famous adherent was Emperor Marcus Aurelius (121–180 CE). It was similarly a materialist-based system but which divided into two tendencies: one whose purpose was to investigate and integrate all forms of knowledge; and one that prioritised ethics with a view to helping people to live a better life. Its ethical positions diverged markedly from Epicureanism in a number of respects, most of all in its attitude towards public duty. An understanding of what constituted a good life embraced the political as well as the personal. Human beings are social animals, and so virtue needed to be considered within a broader social and less individualistic frame. Stoics choose to be virtuous not because it may improve their happiness in some tangible way but because it is a self-contained good. It is how people ought to be, and as such it is in tune with the nature of a rational universe as designed by its benign, albeit corporeal, creator. Happiness itself was not a pleasure-optimisation formula but the result of being truly virtuous; it was a goal towards which to strive and might entail considerable sacrifice. This more exacting, altruistic outlook was a much easier fit with traditional Roman values. Stoics agreed with Platonists that the core virtues were courage, justice, moderation and wisdom.

This leads us on to the biggest beasts in antiquity's philosophical jungle who were, of course, the trio Socrates (c 470–399 BCE), Plato (c 427–c 347 BCE) and Aristotle (384–322 BCE), whose material and non-material dualism was to be incorporated into Christian theology, described by Casanova as a 'monstrous coupling'.[30] Much of what we know about Socrates is derived from Plato so it is not always clear where Socrates ends and Plato begins. Bearing that in mind, for Socrates happiness seems to be tied to the possession and practice of the four virtues listed above – courage, justice, moderation and wisdom – qualities which are intrinsically good and the most important of which is justice. A moral person will behave in accordance with what is just, while such behaviour in turn relies upon wisdom, courage and moderation. Socrates goes further and claims that to be knowledgeable of the good is to be virtuous, suggesting that possession of that knowledge entails in some way an alignment between your actions and your soul, and the submission of wayward desires. He is clear that improving your soul should be your chief concern rather than storing up possessions or hankering after social prestige. For Socrates an immoral life is not worth having, and virtue, specifically wisdom, is all that is required to attain happiness.

Plato explores more deeply the relationship between the virtues, the soul and happiness, and develops his theory of forms. The latter constitute the basis of reality and exist in a non-material realm. Everything that is material is an imperfect representation of these immutable archetypes. In the *Republic* he sets up an analogy between the soul and the city, and debates whether justice is a virtue or nothing more than a social practice instituted by rulers for their own self-interest. Roughly speaking he examines the interplay between justice, wisdom, courage, moderation, knowledge, desire and reason. Justice is appointed the prime virtue. Reason and courage are responsible for controlling desire, and wisdom supplies reason with knowledge of what is beneficial. Unlike desire, reason by its nature is allied to the good, and reason experiences pleasure when it acquires knowledge. Desire is not bad in itself but when it gets out of hand, for example, as in greed for power or riches, injustice is the result. Moderation exists as the expression of harmony between reason, courage and desire. As well as oiling the wheels of virtue, knowledge of the forms will also provide happiness, a happiness superior to the mere fulfilment of bodily appetites.

Aristotle's contribution to ethics follows a similar path to that of Socrates and Plato in its examination of virtue, most notably in his influential *Nicomachean Ethics* (c 340 BCE). For Aristotle the principal good is happiness and, as with the other virtues, it is not pursued for any end other than itself. We achieve happiness through the excellence with which we fulfil our innate function. In the same way that a musical instrument or tool exists for a purpose so do the faculties of the human soul, in particular that of reason. He explains how a virtue lies somewhere between the excess that characterises one vice and the lack that characterises another. So, generosity lies between wastefulness and miserliness. The extent to which a person is virtuous is a measure of the fulfilment of the function of the soul. Virtuous excellence is a necessary condition for true happiness but does not guarantee it; happiness might be undermined by external shocks, such as the death of a loved one. Like Plato, the highest virtue relates to the exercise of reason as it is in charge of desires and can acquire knowledge of the divine. Necessarily, happiness cannot be achieved without the excellent use of reason.

More hard-core hedonists were the Cyrenaics, precursors to Epicureanism, whose founder was Aristippus (c 435–356 BCE), a disciple of Socrates. For them pleasure was an intrinsic good and happiness was the sum of short-term pleasures. These are what an individual should seek. Bodily satisfaction was deemed to be more intense than that of the mind but otherwise it was believed that particular pleasures differed little from the one to the other. The more certain and easily obtainable an enjoyment the better, a perspective that would seem to be echoed by Horace's advice on the topic of adultery. Needless to say, one should avoid pain. Cyrenaics endorsed the importance of prudence in decision-making but nonetheless rejected the idea of foregoing gratification in the present for a potentially greater reward in the future. Why they held that view is unclear. Part of the answer may have been that the future is never certain and that anticipated rewards carried the risk of not materialising.

Another minor Socratic school were the Cynics whose governing principles were freedom, reason and self-sufficiency, and who were famously given to eccentric behaviour such as barking, living in a jar and masturbating in public. They embraced a primitivist ethos that was guided by nature and entailed satisfying only one's basic bodily needs. The Cynics were critical of social conventions and valued a willingness to express uncomfortable and subversive ideas. This is risky behaviour in any society but especially those prior to modern times. The Cynics regarded as delusory the pursuit of goals such as riches and glory in the hope of attaining one's best life. Liberation of the true self could only be achieved by divesting oneself of the trappings of society, mental and material, and so they conditioned themselves to endure lives of deprivation and hardship.

Casanova

Casanova had encountered Horace at least by his early teens and probably earlier. For centuries the poet had been employed as a model for students in their study of Latin, and it may well be that he had been introduced to him by Dr Gozzi who began tutoring him from the age of 9. Horace's stylistic advice and craftsmanship would have been an invaluable resource as the young man honed his own writing skills, and whether under Gozzi or later he would undoubtedly have made use of him. When Casanova was 15 and training for the priesthood, he planned to use an extract from Horace for a sermon he was to deliver but was persuaded to exclude it by his patron Senator Malipiero who described Horace as a 'scoundrel'.[31] When he was 17, he and a fellow seminarian would spend time together discussing the *Odes*. Written by Casanova in his late 60s, he models his substantial philosophical composition, *Philocalies on the Foolishness of Mortals*, on Horace's third satire of Book 2 in which the poet describes a humorous encounter with a recent Stoic convert called Damasippus.[32]

While it is sometimes tricky to untangle the extent to which Horace directly influenced Casanova's opinions and character or simply reinforced predispositions that he already possessed, he is either way likely to have felt an affinity with him. Most readers of Horace have found him to be an appealing character but for Casanova one aspect of his biography would have resonated strongly. This poet whose exceptional talent enabled him to rise to the highest echelons of Roman society and befriend the most powerful man in the world bore the stigma of being the son of a freed slave, or so the poet tells us. Casanova was acutely aware of his own humble background and the social obstacles that lay in the way of success. It is no surprise that he took note of Horace's advice on how to navigate the niceties of high society and patronage. In fact, there are remarkable similarities between the culture of the Paris salons frequented by Casanova and that of the Roman symposium. It was, explains Alessandro Barchiesi, 'the place for exchange among unequal individuals: the traffic included material gifts, rewards in terms of power, visibility, intellectual success, protection, continuation of "friendship"; the interactive behaviour could move through a spectrum of flattery and praise, vituperation and mockery, entertaining performance and poised self-control: a social game.'[33] How to be a friend of the rich without being dismissed as a flatterer was as tricky a line to tread in antiquity as it was in the eighteenth century. Evidence that Casanova had been paying careful attention to the poet's guidance can be found during the event in Warsaw referred to at the beginning of the chapter. One of Casanova's contributions on the topic of Horace was to proffer this piece of advice from epistle 17 of Book 1 as an example of the ancient Roman's delicacy and decorum: 'Those who don't talk about their needs [to their patron] will get more than those who do.'[34] The king took the hint and a little later discretely slipped Casanova 200 ducats.

In other ways, too, he would have found a connection with the poet. Horace's attitude to sex, including pederasty, was a far cry from the Christian norms that so infuriated Casanova, and was very much in accord with his belief that sexual pleasure was a gift from God, fundamental to human nature and, as such, a moral good to be welcomed. A recurring theme in *History of My Life* is the conflict between reason and desire, which Casanova highlights more than once using Horace's maxim, 'Rule your passion, which commands if it does not obey.'[35] Casanova's favourite maxim was also penned by Horace: '*Carpe diem quam minimum credulo postero*.' To the anguish of some classicists this is most famously (or infamously) translated as 'Seize the day, trusting as little as possible to the day to come.' Preferred by David West is 'Harvest the day, and leave as little as possible for tomorrow,' meaning that we should use today to prepare for tomorrow rather than leaving things to chance.[36] Casanova could read, write and speak Latin, so he may well have been intending it in its less impetuous second sense. Either way, making the most of the present was very much one of Casanova's guiding principles. Casanova could relate to Horace's determination to maintain his personal independence and resist the encroachment of others upon his freedom, from Maecenas and Augustus in particular. In his youth Casanova chaffed against restrictions placed upon him by his guardians. Later he resisted the temptations of marriage. And even in old age his instinct to assert his autonomy remained undimmed. Like Horace he was prone to bouts of short-lived anger, both were unmarried and both were nearly drowned in a storm. Consistent with Aristotle, and typical of many other ancients, Horace was a believer in the middle way, and so was Casanova, even if he recognised that at times he found it a difficult virtue to manage.

In line with his contemporaries, the older Casanova seems to have preferred Horace's *Satires* and *Epistles* over his *Odes* and *Epodes*, the *Epistles* most of all. The latter make up the large majority of references to Horace in *History of My Life*. Their focus on ethics supplied him with a fund of aphorisms and memorable turns of phrase which he could use to underscore some moral point that he wished to make. But Horace was more than a handy source of maxims; he influenced Casanova's general moral outlook. Recounting an adventure in Pesaro when Casanova was separated from his lover Bellino, he digresses for a page or so on to the topic of pain, pleasure, happiness and philosophers. Addressing his reader directly, Casanova rejects the suggestion that suffering in life outweighs happiness. During his discussion he engages in speculation which appears to endorse the Epicurean position that pleasure can simply be an absence of pain and he goes on to make the very Epicurean observation that 'pleasure … is always pure; pain is always tempered.'[37] Then a few lines later, in a reference to Horace's first epistle of Book 1, he switches to the Stoics: 'Do you see, my dear reader, the consequence of this reasoning? The wise man, believe me, can never be entirely unhappy. Indeed he is always happy, says my master, Horace.'[38] Horace does indeed appear to endorse this Stoic position but in the epistle gently undercuts it a little, and Casanova is fully aware of this. The passage nicely illustrates Casanova's philosophical instincts and how much they seem to agree with Horace. Like Horace he was reluctant to tie himself to any particular belief system although, again like Horace, he was more sympathetic to the utilitarian individualism of the Epicureans than the dutybound sobriety of the Stoics. This does not mean that Casanova did not value the importance of duty. He certainly did. But he was averse to anything that smacked of fanaticism.

Casanova's familiarity with Epicureanism and ancient philosophy extended well beyond his readings of Horace so it would be reasonable to assume that he was able to recognise the philosophical allusions in Horace's poetry even when they were not made explicit. Casanova was familiar with the work of Pierre Gassendi and had almost certainly read Lucretius. He had, after all, bought a copy of it for one of his lovers. Early in his preface to the memoirs, he appears to accept Lucretius's criticism of Platonic and Christian dualism and, by implication, that if we follow logic alone then we must conclude that all existence is material, including souls and the divine. This was the position of both the Stoics and the Epicureans. 'How an immaterial substance which can *nec tangere nec tangi* [neither touch nor be touched] could be,' Casanova declares, quoting Lucretius, 'there is no man who can explain it.'[39] That said, elsewhere Casanova does refer to God as 'immaterial', an example of him elevating faith above reason.[40]

Casanova may have been seriously interested in the ideas of the ancients but he was not uncritical. In one revealing passage when he recounts his time in the prison of the Venetian Inquisition, he dismisses the claims of both Epicureans and Stoics that it is always possible with sufficient training to obtain tranquillity. For Casanova this is a belief that could only be pushed so far: 'The material pains which afflict the Stoic will not be less than those which torment the Epicurean; and the sorrows will be all the more painful for he who hides them than for the other who obtains real relief by complaining. The man who wants to appear indifferent to an event that determines his state only appears to be so, unless he is an imbecile, or enraged. He who boasts of perfect tranquillity lies, and I beg from Socrates a thousand pardons.'[41] For Casanova the final authority for such a claim was personal experience: 'Any man called upon to judge of a moral possibility or impossibility [i.e. the probability of an empirical truth claim related to human society] is right to start only from himself, for he cannot in good faith admit an inner force in anyone unless he feels the germ of it in himself. What I find in myself on this subject is that, through strength acquired by means of much practice, a man can resist his initial instinct and prevent himself from crying out in pain. That's all.'[42]

After reviewing Casanova's interest in Horace, comparisons between *History of My Life* and the *Satires* and *Epistles* become more salient. The content and style of the works share a number of similarities, some of which make the *History of My Life* quite untypical of memoirs of the time and may be indicators of Horace's influence. In some ways it can be read as an Horatian satire of eighteenth-century Europe, particularly given its spotlight on human folly. Like Horace, Casanova creates a very, dare one say, seductive persona. He is intelligent, witty, incisive, self-critical and self-satirising, disarmingly open, revealing the most intimate and personal details of his life no matter how badly they may reflect upon him, incest and all. His prose is sharp, conversational and filled with lively dialogue. Like Horace, too, Casanova is only interested in writing for a highly educated, elite audience. One of his criticisms of Voltaire was that he was not satisfied with a few readers.

While it seems clear that *History of My Life*, like the *Satires* and *Epistles*, is a moral project, it is on the whole more cautious about taking its lead from any ethical system or set of values. Horace's exhortations and descriptions of human behaviour may be grounded in the events of his own life and the behaviour of his contemporaries but by and large they are crafted to illustrate moral conclusions that conformed to contemporary philosophical traditions and norms even if he was happy at times to mock them. Casanova was similarly sensitive to the fallibility of ideological claims but even more so. There was, after all, the additional complication of Christian doctrine and conditioning that Horace did not have to confront. Casanova was sceptical that the human mind could construct comprehensive theoretical models capable of withstanding close contact with reality. The absence of real-world experience made him particularly dismissive of medieval Christian scholarship: 'Unable to study either men or nature, they were reduced to studying books … They dreamed up arbitrary principles from which they drew subtle and useless consequences: they were authors of ingenious and chimerical systems. It was all speculation and subtlety.'[43] He had witnessed often enough how intellectual vanity could lead the most educated people to believe absurdities. When judged at the court of human experience, as evidenced in the *History of My Life*, Stoicism, Epicureanism, Platonism, Christianity and Libertinism are all found wanting.

Casanova's memoirs stand as a rejection of deducible absolutes and the abstract systems that peddle them, especially when applied at the level of the individual. His message seems to be that the case of the dogmatist always collapses at some point in the face of human complexity. While Horace's stories are often used to buttress moral claims, Casanova's are more likely to dissolve them. Certain ideas, like those to do with moderation or pleasure, may help us to navigate towards what is better or worse but we should not attempt to fashion them into anything more than useful rules of thumb. Neither does that make him a moral relativist of the ilk of the Marquis de Sade (1740–1814). That would be another extremist position. From Casanova's perspective, norms, conventions, duties and laws ought generally to be respected for the good running of society but there are times when it is justifiable for the individual to violate them. He was a pragmatic conservative who believed that human nature was inherently flawed. He had come to the fatalistic conclusion that the impulse of human beings to find out things for themselves made them resistant to following good advice: 'Those whom we instruct do neither more nor less than that which we have done, hence the world always stays the same, or gets worse.'[44]

Despite that gloomy prognosis, elsewhere in his writings he did see grounds for hope institutionally. Utilising philosophy in fields such as Government, the Law and Economics could be a great boon to society. Montesquieu's *Spirit of the Laws*, Cesare Beccaria's *On Crimes and Punishments* and Adam Smith's *The Wealth of Nations* would be prime examples. He argues that the subject of history, an area of particular expertise for Casanova, when infused with philosophical understanding becomes transformed from a discipline that otherwise could be barren and pedantic to 'a true collection of moral and political experiences' of value for rulers and ministers in their governance of society. At this governmental level, Casanova suggests, there is a place to resurrect Plato's philosopher prince – rulers who have enjoyed a deep philosophical education.[45] Casanova was in no doubt about the benefits it could bring: 'The people will be happy when the philosophers are ministers and the ministers are philosophers: then we will enjoy all those advantages that nature and art promise us.'[46]

Chapter 3
Ludovico Ariosto: 1474–1533

> 'Not knowing what method to use to force destiny to reveal to me through the Bible the moment in which I would recover my freedom, I determined to consult the divine poem of *The Frenzy of Orlando* by Messer Ludovico Ariosto, which I had read a hundred times, and which was still my delight up there [in the prison of the Venetian Inquisition called 'the Leads']. I idolized his genius, and I believed him to be much more fitted than Virgil to predict my happiness.'
>
> Giacomo Casanova, *History of My Life*

One and a half thousand years later, the twinned presence of Horace and Epicurus crops up in the poetry of Ludovico Ariosto, in both Ariosto's satires and his epic *The Frenzy of Orlando*. Ariosto was sympathetic to Epicureanism, a philosophical system that was to acquire increasing prominence from the seventeenth century onwards following upon the work of Pierre Gassendi. No doubt this aspect of his writing would have resonated with his future Enlightenment audience.

History of My Life is littered with references to the Italian and his work. When Voltaire asks Casanova which Italian poet he likes best, he answers, 'Ariosto: and I can't say that I love him more than the others; because I love only him.'[1] Later in his memoirs he refers to *The Frenzy of Orlando* as 'the masterpiece of the human mind'.[2] Casanova's admiration was not unusual; the poem was regarded as among the greatest literary works of the Italian Renaissance.

The Frenzy of Orlando

Completed in 1532, the poem is set in the eighth century with the Christian forces of Charlemagne besieged in Paris by the Saracen forces of Agramente, the king of Africa and Spain. It is made up of 40,000 lines divided across 46 cantos, comprising three main plots. These are two love stories and the war between Charlemagne and Agramente. The first love story is a triangle in which cousins Orlando and Rinaldo, the greatest champions of France, pursue Angelica, an Asian Princess at Charlemagne's court. But she falls in love with a wounded Saracen infantryman called Medore whom she nurses back to health, and with whom she then runs off, triggering Orlando's frenzy. The second love story involves Rinaldo's sister Bradamante, a female knight who is searching for her love Ruggiero. In an intricate tale that encompasses Europe, Africa and Asia, the poem weaves together the natural and the supernatural. Alongside the life and death adventures of warriors embroiled in matters of honour, glory and the heart, the narrative features such wonders as a magic ring that confers invisibility, enchanted wells of love and hate, invulnerable armour, a hippogriff and lost wits in a bottle.

Ludovico Ariosto, born in Reggio Emilia, lived during a tumultuous period of European history. It was the age of the Renaissance, the Reformation, the wars of religion, the printing press and global exploration – Ariosto was 18 when Columbus set off for the New World. It was a time when the likes of Ferdinand and Isabella, Henry VIII, Francis I, Charles V and Pope Leo X fought to establish their political, religious and territorial authority. For much of Ariosto's life the Italian peninsula was a theatre of war between France and Spain. Trained in law, and a student of Greek and Latin literature, he was the son of the governor of Reggio, and was to work as a diplomat for the Este family of Ferrara. He dedicated *The Frenzy of Orlando* to Ippolito d'Este, his patron. Ferrara was at this time an important Renaissance city able to boast of works by men such as Piero della Francesca, Jacopo Bellini and Andrea Mantegna. Ariosto himself kept the company of artists and scholars. He had direct experience of war and the battlefield – he witnessed the siege of Padua in 1509 and the Battle of Ravenna in 1512 – giving him insights which he was able to draw upon for his writing.

The Frenzy of Orlando is a sequel to Matteo Boiardo's *Orlando in Love* (1495) which is based in turn upon *The Song of Roland* – 'Orlando' is an inversion of the first two letters of 'Roland' which is then Italianized. This chivalric poem, *The Song of Roland*, is the oldest surviving major work of French literature. The limited nature of divine intervention in the narrative means that it cannot strictly speaking be classed as an epic. It was composed around the eleventh century and based upon the Battle of Roncevaux Pass in 778, a battle in which the army of Charlemagne was caught in an ambush by a force of Basque warriors. Charlemagne's rear-guard, commanded by Roland, were massacred to a man but bought enough time for the rest of the army to escape. Roland was to be transformed over the following generations into a legendary hero, the greatest of Charlemagne's knights, and the battle into a conflict between Muslims and Christians. But as any devotee of the superhero genre can testify, death is never an insuperable obstacle to the resurrection of a great character. Boiardo's way around the problem was to insert his own adventures featuring Roland into the time prior to his glorious death at Roncevaux but still within the context of the war between Muslims and Christians.

Apart from the intrusiveness of the divine, another major difference between *The Song of Roland* and the epics of Boiardo and Ariosto is the increased presence of women and the element of love, as the title of Boiardo's work makes clear. No doubt this change was at least partly motivated by the fact that their audience would have included cultivated women who played an active role in the social and intellectual life of Ferrara and the Este court. Those depicted by Boiardo and Ariosto, such as Angelica, Marfisa and Fiordelisa, are a far cry from the medieval ideal of passive and obedient women, respectful of male authority. There is a much greater degree of equality between the sexes. Although we must remain alert to Ariosto's mischievous irony and a narrative voice which is not always reliable, his attitude seems distinctly feminist. Here he condemns sexual double-standards:

> If like desire, and if an equal flame
> Move one and the other sex, who warmly press
> To that soft end of love (their goal the same)
> Which to the witless crowd seems rank excess;
> Say why shall woman merit scathe and blame,
> Though lovers, one or more, she may caress;
> While man to sin with whom he will is free,
> And meets with praise, not mere impunity?
>
> (Canto 4, stanza 66)[3]

Ariosto uses his female characters to explore and subvert the boundaries of accepted categories, both social and literary. In one role-reversal he has

Bradamante rescue her beloved Ruggiero. This allows Ariosto to play with the traditions of romance and epic by presenting figures whose complexity makes them more than simply love objects or warrior heroes.

In *The Song of Roland* women make an occasional appearance but they are a rarity on the whole, their existence often referenced only by their relationship to men (wife of, mother of, sister of). Romantic love is likewise at a premium. In contrast, women are everywhere in the Orlando epics (queens, warriors, sorceresses, supernatural beings, monsters), exerting a powerful influence upon the dramatic narrative. One of Boiardo's innovations was to combine Carolingian with Arthurian legends, thereby introducing themes of love, sexual desire and magic, with love becoming one of the central forces that drives the action. In particular, he tapped into the story of Lancelot and Guinevere. The emotional and psychological world of the protagonists is consequently enriched: there is more interest in the dilemmas and struggles of individuals, and less of a focus on the outcomes of the broader territorial and religious conflicts which are the backdrop of the poem. This reflected the growing humanist outlook of the Renaissance. Temporal considerations, such as the love between men and women, began to displace the centrality of religion in people's understanding of the world and their place in it.

The effect upon storylines can be seen in the creation of strong female characters, good and bad, capable of directing events with regards to their own goals. There are love triangles and errant knights whose desire to win the approval of their lady leads to adventures and quests that test their mettle. There is an increased propensity for duelling rather than battling. There are knights who are seduced by beauty and virtue, bewitched by magic spells, driven mad by love (quite literally, in Orlando's case) and who are victims of treachery and manipulation. *The Frenzy of Orlando* explores the theme of love and sexual desire across a wide range of contrasting scenarios: faithful and unfaithful; heterosexual and homosexual; lust, obsession and infatuation; transvestism; multiple partners, and so on. While the language Ariosto deploys to refer to sex tends to be euphemistic, his descriptions are nonetheless erotic and highly charged.

Boiardo's poem ends abruptly, never reaching the Battle of Roncevaux Pass and Orlando's death. Charles VIII of France (1483–1498) invaded the Italian peninsular early in 1494, and the narrator gives this as the reason that he can write no more. Boiardo died in the December of that year.

But *Orlando in Love* was immensely popular, and there remained an appetite for more adventures, especially on the part of the Este court, so

Ariosto provided them. He continues the saga and Orlando's pursuit of his love interest, Angelica. In *The Frenzy of Orlando* our eponymous hero discovers Angelica's love for another man. Driven to despair, in madness he runs amok through Europe and Africa until eventually he is cured.

In pulling together and resolving the various threads laid down by Boiardo, Ariosto skilfully blends contemporary events, classical themes and references, and the traditions of chivalric poetry epitomised by *The Song of Roland* along with a wide range of other literary traditions. The Christian–Muslim conflicts at the heart of the Orlando epics mirror the existential fifteenth- and sixteenth-century struggles by Europe against the Ottomans. Ariosto draws upon recent geographical discoveries such as the New World and in Africa as locations for his fantastical adventures, and refers to works such as Homer's *Iliad*, Ovid's *Metamorphoses* and Virgil's *Aeneid* along with others. The integration of the contemporary and the mythical is common to both the *Aeneid* and *The Frenzy of Orlando*. In the same way that Virgil traces back the ancestral line of Emperor Augustus to the Trojan hero Aeneas in his recounting of the mythical foundation of Rome, so do the Orlando epics represent its heroes as the mythical founders of the Este dynasty. Just as Aeneas descends into the underworld and witnesses a pageant of his descendants stretching to the present time of Virgil and Augustus, so Bradamante witnesses in Merlin's cave a vision of her own descendants down to the present time of Ariosto and the Estensi. But there are numerous other classical references. Let's take the *Iliad*. Orlando's madness echoes the fury of Achilles. The rivalry between Orlando and Rinaldo for Angelica mirrors the rivalry between Paris and Menelaus for Helen. You have the siege of Troy in the one and the siege of Paris in the other. As you have reviews of the opposing forces in the *Iliad* so you have them in *The Frenzy of Orlando*. The poem contains the best part of 200 characters whose exploits unfold across a complex mesh of plotlines and relationships. To forge so many different components into an engaging and coherent story that had such contemporary relevance was an immense achievement.

Boiardo's *Orlando in Love* has been traditionally regarded as a chaotic assembly of disparate adventures, material which Ariosto goes on to shape into something more intellectually and aesthetically satisfying. But for some, the multiplicity of events and looseness of structure of Boiardo's epic reflects contemporary ideas of the Renaissance man: someone who is a master of every situation, an opportunist who is able to take advantage of contingent events and defy the constraints of fortune or history. Each new adventure that Boiardo supplies pushes further and further away any conclusion to the story of Orlando, and in so doing vanquishes even the possibility of death. That Boiardo never finishes the narrative is quite fitting. By completing the saga, *The Frenzy of Orlando* turns into an ironic rebuttal. Ariosto demonstrates that the temporal stasis in which all these events take place is an illusion that must come to an end. Ultimately, fortune and history cannot be denied, even by the greatest of men.

Ariosto constructs this opposing position by making use of the magician Atlantes, a character introduced by Boiardo. Atlantes wishes to prevent the death of the knight Ruggiero, the mythical founder of the Este dynasty who Atlantes has raised since infancy. The magician's fears are based upon two prophecies: that Ruggiero will father a line of heroes, and that he will be betrayed and murdered shortly after being married. Atlantes constructs a magic garden in which to keep Ruggiero safe in an attempt to avert this fate. Ariosto frees Ruggiero in *The Frenzy of Orlando*, and after numerous adventures the first of these prophesies seems to be fulfilled while the second is ominously foreshadowed. The poem ends with a dramatic climax, Ruggiero victorious in single combat over the Saracen leader Rodomonte on the final day of Bradamante and Ruggiero's wedding celebrations.

Whatever the relationship between the two epics, it is clear that Ariosto did not take the ideals of chivalry as seriously as Boiardo, treating the adventures he described with more playfulness and ironic detachment. Helping him do so is his creation of a self-important Polonius-like narrator – a well-meaning character who is obsequious, gullible and prone to moralising, and who from time-to-time shares with the audience his own tribulations of the heart. Here he is lamenting his bad luck with women:

> Though none for whom I hitherto have sighed
> – Of those so many – have kept faith with me,
> All with ingratitude, or falsehood dyed
> I deem not, I accuse my destiny.
> Many there are, and have been more beside
> Unmeriting reproach: but if there be,
> 'Mid hundreds, one or two of evil way,
> My fortune wills that I should be their prey.
>
> (Canto 27, stanza 123)

Ariosto was infamous for breaking off the narrative at points of crisis, returning to them only much later in the story, inevitably deflating the moment. He includes bawdy scenes and adopts a conversational style, both of which would be inappropriate for a heroic poem. He juxtaposes the solemn against the ludicrous, and piety alongside cynical self-interest. His more light-hearted treatment of the actions of his protagonists, and his ruminations about society, reflect people as they are, with all their foibles, virtues and imperfections, more than how they should be or, at least, how they should be according to Boiardo. When Orlando's comrade Astolfo takes a trip to the moon in a quest to recover Orlando's lost wits – itself a whimsically surreal idea – he is accompanied by St John the Evangelist. On the return journey the saint puts the case that princes should take good care of poets. He argues that it is the poet who will determine a person's reputation after they are dead, whatever the historical reality:

> Homer a conqueror Agamemnon shows,
> And makes the Trojans seem of coward vein,
> And from the suitors, faithful to her vows,
> Penelope a thousand wrongs sustain:
> Yet – would'st thou I the secret should expose? –
> By contraries throughout the tale explain:
> That from the Trojan bands the Grecian ran;
> And deem Penelope a courtesan.
>
> (Canto 35, stanza 27)

So here we have a saint, the author of one of the gospels, essentially telling us that history is a pack of lies conjured up by writers to please their wealthy patrons. This is not to suggest that *The Frenzy of Orlando* is a parody. Much of what Ariosto writes he does so in earnest, such as his descriptions of battle scenes and his reflections on the terrible cost of war. In a reference to the 1512 Battle of Ravenna he observes:

> Our present safety, and life held in fear,
> We see assured us by this victory,
> That saved us from the wintry tempest drear,
> Which would have whelmed us from Jove's angry sky.
> But ill can we rejoice, while yet the tear
> Is standing in full many a widow's eye,
> Who weeping and attired in sable, vents,
> Throughout all grieving France, her loud laments.
>
> (Canto 14, stanza 7)

The legacy of Ariosto's sequel has been profound. Tobias Gregory notes that *The Frenzy of Orlando* 'elevated a popular vernacular genre in the direction of classical epic with such success that the two traditions would be thereafter conjoined by the most talented of Ariosto's many imitators.'[4] It was so successful that it overshadowed Boiardo's epic, which remained neglected until the Romantic Revival of the 1800s sparked renewed interest. It had a particular impact upon the English-speaking world – translated into English in 1591 by Sir John Harrington. *The Frenzy of Orlando* was a major influence upon works such as Edmund Spenser's *The Fairy Queen,* Lord Byron's *Don Juan* and Virginia Wolf's *Orlando.* Christopher Marlowe and the great Bard himself drew upon it for ideas. Ariosto was Sir Walter Scott's favourite poet, rating him more highly than Homer, and he re-read *The Frenzy of Orlando* every year. It influenced Stephen King's *Dark Tower* series and, fittingly, the poem finds its way into *Harry Potter* courtesy of Ariosto's invention of the hippogriff. It was a source of inspiration for painters and musicians as well as writers. Handel wrote three operas about it. Across Europe its impact has been immense. Lope de Vega continued the epic with his own *The Beauty of Angelica*, and it is mentioned in Cervantes' *Don Quixote*. It was the source material for Francesca Caccini's 1625 opera *The Liberation of Ruggiero from Alcina's Island.* There had been almost 70 editions by the mid-eighteenth century. In his *Philosophical Dictionary* Voltaire declares: 'It [*The Frenzy of Orlando*] is at once the *Iliad*, the *Odyssey*, and *Don Quixote* … Every canto is like an enchanted palace, the vestibule of which is always in a different taste; sometimes majestic, sometimes simple, and even grotesque. It is moral, lively, or gallant, and always natural and true.'[5] Like Walter Scott, Voltaire rates Ariosto above Homer. There would have been few educated eighteenth-century Europeans who would not have been familiar with Ariosto's epic.

The impact of *The Frenzy of Orlando* was not restricted to the artistic sphere. It was a vehicle for the transmission of an Epicurean conception of the world that was to have a critical impact upon the moral and scientific direction of Enlightenment thought. From the 1450s onwards, there was a growing interest in *On the Nature of Things* in scholarly circles, notably Florence, Rome and Naples. The 1417 discovery of Lucretius's poem had reintroduced Epicurus to Europe, one implication of Epicurus's materialist philosophy being that there were no moral precepts handed down by a divine entity, Christian or otherwise. As already mentioned, pleasure and pain were the divining rods of the good, and the greatest pleasure was tranquillity, a tranquillity to be achieved, at least in part, by combatting fear through the use of reason, especially fear caused by religion and superstition – these being much the same thing from an Epicurean perspective.

The Frenzy of Orlando is infused with Epicurean ideas. Orlando's descent into madness after discovering that his cherished Angelica loves someone else occurs almost exactly halfway through the epic, and there, in the first three stanzas of canto 24, the narrator comments on the relationship between love and madness:

> Let him make haste his feet to disengage,
> Nor lime his wings, whom Love has made a prize;
> For love, in fine, is nought but frenzied rage,
> By universal suffrage of the wise:
> And albeit some may show themselves more sage
> Than Roland, they but sin in other guise.
> For, what proves folly more than on this shelf,
> Thus, for another, to destroy oneself?
>
> (Canto 24, stanza 1)

The first thing to point out is that Ariosto portrays sexual desire as something which is healthy, in contrast to the Church where earthly pleasures unrelated to religious devotion were treated with enormous suspicion and were actively repressed. He is concerned not so much with an abstract spiritual or platonic love that unfolds in some immaterial realm but a desire whose existence is temporal and derived from nature. Nature itself, from the perspective of Epicureanism, is a material phenomenon shaped over eternity by the collision of an infinite number of atoms. Pleasure is an indicator of the good but only as long as it is moderate. It ceases to be pleasure if taken too far. But love is not an emotion which tends towards moderation. The intensity of Orlando's desire for Angelica has sent him insane. He has become disconnected from reality in the same way that those who are superstitious fail to understand the world as it is and are consumed by anxiety. Man is to be saved by philosophy, not religion. For Orlando, being saved means the recovery of his wits from the moon.

In the third stanza of the canto the author reflects upon his own love-lorn situation, and draws what appears to be a parallel between not only himself and Orlando but between himself and Lucretius:

> One here may well reproach me: 'Brother, thou
> Seest not thy faults, while thou dost others fit.'

– I answer that I see mine plain enow,
In this my lucid interval of wit;
And strive and hope withal I shall forego
This dance of folly; but yet cannot quit,
As quickly as I would, the faults I own;
For my disease has reached the very bone.

(Canto 24, stanza 3)

The hostility of Christianity to Epicureanism had led the Church to attempt to discredit and suppress its ideas. They painted it as a philosophy that endorsed unrestrained self-gratification when the opposite was true. In a biographical sketch about Lucretius, written some thousand years before, St Jerome had claimed, 'After a love-philtre had turned him mad, and he had written, in the intervals of his insanity, several books which Cicero revised, he killed himself by his own hand in the forty-fourth year of his age.'[6] Ariosto's 'lucid interval of wit' is clearly interchangeable here with 'in the intervals of his insanity', while at the same time he describes love as a 'disease'.

'It is religion breeds wickedness,' declares Lucretius.[7] Ariosto worked as a diplomat for the Este dynasty and had witnessed some of that wickedness first hand. In 1510, Pope Julius II had threatened to have him thrown into the Tiber, and on another occasion, along with his master Alfonso d'Este, he had to flee Rome in disguise to escape the same pope's wrath. But it would not have been wise in sixteenth-century Italy for a man to openly express his Epicurean scepticism towards religion, either with regards to its doctrinal claims or with regards to the virtue of its agents on Earth. It is through irony that Ariosto voices his doubts. We have seen how he used St John the Evangelist to impugn the truthfulness of the written word. By implication Ariosto is bringing into question divine revelation as recorded in the scriptures. He also depicts prayer as following a straightforward cause and effect model. God is petitioned by a Christian worshipper and duly obliges, thereby putting divine intervention on a par with the other handy magical devices that populate the story. Its spiritual dimension receives little more than lip-service. In canto 38, Astolfo is amassing an army and requests help. In short order, rocks are turned into horses ready for the men to mount. 'O what things may he do / That in the Saviour wholly puts his trust!' observes the narrator.[8] In canto 14, Charlemagne is surrounded by the infidel. Facing imminent defeat, he sends up a prayer. The Christians should be saved, he argues, not so much because they are any better than the Muslims but because if they are defeated it would make God look bad and undermine his own position on Earth:

> And if that they should suffer is thy will,
> And that they should due penance undergo,
> At least delay thy purpose to fulfil,
> So that thine enemies deal not the blow.
> For, when 'tis given him in his wrath to kill
> Us who are deemed thy friends, the heathen foe,
> That thou art without power to save, will cry,
> Because thou lett'st thy faithful people die:
>
> And, for one faithless found, against thy sway
> A hundred shall throughout the world rebel;
> So that false Babel's law will have its way,
> And thus thy blessed faith put down and quell.
> Defend thy suffering people, who are they
> That purged thy tomb from heathen hounds and fell,
> And many times and oft, by foes offended,
> Thy holy church and vicars have defended.
>
> (Canto 14, stanzas 70-71)

The prayer resembles less a man throwing himself upon the mercy of the Almighty than a client lobbying a prince by pointing out that it would be in God's own self-interest to come to his aid. To make matters worse, God seems responsive and does, indeed, intervene. Shortly afterwards, Archangel Michael, carrying out God's orders, comes across a cloister and discovers, in a dig at the clergy and religious orders, that Piety, Humility, Quietude and Love have been driven out by Greed, Avarice, Cruelty, Wrath, Pride, Envy, Sloth and Discord.

Elsewhere he raises questions about the nature of God's justice, fairness and love:

> God, outraged by our rank iniquity,
> Whenever crimes have past remission's bound,
> That mercy may with justice mingled be,
> Has monstrous and destructive tyrants crowned;
> And gifted them with force and subtlety,
> A sinful world to punish and confound.
>
> (Canto 17, stanza 1)

He goes on to record a long list of tyrants including such figures as Sulla, Nero and Attila the Hun down to his own time with Charles VIII of France. Particularly striking is that God even recruits Muslims to be the servants of this divinely ordained vengeance:

> Now God permits that we should feel the spite
> Of people, who are haply worse than we …
>
> The Christian people with God's placid front
> Must have disturbed with their excesses sore:
> Since them with slaughter, rape, and rapine hunt,
> Through all their quarters, plundering Turk and Moor:
>
> (Canto 17, stanza 5-6)

Sinners are invariably punished and the virtuous rewarded, rather like the uncomplicated cause and effect pattern underpinning petitions to God. Ostensibly this all conforms to what any good Christian would expect and hope for. The complexities, ambiguities and contradictions of human experience, where the corrupt often prosper and the innocent suffer without redress, might prompt the reader to suspect whether the reality described by Christian theology is as fanciful as the mythical world of Ariosto's creation into which it has been seamlessly entwined. This impression could only be strengthened by a depiction of God that bears a strong resemblance to Olympian Zeus, an allusion that is unlikely to have been missed by Ariosto's well-educated audience. Here God gives his commands to Archangel Michael, just as Zeus might send down Apollo to help out the Trojans:

> Find Silence first, and bid him, on my part,
> On this emprise attend thee, at thy side:
> Since he for such a quest, with happiest art
> Will know what is most fitting to provide.
> Next, where she sojourns, instantly impart
> To Discord my command, that she, supplied
> With steel and tinder, 'mid the heathens go,
> And fire and flame in their encampment blow;
>
> (Canto 14, stanza 76)

Ariosto has smuggled into his writing the essential concerns that characterise Epicureanism: irrationality; immoderation and the futile endeavour to satisfy unending desires; and the dangers of false beliefs, notably religious beliefs. But how can a person avoid these hazards apart from taking account of the obvious implication that they should be rational and moderate? The primary goal of Epicureanism is tranquillity – in the sense of an absence of physical and psychological pain – and in canto 24 above he indicates the means to accomplish it: we should 'forego / This dance of folly.' It is this quitting of the dance, of withdrawal and detachment, which is the key. One of the ways Ariosto achieves this in his poem is through the use of irony, as we have already discussed, encouraging the audience to step back and re-evaluate the surface meaning that is presented to them. Another way is the intrusiveness of the narratorial voice. His exordiums at the beginning of a canto speaks directly to his readers, pulling them out of the story and emphasising its unreality:

> I recollect that I was bound to sing
> (I promised so, but it escaped my mind)
> Of suspicion, fraught with suffering
> To Bradamante of more displeasing kind
>
> (Canto 32, stanza 1)

The Frenzy of Orlando and Casanova

In a fascinating passage from *History of My Life* which opened the chapter, Casanova recounts how he used *The Frenzy of Orlando* to choose the date of his 1756 escape from the Venetian Inquisition. It is a typically Casanovan mix, illustrating as it does his ambiguous attitude towards religion, fate and supernatural forces, his Socratic belief in a guiding angel or 'Intelligence' (his oracle) and, of course, his love of Ariosto. Drawing on his knowledge of cabbala to discover the date he should attempt his escape from the Leads, he composes a short question the letters of which he then transforms into numbers and creates an inverted pyramid. By applying a simple formula to the pyramid, he identifies the canto, stanza and line that contains the requisite date: 'Between the end of October and the beginning of November.'[9] And this was the date he escaped. The truth of this tale, of course, is open to interpretation. Was it coincidence, unconscious wish fulfilment arising from a detailed knowledge of the text or a light-hearted satire in the vein of Ariosto himself?

Casanova had been smitten by *The Frenzy of Orlando* since the age of 15.[10] The poem was to be a constant presence in his life, whether it was regaling his lovers with its stories, finding parallels between his own life and those of the epic's protagonists, arguing its merits, berating the inadequacy of translations, reciting it, plagiarising it or identifying its connections with places he visited. He claimed to read it two or three times a year and to know pretty much all 40,000 lines by heart.[11]

So what can we say about his relationship with this poem apart from recognising his great affection for it? Did it have a critical impact upon his ideas and behaviour? Or did it simply reinforce attitudes that he already held? Was it a literary model? We must be cautious not to attribute a simple cause and effect between what we find in *The Frenzy of Orlando* and what we observe in Casanova's life and writing. It has been argued that *History of My Life* was based upon it. This is entirely plausible given the common themes of love, travel, revenge and derring-do. At one point in his memoirs Casanova records how he was separated from his lover Bellino after curiosity led him to mount a horse which then bolted across a military border dividing the opposing forces of Austria and Spain. A similar event occurs in *The Frenzy of Orlando*. In the poem, Ruggiero finds himself separated from his beloved after being lured into trying to capture a hippogriff which then flies off with him on its back. It is not hard to find other parallels. But before drawing too many conclusions we need to recognise that these are both gargantuan texts, constructed around numerous and diverse narratives. Early analysis of *The Frenzy of Orlando* was plagued with scholars crediting Ariosto with religious allegories that he almost certainly never intended. There were many other sources of potential influence upon the young Casanova. His mid-teens were a period of enormous intellectual and social development. By the time he discovered Ariosto, he had already been exploring erotic literature in the library of his tutor Dr Gozzi. When he was 15 he became friends with Senator Malipiero, a septuagenarian who introduced him to elite Venetian society, a sophisticated world in which radical and unconventional ideas would have circulated quite freely alongside more orthodox beliefs. And when he was 16 he graduated from the University of Padua as a doctor of law.

All those caveats accepted, it would still be reasonable to expect *The Frenzy of Orlando* to have left a mark on him given his life-long infatuation with it. A good place to start looking would be chivalry, a moral system associated with knighthood which underpinned romance epics. It originated in the twelfth century, during the period of the early crusades, becoming a popular subject of the literature of the High Middle Ages.

Its devotees were expected to maintain the faith, be of service to others, demonstrate courage and generosity, spurn monetary gain, respect a person's honour, especially that of a woman, as well as possess a heightened sense of their own honour, and be sensitive to courtly etiquette (itself closely tied to conceptions of honour). By the eighteenth century this suite of virtues also encompassed intellectual skill and witty conversation.

Casanova's memoirs reveal countless instances of just such qualities. They are so numerous it is reasonable to conclude that his own moral code had been substantially shaped by the knightly ideals exemplified in *The Frenzy of Orlando*. The words 'honour', 'dishonour', 'honourable' and so forth occur over 800 times in *History of My Life*.[12] Some of these are used as terms of address or expressions of politeness but many do refer to honour in this more chivalric sense. Casanova was an active participant in the duelling culture of his time. He cites revenge as a fundamental principle of sentient life. He rides to the aid of damsels in distress. His attitude to money, honour and assisting others is brought out neatly in an episode where he is the guest of an impoverished noble. The noble was significantly in debt to Casanova financially, including the recent additional cost of two pieces of taffeta for his wife which the count asked him to add to what he owed: 'I replied, embracing him, that he had only to add them on himself, since my custom was never to record that money with which I found myself only too happy to be able to oblige my friends.'[13]

Closely related to chivalry was courtly love, a conception of love that takes place outside of wedlock in which the lover idolises the object of their affections to the extent that they are always possessed by the thought of them and what might please them. It is a secret love which diminishes if it becomes public and is intensified by jealousy. The love object is particularly prized if they are difficult to obtain. A major component of any moral code heavily invested in notions of honour is the etiquette and the skill with which individuals are able to negotiate that particular minefield. Needless to say, Casanova excelled in the elaborate games of manners and conversational interplay between the sexes, in which sensitivity, discretion and deniability were essential.

As with chivalry more generally, *History of My Life* is rich with scenarios and sentiments that underscore Casanova's embrace of the ideals of courtly love. With echoes of *The Frenzy of Orlando*, he talks of his how his love for Henriette has put him into a 'great paroxysm' and that he finds 'the extent of my happiness too much for my faculties'.[14,15] He declares to Henriette that 'I want to be your only lover, on condition … that you will make me worthy of your favours only when I have discovered how to deserve them by my care, and by my attentions, and by all that I will do for you with a submission to which you will have never seen an equal.'[16] He observes that 'it is a great pleasure to do whatever the object of one's love commands.'[17] Again and again, he has to overcome obstacles and resistance to his love. He falls in love with the 'castrato' Bellino when he is 18. Her 'family' drive him to despair by refusing to confirm his suspicion that she is a woman until, eventually, he wins her over. When he falls in love with CC he finds himself confronted by his own carnal desires, a scheming elder brother who is angling to sell her virginity to him, and a protective father. When courting Dona Ignacia the main obstacle to his conquest is religion and her piety. Repeatedly Casanova records how the strain of lost or not-yet-requited love makes him unwell, resonant of the experiences of Ariosto's protagonists. Here is Angelica nursing Medore:

> Her ill [i.e. her love] but festered and increased the more
> The stripling's wounds were seen to heal and close:
> The youth grew lusty, while she suffered sore,
> And, with new fever parched, now burnt, now froze:
> From day to day in beauty waxed Medore:
> She miserably wasted; like the snow's
> Unseasonable flake, which melts away
> Exposed, in sunny place, to scorching ray.
>
> (Canto 19, stanza 29)

Casanova's adoption of the title Chevalier de Seingalt in 1759 is more evidence that he self-consciously identified himself with knightly traditions. 'Chevalier', of course, is French for 'knight'. 'Seingalt', on the other hand, was entirely his own creation, (possibly he was inspired by Voltaire, the man he tried to emulate and who changed his name from François-Marie Arouet):

> 'Why,' he [a German magistrate] asked me, 'do you have a false name?'
>
> 'My name is not false. Find out from the banker Carli who paid me fifty thousand florins.'
>
> 'I know that, but your name is Casanova and not Seingalt – why this last name?'

> 'I take this name, or rather I took it, because it is mine. It belongs to me so legitimately that if anyone dared to use it, I would contest it by all ways and means.'
>
> 'And how does this name belong to you?'
>
> 'Because I am the author.'[18]

And that is about as much as anybody knows. A linguist, accomplished writer and master of cabbala, Casanova revelled in words and wordplay so it may be that Seingalt is an anagram. 'Genitals' has been suggested (although it does not quite fit the French, 'génitales', the Italian, 'genitale' or the German 'Genitalien'). For what it is worth, my own speculative theory is that it is indeed an anagram, but an anagram of 'angelist' as in 'evangelist' (and as in 'Evangelist' in German). An angelist is someone who holds unorthodox views about angels, which was the case with Casanova. Remember, he believed that he was guided by a guardian angel or oracle. At university he very likely studied eudaemonism, a philosophy of ethics with eudaemonia, or happiness, as its goal. 'Daemon' is ancient Greek (which Casanova understood) for spirit and 'eu-' (interchangeable with 'ev-') means good. 'Eudaemonia', therefore, carries a similar meaning to guardian angel. What is more, St John the Evangelist is a character in *The Frenzy of Orlando*. Given that there is some doubt over the consistent goodness of Casanova's angel, it would make sense that 'ev-' is not included as part of the anagram.

A striking similarity between Ariosto and Casanova was their admiration for women, in particular strong and independent women. In the case of Ariosto this may have been pragmatic given that his primary audience at the Este court included a number of women who were highly educated and influential. For Casanova it was an attraction that was more profound. Much of the narrative of *The Frenzy of Orlando* is driven by powerful female protagonists. Bradamante, the sister of Rinaldo, is one of the two greatest knights of Emperor Charlemagne, Orlando being the other. And Bradamante is recognised as being every bit as good a warrior as her brother. In her first appearance she is initially assumed to be a man, dressed in knight's armour and defeating King Sacripante in a duel before disappearing into the forest. Elsewhere she disguises herself as a man and is commonly confused with her brother as they resemble each other so closely. She falls in love with Ruggiero, a noble Saracen warrior with an impeccable pedigree but, being from opposite sides of the tracks, their love appears hopeless, torn as

Bradamante is between her love for Ruggiero and her duty to her family. This becomes the central storyline. After various adventures, eventually they are united and wed, with Ruggiero converting to Christianity.

As for Casanova, recall that two of his great loves, Bellino and Henriette, he met for the first time when they were disguised as men. His love of Henriette was particularly intense, and in a parallel with the Angelica-Medore narrative, there was the tension between Henriette's love for Casanova and Casanova's lowly status. Henriette possessed all the qualities Casanova prized in a woman. She was beautiful, without 'prejudices', accomplished, highly educated, witty, and with refined tastes and sensibility. Above all he admired her courage. Like himself, Henriette was an adventurer, a risk-taker who was prepared to defy social convention despite the enormous potential costs. In short, she was his ideal. It is hard to imagine that Casanova's taste in women was not in some way influenced by *The Frenzy of Orlando*, steeped in its universe and ethic as he was, nor that he did not identify specific similarities between Henriette, Bradamante and Angelica (and himself as the low-born Medore), similarities that would no doubt have made Henriette all the more alluring. Neither would it be surprising if Casanova's knowledge of the poem had shaped his description of their affair, heightening the drama and romance of the tale while at the same time drawing out the parallels between the events of his own life and those of Ariosto's protagonists. A few years later he found himself in thrall to another Bradamantine woman, although this relationship was to be far more of a physical one. That was the nun identified as MM, also an aristocrat. Like Henriette she was beautiful, witty, self-confident, highly educated, a risk-taker who was willing to defy social convention, and even more so than Henriette, without 'prejudices'. And like Henriette, she dressed as a man on occasion.

In other respects, too, we can find similarities between Ariosto and Casanova. The writings of both are characterised by good humour, playfulness and wry observations about the foibles of mankind. When Barbara Reynolds, a translator of *The Frenzy of Orlando*, highlights Ariosto's 'irrepressible laughter … his delight in the absurd … his witty and subtle double meanings … his joy in friendship,' she could just as well be describing Casanova.[19] In the final preface to *History of My Life,* written when he was 72 (the year before he died), he describes his adventures as 'youthful madness' and declares, 'You will see that I laugh at it and if you are kind you will laugh at it with me.'[20] Casanova happily exposes his pretensions, betrayals and self-regard. When he was an adjutant on Corfu the 20-year-old was smitten by a Madame F, the wife of a superior officer, who initially paid so little attention to him that she did not even know his name despite having been in his company for two weeks: 'I found myself all the more piqued, annoyed, and impatient because I could not conjecture that she avoided my eyes by force of premeditated design. That wouldn't have bothered me. But I found myself convinced that for her I was nothing. It was too much. I knew I was something, and I meant for her to know it too. '[21]

Casanova's vivid descriptions and lengthy dialogues draw the readers close to the world of Casanova's past where, like that of *The Frenzy of Orlando*, fate, chance and irony abound. It is a world where a steamy affair with a nun introduces him to a French ambassador who is later chosen by Louis XV as his chief minister of state. That chief minister then becomes Casanova's protector after he flees Venice, introducing him to the French court, with all the benefits from those social connections which ensued. Like Ariosto, Casanova embeds the stories of other narrators within his own account, such as those of his lovers Pauline and Bellino, adding variation of voice and perspective. While the declarations of constancy and eternal love pile up as Casanova duels with the numerous objects of his desire, the audience is pulled into the narration, parsing the likely discrepancy between the spoken intentions of the participants and the probable outcomes. When he declares to Mademoiselle de la M-re, 'You shall be my wife,' and she succumbs to his advances, the reader has a pretty shrewd idea as to the direction of travel the relationship is going to take.[22] 'I was in love with this young lady,' he later observes, 'but Silvia's daughter [Manon] … weakened a love that left nothing more for me to desire.'[23]

Reflections on his affair with Mademoiselle de la M-re brings out another parallel with Ariosto. Casanova opines: 'We complain of women who, in spite of loving us, and being sure that they are loved, refuse us their favours; and we are wrong. If these women love us, they must be afraid of losing us, and therefore they must do all they can to keep alive the desire that we have to succeed in possessing them. If we achieve this, it is certain that we will no longer desire them, because we do not desire what we have: women are therefore right to refuse our desires.'[24] This intrusiveness of Casanova the narrator, to make some broader moral, social or philosophical point directly to the audience, is a feature of Ariosto's own literary style. *The Frenzy of Orlando*'s various plots and numerous characters, with the action often overlapping in time, make it immensely complex. By using a technique called *entrelacement* Ariosto breaks into the narrative to announce a shift in the action (often at critical dramatic moments) and to clarify to the audience what is going on. Likewise, at the beginning of each canto he also steps outside of the narrative. Here, similar to Casanova, he reflects upon the character of men and women:

> A woman for the most part reasons best
> Upon a sudden motion, and untaught;
> …
> But man, of a less nimble wit possessed,
> Is ill at counsel, save, with sober thought,
> He ruminates thereon, content to spend
> Care, time and trouble to mature his end.
>
> (Canto 27, stanza 1)

It is no surprise that Casanova should have found *The Frenzy of Orlando* appealing, not only because he was a proud Italian but because it was so infused with the spirit of Epicurus. This is not to say that Casanova was an Epicurean or that his ideas were not affected by other streams of thought. There is, nonetheless, a clear path that leads from Epicurus to Casanova. At the same time that he was immersing himself in Horace, Ariosto and *The Frenzy of Orlando*, he was also introduced to Pierre Gassendi, the seventeenth-century scholar who attempted to reconcile Epicureanism with Christianity. It can be added that Casanova was also profoundly influenced by sensationalism and libertinism, both of which drew heavily upon Epicurus.

There is a fundamental humanity and tolerance at the heart of Ariosto's writing which corresponds with, and likely helped to form, Casanova's own view of the world. For both men, pleasure and sexual desire are to be embraced as a part of what it is to be human, not scorned as something injurious and corrupt. They recognised, and were fascinated by, the complexities of life, rejecting simplistic generalisations. They also abhorred the suffering inflicted upon the world by superstition, ignorance and religious dogmatism.

Chapter 4
Pierre Gassendi: 1592–1655

> 'The doctrine of the Stoics, and of every other sect, on the force of Destiny is a fantasy of the imagination that is rooted in atheism. I am not only monotheistic, but a Christian fortified by philosophy, which has never spoiled anything.'
>
> Giacomo Casanova, *History of My Life*

Pierre Gassendi was highly thought of by a wide range of key Enlightenment figures, including Diderot and Voltaire. He was a scholar of immense significance, if lesser known than Bacon, Descartes, Hobbes, Newton, Locke and Spinoza. Gassendi connects the philosophers of ancient Greece with the scientists of today, illuminating the transition from the world of the Middle Ages into the modern world. He is important for anyone interested in tracing the materialist ideas that anchored Casanova's libertinism. Casanova was introduced to Gassendi's writings when he was 15 by his patron Senator Malipiero, at least in part as an antidote to the teachings of Aristotle.

Gassendi was born in the village of Champtercier in the south of France, the frail child of a peasant farmer, and went on to study philosophy and theology. He was a gifted student, obtaining a doctorate in theology in 1614 when he was 24. In 1616 he was ordained a priest, eventually rising to become provost of the Cathedral Chapter of Digne in 1634, and in 1617 he obtained the chair of philosophy at the University of Aix-en-Provence where he lectured on Aristotle. Around that time, he lodged with the vicar general of Aix, Joseph Gaultier, an accomplished astronomer. It was from Gaultier that he acquired much of his knowledge of astronomy. Gassendi was subsequently forced out of his post at Aix in 1622 or 1623, along with other non-Jesuits, when the Jesuits assumed control of the university.

In the same year that he was awarded his chair of philosophy, he befriended the nobleman and influential magistrate Nicolas-Claude Fabri de Peiresc, a well-known humanist scholar and amateur astronomer who was to become his patron. The magistrate was sympathetic to Bacon's idea that natural philosophy should be pursued in order to advance the well-being of one's fellow citizens. Taking advantage of the closeness of Provence to Italy, for a period he studied under Galileo in Padua, the two becoming friends. Peiresc was later to intercede on Galileo's behalf in an attempt to have his sentence reduced. Shortly after Galileo discovered Jupiter's four moons in 1610 Peiresc had an observatory constructed at his home and employed Gaultier and Gassendi to record their movements. He recognised that Jupiter's moons might be useful as a way of more accurately establishing longitude. This was a matter of considerable practical importance for sea travel. In 1598 Philip III of Spain had offered a pension to anybody who was able to solve the problem. Unfortunately, the observations of the trio were not sufficiently precise, and the attempt failed. But Peiresc's efforts did pay off in other respects. In 1610 he discovered the great nebula of Orion (although he did not publish his findings).

Peiresc introduced Gassendi to the intellectual circles of Marin Mersenne, a key facilitator of European scholarly debate. Mersenne was a friar, mathematician and polymath, and dubbed 'the secretary of learned Europe'. He engaged and corresponded with the foremost thinkers of the day, including Descartes who was also a friend. Mersenne put scholars in touch with each other, communicated information, raised theoretical queries, translated texts and supplied and published books (including one of Hobbes's optical treatises). It was largely Mersenne who introduced Galileo to France. And it was Mersenne who in 1641 organised the famous scholarly debate around Descartes' *Meditations*. From 1633 Mersenne was at the centre of regular weekly meetings of mathematicians and physicists in Paris, meetings that inspired a number of significant mathematical discoveries. Its attendees were to include luminaries such as Blaise Pascal, Pierre de Fermat and Gilles de Roberval. Known as the Academia Parisiensi, it was a precursor in many ways to London's Royal Society and Paris's Academy of Sciences. These informal networks highlight how new radical theories and ideas were able to sidestep the constraints of formal educational institutions such as universities that were controlled by the Church.

The activities of Mersenne and the scholars with whom he communicated were a symptom of the crisis of authority that had been convulsing Europe since the Reformation. Men such as Mersenne, Gassendi and Descartes were in the vanguard of those trying to work through the implications of the epistemological challenge this crisis raised. How was knowledge possible in the absence of textual authority? One answer, to be found in the works of ancient sceptics such as Pyrrho and Timon, was that it wasn't. Descartes' response, as we have seen, was to attempt to build the foundations of knowledge on the certainty of the existence of the individual self. This epistemological individualism, while discarding the Aristotelian explanation of natural phenomena, accepted Aristotle's premise that scientific knowledge had to be certain and absolute.

From 1621 until 1637 Gassendi was actively involved in international debates, travelling to Paris in 1623 to meet with Mersenne. The two became close and lifelong friends, Mersenne encouraging Gassendi's work and introducing him to thinkers such as Hobbes. Soon after his return from Paris, Gassendi struck up a correspondence with Galileo. In 1628, again in Paris, Gassendi made the acquaintance of the Dupuy brothers who were the keepers of the King's Library. They had travelled throughout France amassing a large collection of books and manuscripts. Under their care were works by Epicurus which Gassendi now began to investigate. The following year he visited the learned and influential Dutch schoolmaster Isaac Beeckman. Beeckman was a natural philosopher who had inspired a young Descartes in 1618. Descartes dedicated his *Compendium of Music* (*Compendium Musicae*) to him, and they worked together on the physics of falling bodies. Beeckman never published his ideas or discoveries but maintained correspondence with important scholars across Europe. Gassendi praised him to Peiresc as 'the best philosopher I have yet met.'[1] Beeckman embraced the Epicurean concept of a mechanistic universe composed of atoms and the void, albeit with reservations about the nature of atoms.

Affected by the death of Peiresc in 1637, and going on to write Peiresc's biography, for the next couple of years Gassendi stayed aloof of public scholarly disputes. But such was Gassendi's growing stature that in a little while he acquired a new and more powerful protector in the form of the governor of Provence, Louis Emmanuel de Valois. In 1640 Gassendi was involved in controversy over whether the Earth was fixed or in motion around the Sun. Correspondence with Galileo make it clear that Gassendi had favoured heliocentrism for many years. He even provided

Galileo with astronomical observations which lent support to the Italian's claims. But in public he was cautious and maintained that he was not committed to Copernicanism. In one dispute he had challenged criticisms of Copernicanism, opening himself up to charges of heresy. His defence highlights the careful line he had to tread, and his reluctance in this case to question the literality of scripture: 'I did this not to assert the motion of the Earth but from a love of truth, to suggest that its rest should be established on firmer reasoning.'[2] This raises the question of the kind of risks Gassendi was running by engaging in such debates. Antonia Lolordo observes: 'despite the fact that he held views that could easily have been seen as heterodox Gassendi never encountered any difficulties with church authorities. This shows how carefully Gassendi formulated his views and how important the patronage networks he belonged to were.'[3]

In 1645 he was awarded the post of professor of mathematics at the Collège Royal in Paris on the strength of his expertise in astronomy. He stayed there for three years until his health deteriorated, conducting lectures and astronomical research, in the latter case with the assistance of the astronomer Jean Picard, the first man to measure accurately the size of the Earth. In 1647 Gassendi published *On the Life and Character of Epicurus* in which he attempted to rehabilitate Epicurus's tarnished moral reputation, subject as he had been to accusations of debauchery and excess by his opponents, pagan and Christian. What else might you expect from a philosophy based on the maximisation of pleasure? It was, of course, a wilful misrepresentation of Epicurus and Epicureanism. In reality, he lived an existence of frugality and moderation. Gassendi sought to show that both the man's behaviour and his ideas were consistent with the doctrines of the Catholic faith. In the same year he published *Astronomical Instruction*, an astronomy textbook which, among other things, dismantled arguments that astrology had the power to predict the weather and the fortunes of men. He pointed out not only the faulty logical basis for its truth claims but how such predictions could be harmful by producing false expectations.

Gassendi also took aim at scholasticism. Along with others, he was critical of its inability to make discoveries and generate new knowledge about the world. Its object was to demonstrate the inviolable truth of what was already known and to teach the logic and tools required to confirm it. But logic itself, Gassendi argued, could not distinguish between what was true and false, a point which was to be echoed by John Locke. Gassendi attacked its concern with definitions and categories, and its failure to examine nature directly. He believed that to understand cause you needed to adopt an inductive method, reasoning from the evidence of effects rather than deduction from abstract ideas and universal principles. He dismissed the value of Platonic forms and essences.

In 1641 and 1642 Descartes had published his *Meditations* which outlined his method of hyperbolic doubt as a way of determining true knowledge, and his claim to be able to prove the existence of God. The two editions included criticisms of Descartes' ideas by a number of eminent scholars along with his replies to them. Gassendi's response was published in the second edition as the fifth set of objections, and in it he attacked Descartes' failure to establish the reality of innate ideas as opposed to an individual's belief in that reality, which could be false. As a defence against solipsism, Descartes had asserted that clear and distinct innate ideas must be true. Gassendi also highlighted the mind-body problem. In response, Descartes posited the idea of a mind-body union which made the question of interaction redundant. A similar causal problem afflicted the Aristotelian-scholastic tradition and some Renaissance Neo-Platonists. By what mechanism could a Platonic form or essence, or particle of an incorporeal world soul in the case of Renaissance Neo-Platonism, interact with material substance? The flaw had been pointed out almost two millennia earlier by Epicurus in his letter to Herodotus: 'those who maintain that the soul is incorporeal are talking nonsense, because it would not be able to act upon or be acted upon if it were of such a nature.'[4]

Gassendi's own approach to the epistemological problem of the foundation of knowledge rejected both the fatalism of the ancient sceptics and the requirement for absolute certainty demanded by Aristotle and Descartes. For Gassendi, scientific knowledge could only be probabilistic, dependent upon the strength of the material evidence and argument that supported it. The stronger the evidence, the more probable the truth claim. But the empirical nature of such knowledge always allowed the possibility of contradictory evidence being discovered at some future point. Gassendi's assertion that he was not committed to Copernicanism was, in this light, a position he could take with a clear conscience. The assertion that knowledge acquired from observation could never be absolute resolved possible tensions between the judgements of human reason and the dictates of faith, in favour of faith. Locke adopted a similarly probabilistic approach to knowledge. It is possible that Gassendi's ideas influenced Locke's thinking, either directly from Gassendi's own works or through the works of, or contact with, others, such as the French physician François Bernier, although the evidence is sparse.[5] Certainly today it is Gassendi and Locke's probabilistic conception of knowledge which dominates scientific thought.

Supporters of mechanical philosophy believed in action by contact rather than attractive forces and action at a distance. It was an understanding of the universe that was at the core of Epicureanism and its desire to reduce human suffering. To combat sources of anxiety such as fear of the gods and punishment in the afterlife, Epicurus sought to rule out divine intervention. He wanted to explain all phenomena in the natural and human world in mechanical and materialistic terms. He rejected the idea that the universe was created by divine beings. Instead, he suggested that an infinite number of eternal and indivisible atoms coalesced according to natural laws to create the forms and structures of nature. The universe was made up entirely of atoms and void; there was no purposeful order underpinning the cosmos, only the incomprehensible determinism of colliding atoms. For all intents and purposes our world was a creation of happenstance. The soul too was composed of atoms. The atoms of the soul provide sensations and the experience of pain and pleasure, and account for rationality. As the soul is constructed from atoms, when the body dies, the soul dies with it, and there can be no pain or punishment after death. There is no essence or abstract form of the good. Pleasure and pain become indicators of what is good or bad. Through our reason we should aim over our lifetime to maximise pleasure and minimise pain. In Epicurean philosophy, virtue and happiness are detached from any spiritual foundation.

Consistent with this materialism, Epicurus contended that truth claims about the world should be based upon empirical evidence mediated by logical deduction. This latter principal contrasted strongly with the practice of scholasticism, whose claims about the world were founded upon abstract theorising. What was important for scholars of the Middle Ages was the internal consistency of their ideas. Aristotle, Plato, the authors of the scriptures and St Augustine, among others, had provided them with a conceptual framework that explained reality both philosophically and theologically. Their job was to demonstrate how natural phenomena fitted into that framework. Evidence from the natural world could not validate or invalidate that framework, it could only illustrate it.

Epicurean philosophy enabled Gassendi to construct alternative solutions to the intellectual challenges bedevilling a world dominated by scholasticism. But although the rehabilitation of Epicurus was one of the major projects of his life, he could not himself be described as an Epicurean. Gianni Paganini observes that, 'In general Gassendi's "Neo-Epicurean" system is no mere recapitulation of ancient material, but takes account both of the new scientific philosophy of the seventeenth century and of Christian doctrine.'[6] Gassendi hypothesised, for example, that desires and emotions that originated in the immaterial mind affected the mechanical operations of the body, central to which was the heart, drawing upon William Harvey's discovery of the heart as a mechanical pump.

In this way, Gassendi accepted some ideas but modified and rejected others. He largely accepted Epicurean hedonism in equating pleasure as a good and, vice versa, the idea that what is good should be judged in terms of the pleasure it generates. Yet he believed that a truly pleasurable life could only be achieved by God. The best that man could hope for would be a relatively good life. Despite his criticisms of scholasticism, he never wavered in his loyalty to the Catholic Church or in his belief in the correctness of its theology. Where Christian theology and Epicurean philosophy clashed, he chose the side of Christian theology.

Borrowing from the Epicurean proposition that the universe was composed of atoms and void, Gassendi provided a coherent account of how macro-level physical structures and behaviour could be related to the inherent properties of atoms at a micro-level, allowing him to ditch the Platonic idea that the motions of animate creatures had an internal cause (the soul). Existence based on atomism appealed to him as it allowed God more flexibility to intervene in creation than did the immutable essences of things as suggested by Aristotelian thought. It meant that Christian belief in a creator could be compatible with understanding nature in terms of its component elements. But he rejected the Epicurean claim that the number and types of atoms were infinite, and that atoms and the void were eternal, as this could imply that God did not have the power to create, destroy and preserve as he so wished. Likewise, he rejected the Epicurean idea that nature exists in the forms it does by a random mechanical process of atoms compounding together. He supported orthodox Christian theology that all creation was a consequence of divine will, and adopted the Aristotelian teleological view that nature behaves the way it does because it has a purpose which is intrinsic to its being. He also diverged from Epicurean thought in other ways: he believed that true happiness required divine providence and that the soul was immortal.

The empirical stance that Gassendi adopts in his criticism of Descartes and the Aristotelians rests upon the relationship between sense perception and knowledge. The only access we have to the natural world is through our senses. All our knowledge about nature is derived from the information they provide. As we cannot perceive essences, universals or immaterial, non-extended entities then we cannot claim to have knowledge of them. They may or may not exist, we simply cannot know. And even the knowledge we can possess will be uncertain to a greater or lesser degree, given the subjective variation of sense experience. Reason is no better, as far as Gassendi is concerned, as its judgements of reality will be undermined by flawed and partial information. Indeed, knowledge derived from reason would be even less reliable as the problem of faulty or incomplete information would be compounded by the fact that reason itself is liable to make mistakes. He does allow for the possibility of knowledge of entities only indirectly experienced, that is, through the effect they have on entities that we can experience. Nonetheless, whatever knowledge we possess about the natural world will still only ever be probable and open to contradiction. Scientific experimentation and observation would allow us to make judgements as to how probable or improbable were any particular claims to knowledge. This was not the same as theologically derived knowledge which he believed did allow the possibility of certainty.

Examples of Gassendi's hands-on interest in empirical science can be found in his work in astronomy, optics and mechanics, with all the practicalities of instrumentation and measurements that entailed. He made extensive astronomical observations to be able to calculate planetary positions, suggesting, as mentioned, that his sympathies lay with heliocentrism. He explored the problem of trying to work out longitude by reference to lunar eclipses. He used a camera obscura to attempt to calculate the diameter of the moon. In Paris on 7 November 1631 Gassendi was able to confirm for the first time Kepler's prediction of the transit of Mercury across the face of the Sun. He observed the event by projecting an image of the Sun through a telescope in a darkened room onto a white screen. Gassendi speculated on the attributes of vision and light, the elasticity of air, and considered the nature of forces acting upon a falling body. In one experiment he confirmed the conclusions of a Galileo thought experiment by dropping a stone from a moving ship, demonstrating that the stone conserved its horizontal speed. Gassendi undertook the earliest attempt to work out the speed of sound by measuring the difference between seeing the flash of a gun and hearing its shot. He calculated it to be 478.4 metres per second (the actual speed is 331.29 metres).

A good example of the exchange and propagation of ideas that was taking place in the seventeenth century beyond formal academic institutions can be observed in the relationship between Gassendi and Hobbes, who became close friends. Hobbes's account of nature rooted in mechanical motion was substantially influenced by his contact with Gassendi and the Mersenne circle in the mid-1630s. It was during this time when Hobbes was visiting Paris that Gassendi was developing his model of a universe based upon inertial and continuous mobility of atoms in a void universe. In 1642, the year of Galileo's death and the year before the birth of Sir Isaac Newton, Gassendi was to be the first thinker to publish the correct formulation of the principle of inertia, this principal being that objects will continue in a straight line at a constant velocity unless acted upon by another force. For Gassendi, the movement of atoms was due to a faculty or force that existed within the atom itself. On this view, matter was not passive but possessed of an intrinsic compulsion to move. This atomic motion, he argued, was an attribute of divine will, its precise nature being dependent upon God's purpose. Hobbes was to argue that by such action of matter in motion both the natural world and the people in it are determined in every respect. A person's behaviour will vary as a response to the external and internal motions of objects acting upon sense perceptions in the same way as the direction of any object of matter will vary in response to the action of another force. The instinct for self-preservation, experiences of pleasure and pain, and the operation of reason will dictate the behaviour of the subject. There is no immaterial soul at play in any part in this equation.

This thoroughgoing determinism inevitably denied the possibility of free will in its incompatibilist sense. The ethical significance for Hobbes was that a necessary cause was a sufficient cause. What an individual desires is what they perceive to be good, and what they have an aversion to is what they perceive to be bad. This self-interest generates a subjective, relativist morality as opposed to an absolutist account of what is good and bad, as is typical of a religion such as Christianity. For Hobbes, individuals left to their own devices would be driven to engage in a 'war of all against all' that could only be avoided by means of a social contract in which men and women cede their freedom to act to a supreme authority such as a sovereign.

As Gassendi's thought was influential in shaping the ideas of Hobbes so Hobbes's account of the operation of pain and pleasure influenced Gassendi. For Hobbes, like inertial motion, a person will aim to continue in a pleasurable state and avoid death, the cessation of movement. Both the behaviour of atoms and the behaviour of people are purely mechanical processes. Gassendi takes Hobbes's concept of pleasure as a phenomenon which shapes human actions and integrates them with Christian metaphysics.

In Gassendi's philosophy pleasure becomes an instrument of providential guidance. As God instils atoms with perpetual motion, so God instils people with a desire for pleasure. Gassendi also gives reason a more dynamic role in decision making than Hobbes's pleasure and pain arithmetic, adopting the free will position of Epicurus. To do so Gassendi must address the dilemma of determinism. If God uses pleasure to guide man to the good, and all actions in nature are based upon atomic mechanical processes, then where is there any space for free will? And free will, of course, was the central Christian defence against the charge that if God created all things then God must also have created evil. Gassendi resolves the problem by drawing on his contention that knowledge of the natural world can only ever be probabilistic. Sense perception, the ultimate foundation of our knowledge of the natural world, would always be subjective and imperfect. Movement toward the good could not be mechanically determined but required the corrective action of reason (itself very fallible).

Gassendi's interpretation of Epicureanism had implications beyond physics.[7] He himself theorised on the deeper political importance of Epicureanism. He took a more positive utilitarian view than Hobbes of people's innate sociability and willingness to cooperate for mutually beneficial ends. Gassendi's Neo-Epicurean perspective drew Enlightenment thinkers along a new path. On subjects such as politics, ethics, justice, the law, medicine and economics, it encouraged scholars to divorce speculation about non-material Platonic forms or the nature and operation of the divine from their examination of society. Pleasure, happiness and the need for self-preservation were seen increasingly as natural forces that directed human behaviour. Moreover, the priorities that these forces engendered acquired a moral significance that could not simply be dismissed by reference to religious doctrines and norms. Gassendi's Neo-Epicureanism represented a conceptual shift that helped to establish the modern idea of universal and inalienable human rights and, via social contract theorists, led to a re-evaluation of the relationship between rulers, the ruled and the institutions of the state. Where the state could not ensure the happiness of its citizens, the state at least ought not get in the way of those citizens' own attempts to obtain it. Whether by stepping aside or being proactively engaged, the state had a utilitarian role to play. The desire for happiness was seen less as a purely individual affair and more as an aspiration that was legitimately connected to the way society as a whole was managed.

In the late 1640s Gassendi released further major works on Epicurus. Around that time, he suffered from a spell of ill health which led him to return to Provence from Paris. His health improved and he continued to work, travelling back to Paris in 1653 where he was to spend the last two years of his life. In 1654 and 1655 he suffered further bouts of illness and despite his objections was subjected to bleeding by his doctors, which likely hastened his death.

Gassendi's reputation, and the importance of his legacy in philosophy and science, is being somewhat rehabilitated having been overshadowed by Descartes. He was well known among British thinkers, and his influence upon major figures such as Hobbes, Boyle, Newton and Hume are being increasingly recognised. Gassendi's role in the rediscovery of Epicurus and the revival of the ideas of the ancient Greek sceptics has led to claims that he had sympathies with atheism and philosophical libertinism. The former is almost certainly untrue and the latter unlikely. After his death, French and English translations of his work (he wrote in Latin) enhanced his reputation, and for several generations his ideas continued to spread, finding their way into the curriculum of educational institutions in France, England, Italy and even North America.

Chapter 5
Libertinism

'In Venice there was not a greater libertine than myself.'
Giacomo Casanova, *History of My Life*

'The mythic character who had so swiftly taken hold as the emblem of libertinism was not merely French, but European: this mythic figure was a man whose life transcended all national cultures, social conditions, and different literary genres. In the final reckoning it is perhaps the figure of Giacomo Casanova that the libertinism of enlightenment Europe has left its most powerful legacy.'
Jean-Christophe Abramovici, *Encyclopedia of the Enlightenment*

God's anarchist

'Libertine' is a term frequently used to describe Casanova, popularly understood today to be 'a person who is unrestrained by convention or morality … one leading a dissolute life' (Merriam-Webster online dictionary). It can also mean, disparagingly, 'a freethinker especially in religious matters' (again, Merriam-Webster) although this usage is probably one with which people are less familiar.

The word arose in the fourteenth century to signify a freed slave or 'freedman' (derived from the Latin *libertinus*) although its negative moral associations did not appear until the sixteenth century and were the result of religious doctrinal and political conflicts triggered by the protestant reformation. 'Libertine' seems to have been first used in a derogatory sense by the second-generation, French-protestant reformer and theologian John Calvin (1509–1564), a central figure in the establishment of the Reformed tradition commonly known as Calvinism. His key work was the *Institutes of the Christian Religion* (*Institutio Christianae Religionis)*, published in 1536, a textbook on the Protestant faith. Calvin's teachings emphasized predestination and that the Bible was the ultimate authority in defining truth. Persecution of protestant dissenters in France led Calvin to flee to Switzerland in 1534, eventually settling in the city-state of Geneva which had recently embraced the Reformation and become a magnet for protestant refugees. There he was involved in the struggle to develop and establish a form of Church government known as Reformed or Presbyterian.

Calvin was opposed by several groups during this struggle in the late 1540s and early 1550s. It was one these, the Spirituels, that Calvin labelled Libertines. This was a reference to the Acts of the Apostles in the New Testament where a group of Hellenistic Jews fell into a dispute with Stephen at the Synagogue of the Freedmen (hence Libertines from *libertini*). Stephen won the dispute but the Jews falsely accused him of blasphemy to avenge their humiliation, leading him to being stoned to death, and becoming the first Christian martyr. The Spirituels attracted particular support from among the social elites of French society, managing to convert several thousand and gaining the favour of Queen Marguerite of Navarre (1527–1549).

It would appear that the Spirituels believed God's grace exempted them from Church or civil law and that they were subject only to their own will and desires. According to Calvin, their interpretation of divine providence denied the reality of free will, and therefore denied the reality of sin, evil and the devil. He claimed that Libertines wanted 'to turn Heaven and Earth upside down, to annihilate all religion, to efface all knowledge of human understanding, to deaden consciences, and to leave no distinction between men and beasts.'[1] First-hand accounts published by members of the sect appear to have been lost so there will always be uncertainty about the doctrine and practices of the Spirituels. Historians are reliant upon the writings of political and theological opponents such as Calvin whose criticisms are unlikely to be impartial. Mirjan Van Veen comments, 'It can be questioned for example whether Calvin's accusation about the libertines' lack of morality and their polygamy was in accordance with the facts. It is very well imaginable that these accusations were part of the reformer's tactic of discrediting his opponents.'[2]

'Libertine' gradually became a pejorative term for unorthodox Christian groups such as Antinomians, Anabaptists, Ranters, Millenarians, Apostolics, Seekers and so on. A range of heretical beliefs could be found among these groups: that the sins of those chosen by God and predestined for salvation could not be described as sins; that sin was a regenerative act; that the differences between religions were unimportant; that there was no hell; that your actions on Earth are irrelevant to whether you will be saved. Sects such as the Seekers were anticlerical, rejecting all forms of organised cults and ceremonies, casting doubt on many aspects of Christian dogma and appealing for unlimited religious tolerance. Philosophical criticism of religion itself arose from among some of these groups. Jean-Pierre Cavaillé notes: 'Free from all forms of power, the libertine is, properly speaking, an anarchist of God, free to do as he pleases, first and foremost to conform or not to the laws and obligations of the cult.'[3]

By the end of the sixteenth century, 'libertine' started to be used in a more generalised sense that was less closely attached to doctrinal disputes. It suggested a certain rebelliousness, an easier going lifestyle and lack of deference to authority. It begins to appear in the works of Shakespeare from 1597, as in *Henry IV: part I* where Hotspur comments on Prince Hal:

> Cousin, I think thou art enamoured
> On his follies: never did I hear
> Of any prince so wild a libertine. (V.ii.69-71)

In *Much Ado About Nothing* Beatrice makes her assessment of Benedick:

> Why, he is the prince's jester, a very dull fool, only his gift is in devising impossible slanders. None but libertines delight in him, and the commendation is not in his wit but in his villainy, for he both pleases men and angers them, and then they laugh at him and beat him. (II.i.114–118)

In England by the beginning of the seventeenth century 'libertinism' increasingly signified debauchery. Some individuals, such as the poet and courtier John Wilmot, Earl of Rochester, were simultaneously philosophical and sexual libertines.

The term 'libertine' now became entwined with the ideas of the Enlightenment. Influenced by the swirl of Reformation and nonconformist 'libertine' ideas was the Dutch philosopher Baruch Spinoza (1632–1677) who, as already mentioned, was to play an important role in the development of the Enlightenment. Spinoza was of Sephardic Jewish descent but expelled from the Jewish community due to his radical ideas. He became interested in an anti-clerical sect called the Collegiants who placed emphasis upon reason as a source and test of knowledge. Spinoza constructed an abstract and impersonal God who was not a transcendent being with directive power over human affairs. He argued that free will was an illusion, 'good' and 'bad' were relative qualities not absolutes, that the universe and all its forms were variations of a single substance, and that God and nature were part of the same reality. Spinoza was a strict determinist who believed that the more we knew, the more like God we became and the freer we were. So far was Spinoza's conception of God from the Judeo-Christian tradition that many accused him of atheism.

This philosophical libertinism questioned the primary religious and moral beliefs of European society, drawing from authors of the pre-Christian world. As we have seen, the latter provided a strong platform upon which to critique the supernatural and to build alternative materialist-based systems of thought. Ancient philosophers had previously been treated as thinkers that pre-figured Christianity, their ideas woven into Christian theology. Christianity adopts from the Platonist tradition the notion of disembodied souls going to heaven. Similarly, eternal Platonic forms are integrated into the story of creation, God using their equivalent as a sort of blueprint. Now these ancient traditions were being rediscovered and utilised to cast doubt on long established religious and metaphysical claims, those of Christianity in particular. Earlier generations of sixteenth-century thinkers were also influential, men such as Machiavelli and Montaigne, thinkers who had encouraged rational scepticism, a rejection of moral certainties, and the intellectual interrogation of previously received wisdom. For Machiavelli, miracles were invented by princes to manipulate the people. Others similarly explored the idea that the development of religion was a product of natural, human and political intervention, not of the divine. If the gap between 'man' and 'God' was widening, the gap between 'nature' and 'God' was diminishing, and Spinoza was reducing that distance still further.

The eighteenth century

These important streams of philosophical thought, including Epicurean materialism, Lockean sensationalism and natural religion helped to nourish the hedonistic creed that characterised the classic eighteenth-century libertine. Christianity, a notoriously sexually repressive religion, had elevated the soul above the body. Materialism, in rejecting the existence of an immaterial soul, undercut the religious prohibitions arising from this. It identified pleasure-seeking and pain-avoidance as fundamental to human psychology, a position Casanova wholeheartedly embraced: 'Cultivating the pleasures of my senses was always my principal concern throughout my life.'[4] Humankind was only different from the rest of the animal kingdom in that it possessed reason. For supporters of natural religion, if pleasure-seeking and reason were intrinsic human qualities created by God then it must have been God's intention for man to maximise pleasure. Hedonism was a virtue, not a sin. Eighteenth-century libertinism also elevated erotic love above romantic sentimentality. Sentimental love and erotic love were seen to parallel the duality of soul and body, the former in each case rejected on the grounds of their immaterialism. Sentimental love was regarded as a culturally manufactured impediment to man's natural sex drive. Libertinism was also disposed to reject conventional social norms more broadly.

By the eighteenth century the morally derogatory connotations of 'libertinism' encompassed sexual promiscuity, atheism and a rejection of religion. But its meaning did not have to be negative. James Turner explains that 'English, French and Dutch usages divide into three main branches: "libertine" may be a largely pejorative term for dissolute sexuality, a neutral or even agreeable description of airy freedom in behaviour and writing, and – prior to and concurrent with these – a religious attitude.'[5] It was never precisely pinned down. Voltaire's sexual libertinism was relatively tame, and he was not an atheist, but in the 1760s he was being attacked for his libertinism by conservative critics. He possessed a 'libertine mind', was irreverent and his free-thinking anti-authoritarianism was corrupting French society.[6] For such opponents a *philosophe* was equivalent to being a libertine. Another way of conceiving of the term that perhaps reconciles this usage is suggested by Abramovici for whom it is 'not so much a concept as an expression of values'.[7] In some respects the term said as much about those using it to criticise their enemies as it did about their enemies themselves.

From the perspective of the French aristocracy, a libertine was similar to a gallant whose sexual escapades were regarded as no more than the light-hearted indiscretions of youth. They were activities to be looked back upon nostalgically. The word also suggested wit and cultivation. But the expansion of the public sphere, and the growing importance of more prosperous commoners, marked a shift in the moral outlook of the times. Such behaviour became regarded not as a bit of harmless entertainment but a threat to family and good order. The libertine was intemperate, prodigal and contemptuous of social conventions – attitudes that were anathema to this group and the Christian ideals many of them valued. For these affluent commoners, it was a discreditable lifestyle.

The inevitable sexual double standard made the opprobrium all the worse for female libertines, who were seen to be transgressing not only the conventions of respectable sexual behaviour but what was expected of their gender. They were regarded by some as a particular threat to social stability, endangering legitimate rights of patrimony and so the very foundations upon which society was based. Libertine women, such as the fashionable British beauty Teresia Constantia Phillips, suffered a degree of social notoriety that men were unlikely ever to experience. Indeed, sexual promiscuity might even enhance the reputations of men among their peers or the general multitude by underscoring qualities of healthy masculinity and independence. The stakes facing a female libertine are highlighted by Casanova when he speculates about the circumstances of Henriette:

> 'Who is this girl,' I said to the air, 'who combines the most elevated sentiment with the appearance of great libertinage? In Parma she absolutely wants to become her own mistress, and I have no reason to flatter myself that she will not impose the same law on me as she imposed on the officer to whom she has already given herself. Farewell my hope. Who is she then? Either she is sure of finding her lover, or she has a husband in Parma, or respectable parents, or by an unbridled spirit of boundless libertinism, confident in her own merit, she wants to defy fortune by plunging into the most hideous precipice if it will not raise her to the peak of happiness by finding her a lover who can lay a crown at her feet: it would be the project of a madwoman or a desperate woman.'[8]

In reality, it seems the aristocratic Henriette was at that moment forging her libertinism into a weapon to use against her oppressive husband and father-in-law, with Casanova her unwitting accomplice. If they did not want a scandal then they would need to come to some sort of arrangement with her, which is what happened.

The emergence of the novel was to help shape this public perception of the libertine whose portrayal was of a figure that was simultaneously fascinating and dangerous. Samuel Richardson's popular novels *Pamela* (1740) and *Clarissa* (1748) both contained libertine aristocrats bent on seducing the eponymous heroines. On the other hand, the libertine novel was itself a genre. It drew attention to the pleasure-seeking lives of the French aristocracy and dealt with familiar anti-clerical and anti-authoritarian Enlightenment themes which were part of the discourse of the earlier generations of philosophical libertines. Filled with villainous nobles and erotic adventures it included works such as *The Sofa: A Moral Tale* (Crébillon fils – 1742), *The Indiscreet Jewels* (Diderot – 1748), and *Dangerous Liaisons* (Pierre de Laclos – 1782). It may have rubbed shoulders with the pornographic novel but there were distinct differences. Most significantly, the pornographic novel appealed to the body, exhibiting its erotic content and addressing the reader directly. The libertine novel was less explicit and appealed to the mind as protagonists sought to overcome the reluctance of their desired object through strategies of persuasion. The Marquis de Sade took extracts from d'Holbach's materialist philosophical text *The System of Nature* (1770) and included them in his own fictional works. The libertine novel was concerned with the material not the metaphysical world, one in which men and women acted in accordance with their nature. Characters responded to their own needs, senses and desires rather than conforming to artificial conventions. Within this moral and intellectual framework, the libertine could be the hero by overcoming such conventions.

If the disapproval by affluent commoners of the sexual antics of their superiors coloured their usage and application of the term 'libertinism', so did their apprehensions with regards to their urban-dwelling inferiors: the unemployed, the homeless, the destitute, those on the edge. This was another group, they believed, which did not abide by the moral codes that ensured a well-ordered society. As a consequence, idleness, prostitution, debauchery and disease thrived among them. In the minds of affluent commoners, it was a manifestation of the degeneracy already observed in the aristocracy. By the mid-eighteenth century 'libertinism' had acquired meanings and connotations most of which would have been treated with suspicion by the mainstream opinion of the time. The entry for 'libertinism' in Dr Johnson's *A Dictionary of the English Language* (Vol. II, 1755) reads, 'Irreligion; licentiousness of opinions and practice'. By the end of the century the notion of a libertine as a person who contested religious dogma had been displaced by predominant meanings of degeneracy and debauchery.

Casanova

So how does Casanova understand the terms 'libertine' and 'libertinism' and what kind of libertine was he? He uses the terms about thirty or so times in his memoirs. Here he describes Count Emanuel Torres: 'Libertine, braggart, habitual liar, bold talker, spiteful, and indiscreet, his company was welcomed because he told stories well, was witty, and made people laugh.'[9] Casanova's negative use of 'libertine' in his depiction of Count Torres is fairly typical of his use elsewhere, and suggests that Casanova has accepted those pejorative connotations of immoral behaviour, both sexually and more generally, that we might have expected from someone writing at the end of the century.

As far as Casanova's own behaviour was concerned, following upon his large slice of good fortune when he acquired the patronage of Bragadin and his friends, he writes: 'I began to live truly independent of anything that could limit my inclinations. As long as I respected the law, it seemed to me that I could disregard prejudices.'[10] This was 1746. By 'prejudices' he meant any attitude or behaviour based upon the prevailing beliefs, taboos, customs and practices of society at large. Casanova's description of himself matches up pretty well with what the word 'libertine' signified to his contemporaries: sexual promiscuity; someone who prioritised the temporal pleasures of the here and now above those of the sacred and the hereafter; and a freethinker who was open to new ideas and experiences.

Although his self-conscious rejection of many of the social mores of the time was not simply about sex, sex was important so we will kick on from there. In terms of partners, he was not that exceptional among men of his social status, especially an unmarried man who was an inveterate traveller and, for periods of time, was either rich or appeared to be so. Ian Kelly calculates that over the period covered by his memoirs he averaged around four partners a year and points out that he resorted to prostitutes less than was the norm for urban men of the period.[11] He was fascinated by sex but he was not a sex addict, and for most of his relationships the sex itself was only part of the attraction. Rather, he was a romantic who enjoyed the exquisite pleasures of seduction and of being in love.

For Casanova, the social dance with all its ingenuity and elaborate subterfuge was as important as the sex. Extramarital relationships could incur serious reputational damage as well as retribution. For many, those risks amplified the pleasure. To seduce then to organise and maintain a clandestine affair required a skill set which Casanova possessed in abundance: charm, wit, nerve, improvisation, intelligence and empathy. In this social dance, a woman needed to be 'read'. Fine judgement was required to assess the extent to which her outward piety and respectability matched her inner desire. In the subtle and sophisticated worlds of the elite society that Casanova was so adept at navigating, excessive virtue (or 'prejudice') and excessive vice were equally reprehensible. Proper behaviour, even for a Mother Superior, lay somewhere in between. It was in the space between the extremes of vice and virtue that the game of seduction was to be played between two (or more) knowing collaborators, and this relative degree of equality casts doubt on the notion that Casanova was no more than a selfish manipulator and exploiter of women. There were occasions when this was true but there were also occasions when it was Casanova who was the one being exploited.

The distance between Casanova's moderate libertinism and those at the Marquis de Sade end of the continuum can be gauged by his attitude towards orgies. He was happy to engage in group sex with willing partners who enjoyed themselves as much as he did but was not aroused by humiliation or physical suffering. He recounts an orgy organised by James O'Bryan, Earl of Lismore. There were twenty-four revellers, all of them drunk after their supper, apart from Casanova who tended not to be a heavy drinker. 'That was when the great orgy began.' After describing the scenes quite unjudgementally, he writes: 'What I have gained from this infernal debauchery is a greater knowledge of myself. I risked my life. I had only my sword, and I would certainly have used it, if the lord in his bacchanalian fury had thought of forcing me to do like the others.'[12] For all its hellishness, it was typical of Casanova's fascination with life not to have regretted attending: 'Despite this, I went to bed very happy to have witnessed a spectacle the like of which I had never seen before that time, and the equal of which I have never seen afterwards.'[13]

Integral to his lovemaking and beyond it, he relished the pleasure that he could obtain from the senses, both raw and refined: 'As far as women are concerned, I have always found that the one I loved smelled good, and the stronger her sweat, the sweeter she seemed to me. What a depraved taste! What shame to recognize it, and not to blush! This criticism makes me laugh. Thanks to my vulgar tastes, I am audacious enough to believe myself happier than others, most of all because I am convinced that my tastes make me capable of more pleasure.'[14] Unsurprisingly, the enjoyment of food was very much an abiding obsession with him: 'I have always loved strong savoury dishes: macaroni made by a good Neapolitan cook, olla podrida [a rich Spanish stew], glutinous Newfoundland cod, gamy meats, and cheeses whose perfection is manifest when the small beings which inhabit them begin to make themselves visible.'[15] Observations about food and drink are a constant theme in his memoirs. Kelly notes: '*History of My Life* … records more than two hundred meals, at least twenty different wines from all over Europe, many dozens of foodstuffs and otherwise lost gastronomic arcania.'[16] He would play a game with his lovers that involved passing oysters between their mouths. Chocolate and champagne were two of his favourite drinks. He describes in detail the menu he had arranged to welcome his lover MM at his casino. It included 'game, sturgeon, truffles, oysters and perfect wines'.[17]

Other behaviours and attitudes also align Casanova with libertinism. As shown by his reaction to the Earl of Lismore's orgy, he welcomed new experiences whether or not they were respectable. Casanova was an avid gambler, at cards as well as in life, and gambling was a typical libertine pursuit. To gamble was to dabble with fate, which was God's domain. It appealed to man's selfish instincts. It encouraged people to aspire above their status and was thereby a threat to the established order. Casanova's fascination with the occult and his membership of freemasonry was also a challenge to religious authority. And he erred instinctively on the side of religious tolerance. Casanova regarded himself as a serious philosopher, a subject that valued reason above dogma and prejudice. Significantly, reason was the means by which the three fundamental instincts that he believed united all creatures were transformed by men into refined pleasures that extended beyond mere brute gratification: 'We suffer hunger the better to savour the ragout: we postpone the pleasure of love to make it keener: and we suspend vengeance to make it more deadly.'[18]

Some of the other associations with the term 'libertine' are not such an easy fit. Casanova was not a political or religious radical. For the most part, his behaviour was relatively restrained, and he himself was critical of other libertines who pushed their behaviour to extremes. 'Happy are those who, without harming anyone, know how to obtain pleasure,' he declares.[19] Peter Cryle remarks: 'Casanova sought an accommodation with virtue. We might say, in fact, that he took care not to be a "grand libertin". His libertinage was quite 'bridled', and perhaps all the more exquisite, all the more typical of its time, for being so.'[20]

Chapter 6
Voltaire: 1694–1778

> '"This," I said to him, "is the happiest moment of my life. Finally I see my master. For twenty years, sir, I have been your pupil."'
>
> Giacomo Casanova, *History of My Life*

Much of the French Enlightenment was dominated by public intellectuals, or *philosophes*, such as d'Alembert, Comte de Buffon, Nicolas de Condorcet, Diderot, Helvétius, d'Holbach, La Mettrie, Montesquieu and Rousseau. But foremost among them was Voltaire. His output (literary, historical, political and philosophical) was prodigious, filling over 100 volumes of published works and over 100 volumes of correspondence. They included satirical novels such as *Candide* (1759), philosophical short stories such as *Plato's Dream* (1756), entries for that great Enlightenment project the *Encyclopedia*, histories such as *The Age of Louis XIV* (1751), poetry such as the *Henriade* (1723), tragic plays such as *Oedipus* (1718) and comedy ballet such as *The Princess of Navarre* (1745). His works brimmed with originality, subtlety and wit, their frequent subversiveness incurring the ire of the Church and state. And it was not just the sharpness of his pen that got him into trouble. His tongue could be just as provocative. He was exiled and imprisoned on various occasions (twice in the Bastille), and his writings censored, banned, confiscated and burned. Voltaire's influence and reach, in France and abroad, was immense. Not for nothing was he known as 'the patriarch' of the Enlightenment. He did much to establish its key battlegrounds: anticlericalism, censorship, deism, ethics, Newton, political oppression and toleration. Despite his various works grounded in philosophy and natural philosophy, he was a reformer and activist (although not a revolutionary) rather than a creator of philosophical systems. The persona of the *philosophe*, as it had come to be understood by the middle of the century, was largely created by Voltaire.

Born François-Marie Arouet in the long reign of Louis XIV, Voltaire was 20 years old by the time of the Sun King's death. The first twenty years of anybody's life is hugely formative but this was particularly the case with Voltaire. The final two decades of Louis' reign had been marked by war, famine, religious persecution and intellectual upheaval. The Edict of Fontainebleau of 1685 stripped the rights awarded to the Protestant minority by the 1598 Edict of Nantes which had allowed them to practise their religion free from persecution. Over a period of more than a quarter of a century, the wars of the League of Augsburg (1688–1697) and the Spanish Succession (1701–1714) ensured that France had enjoyed only a handful of years of peace. Across the channel, the discoveries of Newton, the writings of Locke, and the Glorious Revolution of 1688 with its 1689 Bill of Rights undermined the older political, intellectual and religious certainties. Throughout Europe radical ideas were being discussed in academic societies and circulated by people of letters and learned publications. Journals and journalism proliferated, enabling access to these debates by the more educated members of society. And France was not immune. The Regent of France from 1715 to 1723, Philippe II, Duke of Orléans, was sympathetic to much of this thought, reducing censorship and allowing French citizens to engage with literature that was critical of the established orthodoxies of the state.

François-Marie was born in Paris to an affluent family. His father, also François, was a lawyer whose own family had been successful merchants and businessmen, although Voltaire suspected that he was not his true father. Voltaire's mother, Marie-Marguerite, was from the minor nobility, and there is a possibility she may have had an affair with a higher-ranked nobleman, Guérin de Rochebrune, who was one of her husband's clients. François Arouet bought the lucrative royal office of 'receiver of spices' shortly after Voltaire was born which allowed him to collect taxes levied on the spice trade. On top of this he was a moneylender, a sideline that his son would go on to pursue. Voltaire was encouraged to write poetry from an early age, a highly regarded skill for a gentleman, while his father's wealth and connections meant that he came to know important writers of the day, such as the poet and critic Nicolas Boileau (1636–1711), spurring on his literary ambitions. Also, from an early age, his godfather, Abbé de Châteauneuf, taught him to be sceptical of religious claims.

Voltaire was educated at the prestigious Jesuit college, Louis-le-Grand, a highly competitive environment in which he thrived. He was a pupil there from the age of 10 until he was 17. He received a rigorous intellectual training that incorporated aspects of traditional, theologically based scholasticism with the classical scholarship of Renaissance humanism. It placed great value on debate, poetry, drama and performance, and gave him a handy network of friends who were to become figures of national importance later in life; men such as the Duke de Richelieu, who was to become the Marshal of France, and the d'Argenson brothers, one of whom became the Minister of War, and the other the Minister of Foreign Affairs.

After Louis-le-Grand, Voltaire's father expected his son to go on to study law but instead he spent his time mingling in literary circles and writing. Continuing to push Voltaire in the direction of a more respectable career, his father arranged for him to be secretary to the French ambassador to the Netherlands, but this collapsed when Voltaire caused a scandal by falling in love with a French protestant refugee. From 1714 Voltaire frequented a literary and philosophical society called The Temple to which he had been introduced by his godfather. There he made a name for himself with his satirical verse. The Temple was a centre of free-thinking men and women, and a source of radical ideas, notably deism. Despite not being of particularly exalted birth, Voltaire found himself hobnobbing with the aristocracy, who appreciated his wit and intelligence. He was a regular visitor at the fashionable salon of Louise de Bourbon at Sceaux, and later became friendly with the exiled English aristocrat and deist Lord Bolingbroke, through whom he was introduced to the ideas of Locke, Newton and natural philosophy. In 1717 he was imprisoned in the Bastille for eleven months after penning some scurrilous verse at the expense of the Prince Regent. Voltaire had been exiled from Paris the year before – a rather comfortable one, in the Sully-sur-Loire with clients of his father. Nonetheless, during this time his reputation as a writer was growing, and he was achieving commercial success. In 1718 his play *Oedipus*, written in the Bastille, was staged at the Comédie Française to huge acclaim. Voltaire had made his mark. In the coming years he was to be recognised as the century's greatest French playwright. But, as mentioned, plays would only ever be one part of his prolific output. In 1723 he published the *Henriade*, his celebrated epic poem based on Henry IV, founder of the Bourbon dynasty, which he used to promote the message of toleration.

A few years later he was again on the wrong side of the law or, at least, the law as it was applied according to the arbitrary workings of privilege in the Old Regime. In 1726 he offended the honour of the Chevalier de Rohan-Chabot, a man in possession of a prestigious name and a dubious reputation.

The nobleman was jealous of the writer's increasing popularity at court and mocked his adoption of the name 'Voltaire'. The upstart Voltaire fired back, and matters got out of hand. Rohan-Chabot had Voltaire beaten up. The latter now insisted on a duel which the Chevalier rejected, as he could do without any damage to his honour given his superior rank. Deserted by his aristocratic friends, and facing another spell in the Bastille, Voltaire negotiated a thirty-month period of exile in England.

On a visit to the Dutch Republic in 1722 Voltaire had been struck by the benefits of a more open and permissive culture, and his time in England only reinforced what he had witnessed there. His exposure to English scientific and philosophical ideas, and how the country organised its political, social and religious affairs was to have a major influence upon his thought. Roger Pearson notes: 'This deist reader of Locke and Newton would now become increasingly militant in his campaign against the Catholic Church.'[1] England was also to have an impact upon his writing. Through Bolingbroke, he met Alexander Pope, John Gay and Jonathan Swift who were experimenting with new literary forms such as *Gulliver's Travels* (1726). Voltaire returned to Paris in 1729, and over the next several years a large family inheritance, a fortune made through lottery manipulation, pensions from his aristocratic admirers, income from his literary success, and some shrewd investing combined to make him extraordinarily wealthy. In 1733 he released a collection of essays in letter form on his English experience. It was to be one of his most influential works and a key Enlightenment text. A version was published initially in London and entitled *Letters Concerning the England Nation* before publication in France the following year as *Philosophical Letters*. Such was the outrage that greeted its appearance in France that an order for Voltaire's arrest was issued, and once again he was forced to flee Paris.

In *Philosophical Letters* Voltaire celebrates the seventeenth-century English scientific and philosophical revolutions, disseminating their ideas to an increasingly educated French public. He highlights the achievements of an empirical tradition that was based upon the principles and methods of Francis Bacon. The humanist concern for man's physical well-being, as opposed to spiritual well-being, particularly appealed to Voltaire. He drew attention to the practice of inoculation against smallpox which had been taken up in Britain but which encountered far greater resistance in France: 'What! Aren't the French fond of life? Do their women not care about their beauty? Indeed, we are strange folk! Perhaps in ten years' time we shall adopt this English method if the priests and doctors permit.'[2] He had high regard for the achievements of Descartes but for him the progress in understanding the natural world made by scientists and philosophers such as Newton and Locke was undisputable. Locke's epistemology, that all knowledge was derived from sense experience interrogated by reason, was superior in his view to the rationalism and doctrine of innate ideas of Descartes. For Locke, human knowledge had its limits. The nature of immaterial substances, such as the mind and the soul, lay beyond those limits.

It was not just the scientific and philosophical traditions of England that impressed Voltaire but the environment that allowed them to flourish. In an essay on Newton, he writes: 'When one considers that Newton, Locke, Clarke, and Leibniz would have been persecuted in France, imprisoned at Rome, and burned at Lisbon, what are we to think of human reason? One would swear it was a native of England in the present age at least.'[3] Voltaire used England as a way to critique many of the things he found objectionable about his home country, most notably the restrictions placed upon people's liberty to think, write and act. One of the most striking differences he highlights is religion. In France, religious intolerance had led to Protestants finding refuge in the Dutch Republic, England and Prussia – a commercial gain for those countries and a loss for France. By contrast, in England a wide range of religious communities from Anglicans to Quakers to Presbyterians to Baptists to Ranters lived together peacefully, and even though the rights of Roman Catholics were restricted they were not violently persecuted. For Voltaire, diversity was a positive benefit to society. He pointed to the success of the Quakers in trade and commerce, and the wealth that they generated.

Voltaire compared the relationships between the state and the established Church. In England the Church had far less political power. According to Voltaire, although this was questionable in reality, its focus was to administer to the spiritual needs of its members, with senior Church offices distributed on the basis of devoted service. In France, instead, clerical appointments were a lucrative source of patronage for the aristocracy, and many of those in positions of ecclesiastical authority were notoriously corrupt.

Voltaire explained that the power that English governments wielded over ordinary citizens was more circumscribed than was the case in France, that its laws were less arbitrary, and that all Englishmen were protected by them. Its scholars, philosophers and scientists were treated with respect. Citizens in England were taxed equally, while in France the First and Second Estates – members of the Church and aristocracy – were largely exempt.

In France, trade and commerce was treated as rather demeaning whereas in England it was more highly esteemed. Although he did voice criticisms of the English, on the whole France was depicted as rather backward, despotic and fanatical by comparison. It is unsurprising that *Philosophical Letters* received a hostile reception on the part of many in authority, particularly supporters of Jansenism. Voltaire had attacked the ideas of seventeenth-century Jansenist philosopher, Blaise Pascal, in a letter he had added to his French version. Ironically, the responses to the work confirmed much of what Voltaire had written.

For the next eleven years Voltaire took refuge at Cirey-sur-Blaise in the château of the Marquis du Châtelet. Voltaire, with the Marquis' full knowledge, was the intellectual soulmate and lover of his wife, Émilie du Châtelet: 'At Cirey we cultivated all the arts; it was there I composed *Alzire*, *Mérope*, *L'Enfant Prodigue*, and *Mahomet*.'[4] Émilie du Châtelet was a gifted scholar: a scientist and mathematician, translator of Newton's *Mathematical Principles of Natural Philosophy*, and one of the continent's leading advocates of Newton's ideas – she was known as Lady Newton. During his time at the château, which he restored at considerable expense, Voltaire worked with du Châtelet in championing Newton against the supporters of Descartes. There he wrote philosophical works such as his *A Treatise on Metaphysics* (1734), in which he explores the implications of the philosophy of John Locke, as well as works of history, ethics, drama and poetry.

By 1745, with the help of Émilie du Châtelet's influence at court, Voltaire had managed to rehabilitate himself sufficiently to be able to return to Paris and Versailles. He obtained the position of Historiographer Royal and was elected as one of the 'immortals' to that august cultural institution the French Academy. He also made a useful ally in the form of Madame de Pompadour. But he still had plenty of enemies, especially in the Church, and found himself embroiled in various disputes.

At the end of 1748 du Châtelet became pregnant. She had been having an affair with Jean François de Saint-Lambert for whom she had developed an intense passion. Voltaire knew about the affair which, unsurprisingly, put a strain on their own relationship. But the two remained exceptionally close, and he was devastated when du Châtelet died in childbirth at the age of 42. For much of the following year Voltaire based himself in Paris but he was not as fashionable as he once had been nor as popular at court. Prior to du Châtelet's death the couple had spent quite a lot of time away from Paris at Cirey and at the court of Lorraine where resided Stanislaw Leszczyński, the ex-King of Poland, Duke of Lorraine and father of the Queen of France. It was where du Châtelet had met and fallen for Saint-Lambert. Now back in Paris, Voltaire's latest works were not being well-received – *Orestes* (1750) fell flat and the Comédie Française refused to stage *Rome Preserved* – while the elderly Crébillon was making a successful comeback with his play *Catalina* (1748). Consequently, Voltaire decided to pursue his career elsewhere.

In June 1750 Voltaire left Paris for Prussia and the court of Frederick II, which he had visited for a short time in 1740 and then in 1743. On the latter occasion it was as part of a mission to gather information for the French government. Frederick had been an adoring fan of Voltaire's since his youth. The two regularly corresponded, and Frederick had long been keen to bolster his Enlightenment credentials and that of Prussia by adding this most famous of all *philosophes* to his collection of European intellectuals. Voltaire was to serve Frederick in an official capacity as a chamberlain, for which the Frenchman was to be paid 20,000 livres annually. Voltaire enjoyed the freedom Prussia gave him to write pretty much what he wanted and, as always, he was productive. In 1751 he published one of his satirical philosophical tales. A philosophical tale is a fictional text which through its narratives and characters allows the author to explore important moral and philosophical issues. It was a science fiction one this time, entitled *The Micromégas*. The Earth is depicted as a rather insignificant speck in the universe, and a visiting interplanetary traveller reveals himself to be sympathetic towards empiricism and the ideas of Locke. In the same year arrived his history *The Age of Louis XIV*. Then there were his attacks on Christianity in works such as *The Sermon of the Fifty* (1752). Throughout the 1750s he became heavily involved in the defence of Diderot and d'Alembert's emphatically secular and anti-authoritarian *Encyclopedia*, to which he contributed over a score of entries. It was the *Encyclopedia* which inspired him to write his own *Philosophical Dictionary* (1764).

But before long he fell from grace, involving himself in some shady financial dealings, and having a spectacular rift with one of Frederick's favourites, Pierre-Louis Moreau de Maupertuis (1698–1759). Maupertuis was president of the Royal Prussian Academy of Science, and an erstwhile Newtonian ally who had previously been a tutor of du Châtelet. Ironically, it was Voltaire who had recommended him to Frederick. The two became rivals, jealous of their relative status. The quarrel involved an essay on cosmology by Maupertuis which contained calculations which were disputed by another scholar, Samuel König. König also claimed that the formulation of the concept at the centre of it, 'the principle of least action', which still today is ascribed to Maupertuis, had already been described by Leibniz in 1707. Maupertuis reacted by having the academy condemn König for trying to damage his reputation. According to Voltaire, this was an abuse of power. He publicly attacked the academy's president but in doing so had seriously miscalculated Frederick's response. The king was furious and came to the president's defence. When in a hole, Voltaire was not a man to stop digging. He countered with a merciless satire of Maupertuis, *The Diatribe of Doctor Akakia* (1752). This was too much for Frederick. He had copies of the work seized and burned by the public hangman. It was time for Voltaire to move on.

But where to go. Throwing his lot in with Frederick had upset the French court, making him unwelcome in Paris and Versailles. On the debit side, he remained a famous literary figure and was rich. In the end, he settled on Geneva, a Protestant city-state beyond French jurisdiction. Of particular interest to Voltaire was its flourishing book trade. Materials that were too hot to handle in France were typically printed and published abroad, often under a false imprint, and then imported clandestinely. In 1755 he became a resident of Geneva, and leased Les Délices, an elegant and spacious hillside residence with picturesque views. Setting up home with him was his 43-year-old niece (or, perhaps, half-niece) Madame Marie-Louise Denis. The two had been in a romantic relationship since before the death of du Châtelet but now they became an established couple, if unmarried. A few years later he bought Ferney, an estate that cut across the French-Swiss border which was to be his home for the rest of his life. There he played the role of enlightened ruler, using his wealth to modernise and invigorate its languishing economy. Les Délices and Ferney were to become intellectual and cultural hubs. Streams of international visitors, many of whom, like Casanova, were complete strangers, journeyed to see him. He engaged in voluminous correspondence with people from all walks of life, constructing an extensive network of friends, allies, scholars, statesmen and rulers; contacts that would help him maintain his influence in the wider world and support him in his campaign against the 'infamy' – that is, superstition, intolerance and abuses of power.

Yet for all his activity this was a depressing period for Voltaire. There was the death of du Châtelet, Europe was convulsed by the Seven Years War, and in 1755 there was the horrendous Lisbon earthquake which inspired a poem for which he was publicly rebuked by Jean-Jacques Rousseau. In it he had attacked the optimistic philosophy of Gottfried Wilhelm Leibniz which attempted to tackle the question of how suffering could exist in a world created by a God who was infinitely good – the question of theodicy. Leibniz's conclusion was that the suffering in the world was the least there could be. As only God could be perfect then some degree of suffering had to exist on Earth, and any other possible world that God could have created would have contained even greater suffering. Voltaire's rejection of this conclusion, and his humanistic assertion that it was mankind not God that required man's love, outraged Rousseau whose *Letter to Voltaire on Providence* (1756) argued that Voltaire was challenging the fact of God's perfection (a fact proven by the power of reason), and that man was responsible for evil not God. The Lisbon earthquake was God's message to mankind that cities were a cause of moral degradation. In attacking God, Voltaire was undermining the greatest source of comfort that was available to man to alleviate his unhappiness.

Central to this dispute was a clash of epistemology. Should primacy of authority be given to the deductive theories of Descartes and Leibniz, or to the kind of experientially based knowledge characterised by the English tradition. For Voltaire, the ideas of Leibniz led to fatalism and despair. If what happened in this world was for the best in the best of all possible worlds then what was the point in trying to improve upon it. It denied the human reality of suffering and its fundamental injustice. It was to be several years before Voltaire responded to Rousseau's broadside. He did so in the philosophical tale *Candide*, a powerful demolition of optimistic philosophy that in the figure of Professor Pangloss laid bare its absurdities.

Although Voltaire may not have devised his own systematic philosophy there are, through his active engagement in the key intellectual controversies of the time, a number of recurring themes. Many of these concerns were long-standing preoccupations of Western theology and philosophy given new direction as the Aristotelian-scholastic tradition was eclipsed by the tangible successes of natural philosophy. The age-old tension between reconciling an omnipotent creator of all things with the operation of free will continued to play itself out, but with the determinism of the materialist and immutable laws of nature now placed alongside the determinist implications of an all-powerful God. There was the epistemological tension between the Cartesian and metaphysical claims to certain knowledge against the well-honed doubts of the sceptical philosophical tradition, and the probabilistic claims of thinkers like Gassendi and Locke. In government and law there was the tension between the political ideals of absolute authority and those of popular sovereignty.

With regards to the first of these, Voltaire steers a course between determinism and free will, allowing men some degree of agency where they have the capacity to use reason. He rejects theological certainty, with all its obscure dogmas and doctrines, as well as the deductive metaphysical and philosophical certainties of scholars such as Leibniz and Descartes. For Voltaire, to veer off into deductive, metaphysical explanations divorced from empirical evidence was little more than inventing comforting fairy stories.

Like determinism and free will, so with government: Voltaire opts for a middle way between republicanism and absolutism, preferring a reformed monarchy with restricted powers and more liberty for individuals. Particularly important for Voltaire were toleration and freedom of speech, principles that were essential to the ideals of the Enlightenment. Social and scientific progress required that men and women had the opportunity to reason and debate with each other, and hold opinions that others, especially the institutions of the Church and state, may oppose. Toleration was also a logical consequence of epistemological doubt. If there were no philosophical or theological certainties then there was always the danger of error, and toleration could help to mitigate the consequences of such error. This pattern of adopting a middle way repeats itself again in his attitude towards divinity. Voltaire rejects the authority of the Church and rejects hard-line, materialistic atheism. Instead, he embraces a deistic position. He also felt it was necessary for people to believe in the existence of an immortal soul, a belief to be attained through religion and faith rather than reason. For Voltaire, an acceptance of the possibility of retribution in the afterlife was central to human morality. Why would men behave morally if there was no danger of being punished for one's earthly sins?

Influential in shaping Voltaire's morality was Neo-Epicurean hedonism. As already discussed, this was a philosophy that regarded pleasure as a measure of what was good and directed that a rational person should aim to maximise pleasure and minimise pain. As well as in the conduct of his personal life – although it was not that outrageous – Voltaire expressed this belief both in his libertine literary works, and his attacks upon the sexual repressiveness, self-denial and physical purging that had long been a feature of Christianity, most notably in the celibacy of the Catholic priest. It was an outlook that reinforced his antipathy towards joyless, religious movements such as Jansenism. It was also evident in his defence of commerce and luxury, and their importance in the foundation of civilised society and increased sociability.

Voltaire was to become the most widely read Enlightenment author in the world. He achieved particular renown for his philosophical tales such as that of *Candide*. Philosophical tales were a vehicle perfectly suited to Voltaire's satirical genius. Placing figures with which his audience would be familiar, either barely disguised real individuals or well-known types, such as courtiers, scholars, physicians, kings, lawyers and clerics, in frequently outlandish settings and plots, he was able to debunk institutions and established beliefs. Through mockery he undermined claims to authority and deference. They enabled him to confront his audience with radical ideas without having to commit himself to any position that might leave him vulnerable to prosecution; his readers would be left to draw their own conclusions from the scenarios he constructed. Typical subjects that he dealt with included justice, government, arrogance, greed, superstition, suffering, pacifism, anticlericalism, religious tolerance, the abuse of power, the limits and relativity of human knowledge, the potential of science, and the nature of God.

After *Candide* and his dispute with Rousseau, Voltaire focused his energies more on practical action. From the 1760s he devoted himself to campaigning and writing in the cause of toleration. He was at the peak of his fame and influence. Employing ridicule, reason and appeals to humanity, he made his case to the public through pamphlets, articles, works such as *Treatise on Toleration* (1763) and his *Philosophical Dictionary* (1764) as well as voluminous correspondence with people of letters and political figures across Europe. Voltaire championed the victims of particularly egregious miscarriages of justice such as that of the Huguenot Jean Calas who was accused of the murder of his own son. Calas was convicted and sentenced to be publicly tortured on 9 March 1762. He refused to confess his guilt despite his brutal ordeal, and on the following day he was executed by being broken on the wheel, a hideously painful death. Voltaire's investigation exposed the complicity of the local community in a prosecution that was founded on nothing but prejudice and religious zealotry:

> Some fanatic in the crowd cried out that Jean Calas had hanged his son Marc Antoine. The cry was soon repeated on all sides; some adding that the deceased was to have abjured Protestantism on the following day, and that the family and young Lavaisse had strangled him out of hatred for the Catholic religion. In a moment all doubt had disappeared. The whole

> town was persuaded that it is a point of religion with the Protestants for a father and mother to kill their children when they wish to change their faith.[5]

He succeeded eventually in having the verdict overturned and the family compensated.

As well as toleration, other crusades for which Voltaire fought included the abolition of slavery and serfdom, freedom of thought, free trade, judicial reforms and an end to war. He produced numerous anonymous texts which he had distributed throughout the continent. He was a patron to young writers, and a critic who pronounced on what was worth reading and what was not. Ironically, he was himself quite an intolerant man. In particular, he was antisemitic.

In February 1778 the 84-year-old Voltaire was allowed to return to Paris. He received a rapturous welcome and was feted by both the ordinary peasants and the Parisian elite. But the demands upon him took their toll and, exhausted, on the 30 May he died – followed just a few weeks later, coincidentally, by Rousseau. In 1791, two years after the French Revolution, his body was exhumed and moved to the Pantheon of heroes in recognition of his fight against injustice and abuses of power. However, when the Revolution became more radical it was Rousseau, who had bitterly criticised Voltaire, who became the favoured son.

Newton

By the late eighteenth century, the British mathematician and natural philosopher Isaac Newton had become an iconic figure in France. He had demonstrated spectacularly how the power of human reason could reveal the secrets of nature without the need for divine revelation, biblical or otherwise. In the 1750s the legend was established that it had only been twenty years earlier when a monolithic Cartesian orthodoxy had been challenged, and then overcome, by a young generation of French Newtonians spearheaded by Voltaire and Maupertuis. For the group that was at the heart of the French Enlightenment, mid-century *philosophes* and Encyclopedists such as d'Alembert, this was how France was dragged into modernity. But the reality of the beginnings of the French Enlightenment and Voltaire's place in it was more complex, as made clear by J. B. Shank's *The Newton Wars* (2008) from which much of this section is drawn.

As mentioned previously, a key feature of the Enlightenment and its genesis was an informal network of European thinkers who corresponded at length on matters of scholarly interest. Dubbed the Republic of Letters, this network acquired particular prominence from the mid-seventeenth century onwards. The savants who comprised it were driven by a desire to pursue truth, as far as possible with intellectual honesty. They were governed by a code of courtesy and sociability, rather like salon culture, and attempted to eschew nationalistic, political or religious tribalism. Bitter disputes did arise from time to time but were frowned upon.

Through these networks and learned societies such as the Royal Society of London (1660) and Paris's Royal Academy of Sciences (1666), ideas circulated across international boundaries. The suggestion that French scholars, out of some petty-minded, Cartesian nationalism, had not engaged with Newton or had not found great merit in his discoveries long before Voltaire and Maupertuis was simply untrue. Newton's *Mathematical Principles of Natural Philosophy*, the *Principia*, had been a part of French scholarly discussion since its publication in 1687. The early reception of its mathematics was positive; *Principia*, after all, drew upon mathematical mechanics that had been pioneered by the French. But its implication, by combining mathematics and empirical evidence, that there operated in nature a universal force of gravity, was treated with scepticism. To the scholarly mind of the seventeenth century, attempting to apply mathematical abstraction to the physical world would be rather like trying to smell a circle. The two forms of understanding did not go together. Significantly, the author himself was cautious not to claim outright that gravity was a physical principle. In the following years Newton's mathematics, alongside the ideas of contemporaries Nicolas Malebranche and Leibniz, exerted an important influence upon French mathematicians, particularly in the study of motion. It is worth pointing out that Newton became a member of the Royal Academy of Sciences.

Despite the concern with gravity, it was not until forty years later that these ideas became a matter of partisan dispute among rival Newtonian and Cartesian camps. Instead, debate had divided across a range of philosophical, mathematical and religious issues. Contestants could disagree in one area but agree in another. It had not been a matter of tribal allegiances. Questions raised included the status of God. Was God an interventionist force in nature or did the Creator put in place the rules of existence and let it go merrily on its way, as Newton's laws of motion might suggest? Did God stand outside the universe, was God part of it, or were God and the universe one and the same, as the supporters of Spinoza would have it? How were miracles to be understood? Was God being displaced entirely by a materialistic universe? Was Newton the harbinger of an irreligious and atheistic future? What were the consequences for faith, doctrine and the institutional power of the Church? Then there was the philosophical question of causality. Did, as Newton believed, matter contain within itself an active force, an inherent creative power that did not require an external cause? Descartes had battled to replace the old scholastic tradition of intangible, unmeasurable, qualitative essences with explanations of nature that were quantifiable and mechanical. Then along came the Englishman demonstrating that objects attract each other across the void of space without any causal explanation. It looked like a return to scholastic woo-woo nonsense. Few in Europe before 1710, even in England, were prepared to go along with that. Mathematical proofs may be all well and good – everyone acknowledged the Englishman's mathematical genius – but where was the 'how'? For Newton himself it was a matter of divine will. Descartes' explanation for the motions of the cosmos lay in the mechanical concept of vortices and three different types of matter: stars composed of luminous matter, planets of denser opaque matter, while space was filled with transparent matter. Planets would orbit stars because of systems of vortices, rather like whirlpools. It was a step up from Aristotelian cosmology but its practical, explanatory power was limited and required complicated mathematical systems of calculation. Inevitably, thinkers from different intellectual and religious perspectives took up different positions on all this. And the originality and sophistication of Newton's ideas added further dimensions to the debate.

From 1699 reforms at the Royal Academy saw it become more outward looking, an indication of the growing significance of the public sphere. Central to this new direction was the appointment as its secretary of Bernard le Bovier de Fontenelle (1657–1757) who attempted to make science accessible to a non-specialist audience. He became well known for his writings on nature and the universe, notably his *Conversations on the Plurality of Worlds* (1686). Each year he would provide a written account of the Academy's scholarly work, address public assemblies, compose academician obituaries and engage in correspondence. This public face of a royal institution increased its political importance, making Fontenelle a key figure in the framing of scientific debate within France and, more broadly, the Republic of Letters. As far as cosmology was concerned, Fontenelle's sympathies lay with Descartes, and while he worked to paper over intellectual disputes within the Academy to avoid conflicts that might damage its reputation, in his writings and public presentations he favoured work that supported or could be interpreted to support the concept of vortices. This gave the impression to the outside world that vortical mechanics was more important to French science than was the case. Shank observes: 'Fontenelle in effect fostered the perception that a Cartesian unity existed in France when diversity was really the norm.'[6] In reality, as early as the first decade of the eighteenth century, there were signs within the Academy of some sympathy for the idea of a gravitational force, notably on the part of the chemist Étienne François Geoffroy (1672–1731). But when Fontenelle commented on universal gravity he maintained that it was a mathematical idea not an actual physical force, and that in this respect Newton had erred. He also supported the primacy of Cartesian deductive analysis in providing scientific truths over the Newtonian emphasis upon inductive analysis, based upon experiment and observation, which was intrinsically more uncertain.

Over the following years the complex interplay of various factors resulted in a debate that became increasingly controversial and a matter of broader public interest whereas previously it had been largely confined to the polite circles of academia and the Republic of Letters. An early example of this shift, and a reflection of the unusually partisan and nationalistic quality of English political culture, was the calculus priority dispute that broke out between Newton and Leibniz. Both men had independently invented their own form of infinitesimal calculus but Newton's supporters accused Leibniz of plagiarism. Public displays and courses of experimental science grew in popularity from early in the century, heightening public engagement in scientific debates. Then there was the growth in Europe of scholarly journals, originating in the Dutch Republic in the late seventeenth century. Such journalism was less restrained by the decorous culture of the academies and Republic of Letters, and more willing to be openly critical. They were also influential in shaping debates. In its review of gravitational attraction, the Jesuit *Journal de Trévoux* associated Newton with Spinozan, pantheist materialism, an alarmingly heretical philosophy from a French perspective. Neither was it an altogether unreasonable connection to make given the works of the Irish philosopher John Toland (1670–1722) who yoked together Newton and Spinoza. This had the effect of increasing the sympathy of the Jesuits for the mechanical physics of Descartes, reinforcing a growing perception of a generalised Cartesian-Newtonian divide. Journalistic offerings became more sensationalist as they looked to secure an audience and began to take a nationalistic turn. There were claims that in England Newtonian philosophy was undermining religion. By 1730 the public sphere and its political importance had expanded considerably.

It was in this more polemically charged, public and nationalistic environment that Voltaire and Maupertuis' careers as French champions of Newton, and facilitators of the French Enlightenment, took flight. Maupertuis had the authority of being a respected academic with diverse scholarly interests, including mathematics, experimental physics and natural history. He was a member of the Academy, an elegant writer, wealthy, well connected, and a worldly habitué of Parisian salon culture. In 1728 he visited London, making the acquaintance of several Newtonian scholars and becoming a member of the Royal Society. He was also one of a group of French academicians embracing Newton's ideas, the awkward implications of whose work, from a Cartesian standpoint, Fontenelle was trying to sideline. Nonetheless, despite his Newtonian sympathies, by 1731 Maupertuis had become a man of importance in the Academy. But although his authority had been established in academia, he did not entirely restrict himself to an academic audience. The work of Fontenelle, journalists, experimental demonstrators, and an expanding print culture had generated interest among the educated general population. It was this public that Maupertuis addressed, bolstered by a carefully honed reputation as a man of intellectual integrity. In 1732 he published his *Discourse on the Different Figures of the Planets*, a refutation of Cartesian critiques of gravitational attraction in a way that appealed to French sensibilities and defused religious anxieties. It made him at the time the most prominent French defender of Newton.

Voltaire's authority was of a different kind. He was a man of letters and a celebrated literary figure. Although Voltaire was to engage in experimental research with du Châtelet he was never to be a distinguished natural philosopher. The increasing significance of the public sphere, however, gave him the opportunity to fashion an image as a public intellectual. In the process he reinvented the persona of the *philosophe*, helping to establish an influential class of independent thinkers who were to become the principal agents of the French Enlightenment and of its central project, the *Encyclopedia*. Until Voltaire, a *philosophe* was generally perceived as irreligious and self-centred, a marginal figure of low status. But they could be associated with virtues such as reason and moderation, impartial enquiry into truth, and a willingness to question authority and to denounce prejudice, hypocrisy and injustice. It was these virtues that were to define Voltairean *philosophes*, turning them into servants of the public good. Shank comments on how in this reshaping of the identity of the *philosophe*

Voltaire was 'infusing the much older tradition of aristocratic libertinism and intellectual independence with the new discourses of philosophical and political liberty coming out of England and the Low Countries.'[7]

Partly encouraged by *Discourse on the Different Figures of the Planets*, Voltaire pushed ahead with his own venture, *Philosophical Letters*, contacting Maupertuis directly to clarify Newton's ideas. Part of the exercise was to project an image of Voltaire as a man to be taken seriously on matters of political, religious and philosophical importance; he needed to be recognised as more than a poet and libertine wit. Influenced by the freer critical and intellectually combative environment of England, to a significant degree, but by no means entirely, Voltaire eschewed the decorous and playful tone that was typical of French discourse. Here is his blunt comparison of Descartes to Newton: 'I don't think we really dare compare in any way his philosophy with that of Newton: the first is a sketch, the second is a masterpiece.'[8] Additionally, unlike Maupertuis, his defence of Newton drew on an Anglo-Dutch materialist tradition more likely to cause concern among the faithful. Beyond Newton, his observations in *Philosophical Letters*, while not in themselves particularly original, were an unvarnished challenge to core French institutions, values and beliefs. It was a call to transform French and European society which he was to pursue with unrelenting vigour for the next four and a half decades. As part of his quest to be taken seriously as a philosopher, in 1738 he published *Elements of the Philosophy of Newton* jointly with du Châtelet. In the same year he had achieved recognition from the Royal Academy of Sciences for a paper he submitted on the subject of fire.

During this period Voltaire and Maupertuis had met on several occasions. In 1734 Maupertuis visited Voltaire and du Châtelet at Cirey where Maupertuis tutored du Châtelet, and the two briefly became lovers. But the two Newtonian allies had different personal and strategic priorities. Voltaire was looking to acquire respectability as a philosopher, and so was keen to associate himself with Maupertuis. Maupertuis, on the other hand, was wary of his scholarly reputation being tainted by too close a connection with a man frequently mired in controversy. Despite *Discourse on the Different Figures of the Planets*, the main focus for Maupertuis in the 1730s was the Republic of Letters and the Academy, a time when Voltaire was having to defend himself against some hostile anti-Newtonian journalism as well as attempts to delegitimise his voice by attacks on his integrity. In his memoirs Voltaire records how in 1740, when he first met Frederick II, 'I was praised by a king, from the crown of my head to the sole of my foot, at the same time that I was libelled, at least once a week, by the abbé Desfontaines, and other Grub-street poets of Paris.'[9] This dynamic changed in the 1740s. Maupertuis's scholarly reputation was secure, and he now devoted more attention to the world outside academia. He had a brilliant success with his anonymously published *A Disinterested Examination* (1740) about the shape of the Earth, a key battleground in the Cartesian-Newtonian debate and one which had grabbed the interest of broader society. His image as a public intellectual and fashionable libertine wit grew closer to that of Voltaire's. He became less cautious in his pronouncements on gravity, adopting Voltaire's stance that it was an empirically proven fact. Shank remarks: 'For Voltaire, Maupertuis' success, and the wider acceptance of their shared Newtonian positions, translated into increasing public acceptance and support.'[10] In 1745 Maupertuis departed France for Berlin, head hunted by Frederick II to become president of the Royal Prussian Academy of Science.

But the tide was already turning, and by 1750 the Newtonian-Cartesian debate was resolving itself in favour of Newton. An important intervention by the young and gifted mathematician Jean le Rond d'Alembert had undercut Leibnizian metaphysical speculation, with the religious implications that entailed, by demonstrating that it was an unrequired complication. Newtonianism was now ascendant within the Academy of Sciences, and within the journalistic arena too it had largely been accepted. In 1746 Voltaire's intellectual respectability had been endorsed by becoming a member of the French Academy. The curtain was about to rise on the next, great, decades-long struggle of the French Enlightenment, sporting a new generation of protagonists: the creation of the *Enyclopedia*.

Casanova

Voltaire was one of the most significant figures in Casanova's life. The Venetian aspired to be recognised as a serious man of letters, and it was Voltaire against whom he sought to match himself. On the surface it might appear absurd to the point of delusional for Casanova to seek to rival this European colossus. Yet if he did fail to match Voltaire it was because Voltaire achieved so much not because Casanova achieved so little. By any other standard he was a considerable intellectual and literary figure.

Like Voltaire, Casanova was an accomplished writer across a wide range of genres, styles and topics including his memoirs, poetry, drama, science fiction, parody, essay writing, literary criticism, satire, philosophy, religion, mathematics and history. Like Voltaire, he was a pamphleteer and avid letter writer. In his last period of stay in Venice (1774–1783) he wrote his own monthly journal. He did not match the industrial scale of Voltaire but his output was pretty impressive nonetheless, in terms of both quantity and quality. His memoirs are recognised as one of the great works of European literature, skilfully crafted, and full of intelligence, humour and psychological insight. It is also a philosophical work – an examination of freedom and morality. In this respect it resembles Voltaire's philosophical tales, such as *Candide*, which make use of character and narrative to explore questions about the nature of society and, indeed, reality as a whole. Readers of *History of My Life* are treated to a parade of folly and iniquity perpetrated by men and women from every walk of life, most notably the rich and powerful. Respectability, authority and the institutions of the state in this way are all subverted. Another monumental work (another philosophical tale) was Casanova's five-volume science-fiction novel *Icosameron* (1788). In the *Encyclopedia of Italian Literary Studies* (2007), Mattia Begali notes: 'With an imagination comparable to Jules Verne's, Casanova foresaw the motorcar, the airplane, television and several other inventions that were not realised for more than a century.'[11] In addition, he composed philosophical dialogues such as *The Philosopher and the Theologian*. He had his own European blockbuster, *History of My Escape from the Prisons of the Republic of Venice*, which according to Begali, was 'one of the most engaging and suspenseful texts of eighteenth-century literature'.[12] Like Voltaire, Casanova wrote histories, (notably *History of the Polish Troubles*, 1774) and in terms of the use of original sources and objectivity was arguably closer to the standards of modern historical scholarship than Voltaire, who found it difficult to avoid the urge to convey his own vision of the past. Polish historian Maciej Forycki describes Casanova as 'a refined observer of political culture and the daily life of Polish elites in the 1760s … an incontestable erudite and philosopher, going completely against the current of widespread contemporary opinions on the subject of Poland' and that included the opinions of Voltaire.[13] He translated much of Homer's *Iliad* – although a lack of financing meant he was unable to complete it – and, it would appear, he played a small part in Mozart's production of *Don Giovanni* (1787).

As well as their intellectual and literary interests the lives of the two men overlapped in plenty of other ways. Although Voltaire was considerably older than Casanova, they were contemporaries whose careers coincided with the High Enlightenment (1730–1780). They were both long-lived by the standards of their day despite neither being expected to survive childhood. They were both self-made men, believed themselves to be illegitimate, and were driven by a need to prove themselves. Both were regularly in trouble with the authorities and spent most of their adult lives in exile from their places of birth. Both were extraordinarily well travelled and kept the company of the great and the good throughout Europe. Both were jealous of their own reputations as scholars, and neither was averse to ingratiating himself to those in power when it suited his own ends. Both made fortunes from Paris lotteries. Both were entrepreneurs (Casanova a far less successful one, for the most part, than Voltaire) and spies. In terms of free-thinking and challenging the social and religious norms of the time both were advocates of libertinism although the Frenchman was not quite such a dedicated practitioner as the Venetian. They were similarly attention-seekers, charismatic, combative, opportunistic, generous, pragmatic, at times reckless, great conversationalists and possessed with phenomenal energy. And both fled England on account of shady financial dealings that carried the death penalty.

So how did Voltaire influence Casanova? Before attempting an answer, as with Ariosto, it is worth sounding a note of caution. There is no doubt that Voltaire did have a major impact upon Casanova but we need to bear in mind that both men were subject to the influence of common trends and sources of ideas available to the educated public. Venice was a centre of the book trade which meant that the works of a wide range of thinkers and scholars would have been readily accessible, either in Latin or in translation. Ideas that may have underpinned Casanova's hedonistic morality were as likely to have sources in the philosophy of Epicurus and Gassendi as the works of Voltaire.

Back to the question: How did Voltaire influence Casanova? First, Casanova can be described as a Voltairean. By this we mean that he was preoccupied by the themes and ideas pursued by Voltaire, sometimes in agreement, sometimes in bitter opposition. One of Voltaire's central interests that engaged Casanova's attention was the nature of the soul, morality and the existence of God. For Voltaire, as mentioned, morality required the existence of God, a belief in an immortal soul, and some form of heaven and hell. This was an issue to which Casanova kept returning. Casanova did not question the existence of an immaterial God but his understanding of the nature of the relationship between the soul and the body was more nuanced and led him to reject the idea of divine reward and punishment after death. Likewise, Voltaire's Enlightenment quest to create a secular morality is echoed in

Casanova's memoirs and works on history which are, in part, meant to be read as studies of human nature. These are accounts of human psychology, motivation and behaviour from which it is possible to draw conclusions without relying on explanations rooted in the designs of the Almighty.

The second important way in which Voltaire was a major influence was as a role model. Voltaire was the quintessence of a man of letters, and repeatedly we see genres which Voltaire either pioneered or with which he was strongly associated being taken up by Casanova, such as his philosophical tale *Icosameron*. This was intended to be a defining masterwork with which he hoped to establish his name as a serious scholar worthy of public recognition. We witness a similar pattern with his histories and philosophical dialogues. But on occasion Casanova went beyond mere emulation and would lift material directly from Voltaire's works to use for his own (Voltaire was equally free and easy with the writings of others). This was the case for some of Casanova's philosophical dialogues. Another similarity can be found in Casanova's libertine writing style. Works such as *Candide* and *History of My Life* are both characterised by a polite, decorous tone frequently employing euphemisms, innuendo and understatement that ironically belie their erotic content and social critique. During the gruesome execution of Robert Damiens, Casanova records the behaviour of guests he had invited to witness the event by means of a staircase window which overlooked the scene, and that he had hired especially for the occasion:

> At Damiens' torment, I had to avert my eyes when I heard him screaming, having only half of his body left; but La Lambertini and Madame XXX did not look away; and it was not due to the cruelty of their hearts. They told me, and I had to pretend to believe them, that they could not feel the slightest pity for such a monster: they loved Louis XV so much. It is true, however, that Tiretta kept Madame XXX so singularly busy throughout the whole execution that it may have been only because of him that she never dared to move or turn her head. [14]

For comparison with Voltaire, here is Professor Pangloss's account of how he contracted syphilis:

> 'My dear Candide! You must remember Paquette, the pretty lady's maid to our august Baroness; well in her arms I tasted the delights of paradise, which in turn provoked the torments

> of hell by which you see me devoured; she was herself infected, and may now be dead. Paquette received this present from a very learned Franciscan, who could trace it back to its source: for he had been given it by an old countess, who in turn had it from a cavalry captain, who was indebted for it to a marquise, who caught it from a page-boy, who contracted it from a Jesuit, who, while a novice, had inherited it in a direct line from one of the shipmates of Christopher Columbus. As for me, I will pass it on to no one, for I am dying of it.'[15]

At the age of 35, Casanova had the opportunity to meet the great man at Les Délices. In 1759 Casanova was rich but an extraordinarily lavish lifestyle combined with some poor business dealings meant that he was quickly burning through much of this fortune. His social standing in Paris and the Dutch Republic had also begun to fall, his position made worse when his powerful protector, Abbé de Bernis, was sacked by Louis XV and packed off to Rome. After a failed attempt in Amsterdam in 1760 to raise a loan for the French government, Casanova decided to travel east. This is when he visited Voltaire. It does not appear that he had any difficulty in getting access to him even though at this time Casanova had produced little of scholarly or literary interest. In his memoirs he comments that 'everyone wanted to give me letters for Monsieur de Voltaire.'[16] The precise date of Casanova's visit is unclear. Casanova claims it was August 1760 but evidence from Voltaire's correspondence suggests it was probably May.

'"This," I said to him, "is the happiest moment of my life. Finally I see my master. For twenty years, sir, I have been your pupil." "Honour me with another twenty, and then promise me you'll come and bring me my wages."'[17] So went the opening salvo between the two men as recorded in *History of My Life*. Over the following few days, Casanova went to dine with Voltaire and Madame Denis, along with a range of other guests, while at night cavorting with 'three nymphs' thanks to an unnamed 'Epicurean'. The picture painted of Voltaire was of an incredibly learned man who could recite from memory lengthy passages of poetry, including Ariosto, and who was a witty, generous and hospitable host. Casanova notes approvingly: 'He maintained a residence that could not be more noble, and the only good food was at his house.'[18] Curious about the world and eager to obtain information from his visitors, Voltaire quizzed his guest about people he knew such as the Venetian playwright Goldoni. There is also evidence in the account of Voltaire's copious letter-writing: 'He [Voltaire] opened a door, and I saw an archive of almost a hundred large packages. "This", he told me, "is my correspondence. You see about fifty thousand letters to which I have replied."'[19]

But Casanova also depicts a less flattering side to his host, a man who is 'greedy for praise', who loves playing to his audience, who can be fault-finding, sarcastic and disingenuous. At one point, Voltaire claims he wishes he were English to a couple of English visitors. 'A poor compliment,' Casanova chides, 'because he forced them to answer him that they would like to be French, and they may not have wanted to lie, or they might be ashamed to tell the truth. It is permissible for the man of honour, it seems to me, to put his own nation above others.'[20]

Perhaps the most striking feature of Casanova's account is the exchanges between the two men, and a sense of incessant point scoring. He seems to go to enormous pains to demonstrate to his audience that he was a match for the great man's wit and learning, at times even correcting him. Casanova describes them as both being equally capable of moving their listeners to tears through their renditions of Ariosto, and several times they have lively discussions on the merits of various literary works and forms. Here is an example of Casanova putting Voltaire straight on a translation into Italian of the work of the playwright and poet Prosper Jolyot de Crébillon, whom Casanova happened to have known well:

> [Voltaire] "Martelli proves that his verses sound to Italian ears the same as the French alexandrines to the French."
>
> [Casanova] "He is grossly mistaken, and I want you to judge. Your masculine verse has only twelve syllables, and the feminine has thirteen: all Martelli's verses have fourteen except those which end in a long syllable, which at the end of the verse is always worth two. Observe that the first hemistich of Martelli is eternally seven, while, in the French alexandrine it is always always six."[21]

Overall, you do get the impression that Casanova has tried to give an honest and even-handed description of Voltaire, taking care to illustrate both his vices and virtues. One of the aims of *History of My Life*, after all, was to try to give a truthful insight into human nature. Unfortunately, Casanova's final visit ended on a rather tetchy note, with Voltaire being in a bad mood – according to the Venetian, because he had refused to extend his time at Les Délices. They had also clashed over what role religion and the people should play in the governance of society. Voltaire, as described by Casanova, was more hostile towards religion and more democratic whereas Casanova himself, taking a Hobbesian line, and conscious of human failings, argued that the masses needed a sovereign buttressed by the Church.

Casanova was subsequently to become highly critical of Voltaire, and seemingly obsessed by him. What caused that rankling feeling? Perhaps it was jealousy of Voltaire's towering genius, and the world's recognition of it. Possibly he felt that Voltaire had been condescending towards him, and his intellectual pride and sensitivity had taken it badly. Casanova records that in 1762 he returned to Geneva but refused to visit Voltaire, who had now moved to his new estate at Ferney and was apparently hoping to see the Venetian. Since their meeting, Casanova had translated Voltaire's play, *The Scotswoman*, into Italian, and sent it to him. He had not received a reply but had learned from a friend that Voltaire thought the translation was poor, an opinion that Casanova no doubt feared would have been shared with others to the detriment of his reputation. But his public hostility may not all have stemmed from injuries to his self-esteem. There were genuine philosophical differences between the two men.

Whatever the reason for Casanova's unhappiness, from 1766 onwards he attacks Voltaire and his ideas in his letters and writings. In Casanova's *Refutation* of 1769, he castigates Voltaire's defence of suicide and seeks to prove that the logical conclusion of his arguments about God was atheism. In 1779, the year after Voltaire's death, he orchestrated *Scrutiny of the Book 'Praise of M. Voltaire' by Different Authors*, including more criticisms of Voltaire's views on religion and suicide. But at the end of his life Casanova recognised that he had been unjust to a man who, in reality, he had greatly respected and whose writings and ideas had hugely influenced his own. He reflects on his visit to Les Délices:

> I repent of it today, although when I read what I published against him I find that I was right in my criticisms. I should have stayed quiet, respected him, and doubted my opinions. I think that without the taunts with which he displeased me on the third day, I would have found him sublime in everything. This reflection alone should have silenced me; but an angry man always imagines he is right. Posterity, reading me, will place me in the number of the Zoiluses [an ancient Greek rhetorician who criticised Homer] and the very humble reparation I make to him now will perhaps not be read.[22]

Chapter 7
Denis Diderot: 1713–1784

'There is no man in the world who manages to know everything; but every man must aspire to know everything.'

Giacomo Casanova, *History of My Life*

A prominent Enlightenment figure, Denis Diderot was the prime mover behind the *Encyclopedia*, one of the great intellectual accomplishments of the age. According to biographer Andrew Curran, Diderot was 'the most creative and noteworthy thinker of his era', high praise indeed given the standard of the competition.[1] He was a member of an informal network of brilliant minds centred on the Parisian salon of Baron Thiry d'Holbach (1723–1789). A relentless critic of Christianity who was eventually to become an atheist, in 1749 Diderot was imprisoned in the fortress of Vincennes after publishing a work which questioned the value of believing in a creator God. He was released after four months, partly on the understanding that he would not write any more such blasphemous works. Given the punishment to which authors and possessors of anti-Christian works could be subject, Diderot now had to be more discrete, at least in public. Henceforth he communicated his ideas through entries in the *Encyclopedia*, through literary works, through writings for the 'drawer' to be read only by friends and to be published after his death, by helping to shape and edit the texts of others, and through private conversation.

Casanova had two extended visits to Paris, in his mid-20s and early 30s: 1750–1752 and 1757–1759. It was a period when Paris was the nerve centre of the Enlightenment: an intense, restless city, fizzing with controversy and radical ideas that challenged the established order. Recently published, and generating tremendous outrage, was La Mettrie's *Man a Machine* (1747), which argued that the mind was a consequence of the complex

Antiquity

The importance of classical civilisation to the development of the Enlightenment can hardly be exaggerated, to the extent that the historian Peter Gay describes Enlightenment thinkers as 'modern pagans'.

Right: *Johann Joachim Winckelmann* (1717–1768) ca. 1777 by Anton Raphael Mengs. (Public Domain / The Metropolitan Museum of Art)

Below: *The Death of Socrates*, 1790, Pierre Peyron. (Public Domain / The Metropolitan Museum of Art)

Above left: Title page: volume IV, 'The Antiquities of Rome', 1756, by Giovanni Giambatista Piranes. (Public Domain / The Metropolitan Museum of Art)

Above right: *Artist Among Ruins*, eighteenth century by Antonio Zucchi. (Public Domain / The Metropolitan Museum of Art)

Left: Capriccio with an Ancient Temple, 1756, by Hubert Robert. (Public Domain / The Metropolitan Museum of Art)

Above: Composition with antiquities, 1782–1784, by Jean Jacques Lagrenée. (Public Domain / The Metropolitan Museum of Art)

Right: Marble grave stele with a family group, Greek, Attic, ca. 360 BCE. (Public Domain / The Metropolitan Museum of Art)

Terracotta amphora, ca. 530 BCE, by Andokides. (Public Domain / The Metropolitan Museum of Art)

Marble statue of a girl, Roman, first or second century CE. (Public Domain / The Metropolitan Museum of Art)

Enlightenment Roots

For medieval Christian societies the moral, the spiritual and the supernatural were dimensions of human experience that were woven into the very fabric of the universe. This conception of the universe was to be increasingly questioned from the late Middle Ages onwards by philosophers, scientists and humanist scholars.

Above: *The Last Judgement*, 1558, by Pieter van der Heyden. The right hand of God directs the saved to heaven while the left hand directs the damned to hell. The left (for example left-handedness) was regarded as morally inferior to the right. (Public Domain / The Metropolitan Museum of Art)

Right: *Burning of a heretic in Mantes-la-Jolie*, 1700, etching by Caspar Luyken. Under Christianity the torturing, burning or hanging of witches and heretics were widespread. Punishments of the most gruesome kinds were meted out in rituals of purification and redemption. (Public Domain / Wikimedia Commons)

DAIMONOMAGEIA.

A Small

TREATISE

OF

Sickneſſes and Diſeaſes

FROM

Witchcraft,

AND

Supernatural Cauſes.

Never before, at leaſt in this righ compriſed Order, and general Manner, was the like publiſhed.

Being uſeful to others beſides Phyſicians, In that it Confutes Atheiſtical, Sadduciſtical, and Sceptical Principles and Imaginations.

LONDON, Printed by *J. Dover*, living in St. *Bartholomews-Cloſe*, 1665.

Daimonomagia. A small treatise of sicknesses and diseases from witchcraft, and supernatural causes. 1665. (CC BY 4.0 / The Wellcome Collection)

Reliquary, Spanish, sixteenth century. The everyday belief in supernatural forces is nowhere more apparent than in the cult of relics and the miraculous powers they were believed to harness. Pilgrimage to sites where such relics were housed was of major economic and political significance for many communities. (Public Domain / The Metropolitan Museum of Art)

Right: *Epileptics Walking to the Left from Pilgrimage of the Epileptics to the Church at Molenbeeck*, 1642, by Hendrick Hondius. (Public Domain / The Metropolitan Museum of Art)

Below left: *Saint Antony of Padua: the miracle of the amputated foot*. Engraving by V. Lefebvre and G. Seuter after Titian (c 1488/90–1576). (Public Domain / The Wellcome Collection)

Below right: *Great chain of being*, 1759, from *Retorica Christiana*, print, published by Diego Valdes and signed as F. Didacus. (Public Domain / Wikimedia Commons)

M. TULLIUS CICERO

OF THE

NATURE

OF THE

GODS.

In THREE BOOKS.

With Critical, Philoſophical, and Explanatory NOTES.

By the Rev. DR. FRANCKLIN.

A NEW EDITION.

To which is added,

An ENQUIRY into the *Aſtronomy* and *Anatomy* of the ANTIENTS.

WITH

A CHRONOLOGICAL TABLE and REMARKS on the THEOLOGY of the GREEK PHILOSOPHERS.

LONDON:

Printed for T. DAVIES, in Ruſſel-ſtreet, Covent-Garden.

MDCCLXXV.

Above left: *Thomas Aquinas*, 1476, by Carlo Crivelli. Thomas Aquinas (1225–1274) was one of the key figures in the development of scholasticism, a method of learning that was to dominate university teaching from the High Middle Ages and into the Enlightenment. (Public Domain / Wikimedia Commons)

Above right: *Of the Nature of the Gods* by Marcus Tullius Cicero. Cicero was one of several ancient thinkers whose authority was beyond question and whose works formed the basis of the practice of scholasticism. (Public Domain / The Metropolitan Museum)

Francesco Petrarch (1307–1374), one of the influential early figures in the development of the Renaissance, humanism, and the reorientation of scholarly thinking away from the contemplation of God to greater consideration of human society and individual agency. (Public Domain / Wikimedia Commons)

Important Pre- and Early Enlightenment Thinkers

In the seventeenth century, a number of influential philosophers laid much of the intellectual groundwork that was to be drawn upon by later Enlightenment writers who went on to challenge established beliefs, ideas and institutions.

Francis Bacon (1561–1626), line engraving after Blyenberch. (Public Domain / Wellcome Collection)

Thomas Hobbes (1588–1679), 1668 line engraving by William Faithorne. (Public Domain / National Gallery of Art)

Above left: René Descartes (1596–1650), engraving by Jonas Suyderhoff, after Frans Hals. (Public Domain / National Gallery of Art)

Above right: John Locke (1632–1704), 1697, portrait by Godfrey Kneller. (Public Domain / Wikimedia Commons)

Left: Baruch Spinoza (1632–1677), 1765?, line engraving by E. Fessard. (Public Domain / Wellcome Collection)

Influential Figures in Casanova's Intellectual and Cultural Development

Horace (65 BCE–8 BCE), poet as imagined by Anton von Werner. (Public Domain / Wikimedia Commons)

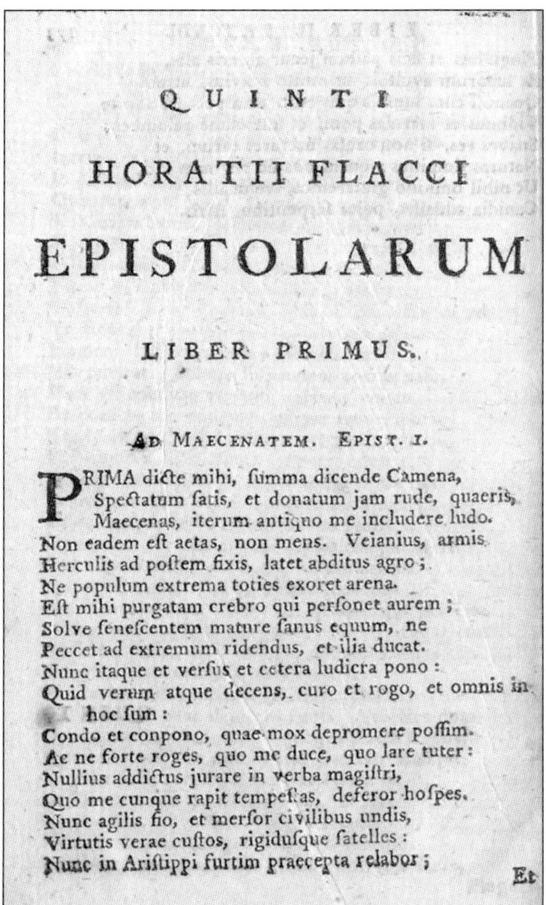

QUINTI

HORATII FLACCI

EPISTOLARUM

LIBER PRIMUS.

AD MAECENATEM. EPIST. I.

PRIMA dicte mihi, summa dicende Camena,
Spectatum satis, et donatum jam rude, quaeris,
Maecenas, iterum antiquo me includere ludo.
Non eadem est aetas, non mens. Veianius, armis
Herculis ad postem fixis, latet abditus agro;
Ne populum extrema toties exoret arena.
Est mihi purgatam crebro qui personet aurem;
Solve senescentem mature sanus equum, ne
Peccet ad extremum ridendus, et ilia ducat.
Nunc itaque et versus et cetera ludicra pono:
Quid verum atque decens, curo et rogo, et omnis in
hoc sum:
Condo et conpono, quae mox depromere possim.
Ac ne forte roges, quo me duce, quo lare tuter:
Nullius addictus jurare in verba magistri,
Quo me cunque rapit tempestas, deferor hospes.
Nunc agilis fio, et mersor civilibus undis,
Virtutis verae custos, rigidusque satelles:
Nunc in Aristippi furtim praecepta relabor;

Et

The opening page of Horace's first book of Epistles. (Public Domain (Antiquarian Books of Scotland)

Ludovico Ariosto (1474–1533), poet and author of *The Frenzy of Orlando*, by Domenico Poggini. (Public Domain / National Gallery of Art)

Canto 42, Stanza 64, from Ludovico's Ariosto's *The Frenzy of Orlando*. (Public Domain / The Metropolitan Museum of Art)

Pierre Gassendi (1595–1655), by Robert Nanteuil. (Public Domain / National Gallery of Art)

1636 engraving commissioned from Claude Mellan by Pierre Gassendi and his patron Nicolas-Claude Fabri de Peiresc who were both keen astronomers. (Public Domain / The Metropolitan Museum of Art)

Voltaire (1694–1778), after a model by Jean Antoine Houdon. (Public Domain /The Metropolitan Museum of Art)

Illustrated scene from Voltaire's *Candide, or Optimist*. Artist Jean-Louis Delignon after Jean-Michel Moreau. (Public Domain / Wikimedia Commons)

Denis Diderot (1713–1784) by Pierre Michel Alix. (Public Domain / Finnish National Gallery)

The engraved titlepage to the *Encyclopedie* of Diderot and d'Alembert. Engraving by B. L. Prevost, 1772, after C. N. Cochin, the younger, 1765. (Public Domain / The Wellcome Collection)

Jean-Jacques Rousseau (1712–1778), 1766, by David Martin after Allan Ramsay. (Public Domain / National Gallery of Art)

THE SOCIAL CONTRACT

OR

PRINCIPLES OF POLITICAL RIGHT

BY

JEAN JACQUES ROUSSEAU

Translated with an
HISTORICAL AND CRITICAL INTRODUCTION AND NOTES
BY
HENRY J. TOZER, M.A. (LOND.)
WITH A PREFACE BY
BERNARD BOSANQUET, M.A. (OXON.)
Formerly Fellow of University College, Oxford

Fœderis æquas
Dicamus leges.
Virgil, *Æneid* XI. 321–2.

London
SWAN SONNENSCHEIN & CO
NEW YORK: CHARLES SCRIBNER'S SONS
1895

The Social Contract by Jean-Jacques Rousseau. (Public Domain / The British Library) organisation of matter not the mysterious operation of the soul. La Mettrie had lived and worked in Paris then moved to Leiden in the more tolerant Dutch Republic after an outcry following upon a previous work *Natural History of the Soul* in 1745. But *Man a Machine* was too much even for the Dutch, and so he fled to Prussia. Montesquieu's pioneering *The Spirit of the Laws* (1748) had also recently been published and was causing a stir (it was banned by the Catholic Church in 1751). That mighty undertaking, the *Encyclopedia*, was under way and provoking considerable opposition, the first volume released, as it happened, in the same year that *The Spirit of the Laws* was banned. Rousseau was making a name for himself with his 1750 winning essay *Discourse on the Sciences and Arts*, followed up in 1754 with *Discourse on the Origin and Basis of Inequality Among Men.* Voltaire was banned from Paris in 1754. Claude-Adrien Helvétius raised a storm in 1758 with his publication *On Mind*, which questioned religion as the basis for morality. Grounded in sensationalist philosophy, he argued that the actions of men were guided by a self-interested desire to maximise pleasure. The book was condemned as heretical and publicly burned by the Paris hangman. Meanwhile, d'Holbach was working on *Christianity Unveiled*, to be published anonymously in 1761, a swingeing attack on Christianity. Those who were discovered to possess the book could be sent to the galleys or incarcerated in a lunatic asylum for the rest of their lives as in the case of at least one poor woman.

The intellectual, political and religious cauldron that was Paris, was a close-knit world, at least among its higher echelons, and Casanova will have met a number of significant Enlightenment figures, including Fontenelle, as discussed, secretary of the Academy of Sciences and science populariser, and d'Alembert, joint editor of the *Encyclopedia*. Illustrating the closeness and interconnectedness of Parisian society, Diderot, in his role as an art critic, was to review the paintings of an up-and-coming artist called Francesco Casanova, one of Giacomo's younger brothers. Indeed, references to Francesco in Diderot's letters to his lover Sophie Volland suggest that Francesco and Diderot were friends, at least to some degree. Our Casanova was later to claim that he identified himself with d'Alembert and Diderot, comparing them to stars that illuminated the whole universe.[2] D'Alembert also had a hand in the creation of the Paris lottery in which Casanova played such a pivotal role (and Diderot may have been involved as well).

Diderot was born in 1713 to a devout, prosperous family in the city of Langres, 275 kilometres south-east of Paris. His father was a master cutler and wanted his son to join the priesthood with an aim to replace his uncle,

Didier Vigneron, as canon in Langres cathedral (a plan which quickly fell through). Denis himself was an exceptionally bright and gregarious child albeit with a marked rebellious streak, his aversion to authority, institutional and intellectual, becoming a lifelong disposition. He joined Langres' Jesuit college when he was 10 years old, and at 12 received minor orders. In 1728 he moved to Paris where he studied for three years at the Collège d'Harcourt before moving on to the Sorbonne college of theology. He would have become familiar not only with Christian theology but the far more dangerous ideas of pagan philosophers, including the materialism of Epicurus. By now Epicurean ideas had become entwined with a range of '-isms', such as deism, atheism, libertinism and the sensationalism of John Locke.

A direct assault upon Christianity arrived in the form of *The Testament of Jean Meslier* (1729). In public Jean Meslier lived an unremarkable life as a local priest but in private he authored a more than 500-page philosophical denunciation of organised religion. Pinning his colours firmly to the mast of materialism, he denied the existence of God, the soul and free will. For Meslier, Christianity had started out well intentioned enough but had long since been corrupted to serve the interests of rulers. His writing was discovered and circulated in various clandestine forms after his death in 1729. In Diderot's poem *The Eleutheromanes* (1772) he is quoting from Jean Meslier's *Testament* when he writes, 'And its [mankind's] hands would weave the entrails of the priest / For the lack of a cord with which to strangle kings.'[3]

In contrast to those who contested the foundations of Christianity by proposing alternative explanations of reality, there were others who cast doubt upon the utility of rational enquiry, at least insofar as understanding God was concerned. Most notable was the sceptic Pierre Bayle and his influential *Historical and Critical Dictionary* (1697) already mentioned in Chapter 1. Add all this to the pantheistic philosophy of Spinoza, who was a strong influence upon Meslier, plus the works of older contemporaries such as Montesquieu and Voltaire, and by the mid-eighteenth century Diderot had access to a suite of powerful intellectual resources that would enable him to fashion his own criticisms of the Christian orthodoxies of his day. In the late 1730s Diderot learnt English and began digging into the ideas and discoveries of men such as Bacon, Newton, Locke and the third Earl of Shaftesbury, exploring for himself their radical implications for man's relationship with nature and God. In 1745 he produced a translation of Shaftesbury's *An Inquiry Concerning Virtue or Merit* (1699).

By the end of his time at college, Diderot was clear that he did not want to follow a career in the priesthood. He had been appalled by the popular miracle cults of the late 1720s and early 1730s, notably the convulsionnaire phenomenon that flared up after the death of the Parisian Jansenist, François de Pâris, in 1727. Pâris was a well-known deacon and ascetic who lived an austere life, going barefoot, eating one meal a day, and giving generously to the poor. His funeral was a conspicuous event that attracted large numbers of mourners. Miracles were reported at the site of his tomb, and it quickly became a popular destination for pilgrims. Extravagant behaviour excited the interest and imagination of the public. Accounts circulated of people convulsing, shouting, screaming, barking, foaming at the mouth, and even being lifted into the air. These convulsionnaires, as they came to be known, increasingly scourged and tortured their flesh, regarding their bodies as a source of corruption. For the *philosophes* there could be no better example to illustrate the fraudulent nature of religion and all the superstition and ignorance that was wrapped up in it. Diderot describes monks as 'vermin which gnaw at her [France] and which will gnaw at her until extinction.'[4] Then there were the internecine quarrels, notably between the Jansenists and Jesuits, which served to highlight the divisiveness of religion and the bloody conflicts that frequently ensued as a consequence. In his correspondence with Sophie Volland, Diderot observes: 'I believe that a Jansenist would trample a crucifix underfoot, on condition of slitting the throat of a Jesuit with impunity.'[5] But if such external factors motivated Diderot's disaffection there was an inward cause as well. The stirrings of sexual desire, and his struggles against them, made a life of priestly celibacy unappealing.

With the Church no longer on the cards, Diderot's father tried to persuade him to move into the legal profession, and so for a short time he studied law as an articled clerk. In reality, Diderot had little enthusiasm for any kind of profession. His passion was for the theatre, literature and intellectual pursuits. He fell out with his father who at one point had him locked up in a monastery. Diderot escaped by climbing out through a window in the early hours. Disowned by his family, and trading financial security for independence, he embarked upon the precarious existence of a hack writer, translator, tutor and even an occasional con man. In 1743 he married a lowly seamstress and devout Catholic, Anne-Antoinette (Toinette) Champion. Unconventionally for the time, he married her for love. They had four children but only one survived, Angelique, upon whom he doted. Although the marriage endured until Diderot's death, the couple had little in common. He was frequently unfaithful, and his increasing rejection of God only soured their relationship further.

It was during this period of hand-to-mouth existence that Diderot became involved in the project that was to dominate the next quarter century of his life. In 1746, initially as a translator and then as joint editor, he was offered the job of producing a French version of Ephraim Chambers' 1728 two-volume English *Cyclopaedia.* At Diderot's instigation the project was to become much more ambitious. His aim was to create a work that comprised nothing less than all the world's knowledge, constructed upon those three pillars of the Enlightenment: freedom of thought, reason and empirical evidence. It would help to sweep away religious superstition and dogma, challenging the legitimacy of religious authority. Around this time Diderot met d'Holbach, the two becoming close friends and allies. They were to be fellow travellers along a more radical Enlightenment path, elucidating a thoroughgoing materialistic concept of existence in contrast to the older, more moderate generation of deistic *philosophes* typified by Voltaire. For d'Holbach, and eventually Diderot, there was no need for God, the supernatural, and all the speculative baggage that came along with it to explain the workings of the universe. The laws of nature would be sufficient.

Staging posts along Diderot's transition from believer to non-believer were his series of short essays called *Philosophical Thoughts* (1746), in which he problematised the traditional Christian view that posited the bleakness of human existence after its fall from grace, and his essay *Letter on the Blind* (1749). The latter moves on to challenge the existence of God and contains alternative materialist explanations of life that have unmistakable parallels with Lucretius's *On the Nature of Things*.

Letter on the Blind was inspired by the case of a girl whose eyesight had been restored following a cataract operation. It raised questions for Diderot about the relationship between knowledge and the senses, questions previously raised by Locke's *An Essay Concerning Human Understanding* (1689). Did man have innate knowledge, as argued by Descartes, or did all knowledge about the world have to be constructed from the information received by the senses, as argued by Locke? If the latter, then how might a person's understanding of the world be changed if they are missing one of the senses used to collect data. Diderot's *Letter* is an extended monologue in which an unnamed correspondent addresses its unnamed recipient. The writer points out that different behaviours are judged differently by the blind. Consequently, morality is relative and not a divine given as Christian dogma would have it: someone's state of undress is of little significance to the sightless whereas theft, which exploits a person's blindness, is a far more serious crime.

Envisioning the deathbed scene of the famous blind English mathematician, Nicholas Saunderson, he constructs a dialogue between the scholar and a priest in which the priest attempts, but fails, to persuade the dying man of God's existence. The priest draws attention to the 'admirable mechanism' of his sense organs (a proof of intelligent design) which Saunderson does not find all that impressive, certainly not enough to convince him of the existence of a 'supremely intelligent being'. The priest also refers to the 'wonders of nature'.[6] This evidence, as Saunderson explains, cannot be comprehended by a blind man. It is of no aid to his understanding. Likewise, assuming the existence of an unfathomable creator God is of no aid in understanding creation – it is simply offering a solution to a difficulty which is more inscrutable than the difficulty itself, a point which Diderot reiterates twenty years later in *D'Alembert's Dream* (1769). Diderot questions the idea that the world was created by God in its present state at a single point in time and advocates a materialist alternative. Saunderson gives an evolutionary explanation of existence (of both planets and species) that allows for the gradual change of matter, including a process of mutation. He contemplates a distant past in which 'monsters have successively destroyed each other, that all the faulty combinations of matter disappeared, only those remaining, the mechanism of which was no important contradiction, which could subsist and perpetuate themselves,' and goes on to observe that 'amidst all this so perfect order, monstrous productions come forth now and then.'[7]

Both *Philosophical Thoughts* and *Letter on the Blind* were condemned upon their publication, but in an atmosphere of mounting political tension in Paris it was the latter which was deemed to have overstepped the line. It was the *Letter on the Blind* that led to Diderot's imprisonment in Vincennes (the Bastille was full). The works had been anonymous but the authorities knew full well who was their author. He was to remain incarcerated for three months before being released on the understanding that he would be locked up permanently if he published any further subversive material. Diderot took the message on board and was far more cautious from then on. For the next twenty-three years most of his phenomenal energy, in public at least, was devoted to the *Encyclopedia*.

Another key philosophical work that Diderot was to write two decades after *Letter on the Blind* was *D'Alembert's Dream.* Unlike *Letter on the Blind*, it was not published until after his death although it did appear in

1782 in *The Literary Correspondence*. This was a handwritten, cultural newsletter aimed at a highly select readership that included European aristocrats. It counted Catherine II of Russia and Stanislaus II of Poland among its subscribers. The newsletter was organised by Diderot's close friend Friedrich Melchior Grimm to whom he had been introduced by Rousseau.

D'Alembert's Dream is a fictional piece comprising three philosophical dialogues. There are four protagonists: Diderot himself, d'Alembert, Mademoiselle Lespinasse (d'Alembert's mistress) and a Dr Bordeu. Diderot uses the dialogues to expound further his materialist understanding of existence, in particular that matter can change form, that complex organisms can develop from simpler ones, and that species can evolve by dint of natural laws without the need for divine intervention. Diderot opens the first dialogue by illustrating to d'Alembert how marble can be transformed from an inanimate to an animate material by being ground into powder and sowing it with seeds, the plants from which can then be eaten and transformed into flesh. Like La Mettrie, he refers to human bodies as machines and describes their mechanical operations. He declares: 'And anyone lecturing to the Academy on the stages in the formation of a man or animal need only to refer to material factors, the successive stages of which would be an inert body, a sentient being, a thinking being.'[8]

One issue that Diderot raises in the second dialogue of *D'Alembert's Dream*, which is of particular relevance to Casanova, is that of identity. How is it possible for any creature in a state of constant change, a machine composed of numerous different parts, to be able to possess an awareness of whom they are as a single, independent being? Our senses, by which we obtain information about the world, are only proof of our existence in the present. For Diderot, the answer lies in memory. That is where our past perceptions are stored. Through the character of Mademoiselle Lespinasse, Diderot describes the body as a network of interconnected threads and compares it to a spider's web: 'Imagine a spider in the centre of his web. Disturb a thread and you will see the creature rush up on the alert. Now suppose that those threads that the insect draws from its own body, and draws in again at will, were a sensitive part of itself?'[9]

A little later in the dialogue these threads, or strands, are discussed in terms of an evolutionary mechanism, taking on a role strikingly like that of DNA. Within the animal machine 'regular or irregular formation depends upon a collection of fine, slender, flexible threads,' summarises Lespinasse.[10] 'Take another thread away from the bundle, the one destined to form the nose, and the creature will become noseless. Take away the one that should form the ear and it will have no ears or only one ear, and the anatomist in his dissection won't find either the olfactory or auditory threads, or will only find one of the latter instead of two.'[11]

The characters discuss how inherited abnormalities and changes can be traced across generations. The threads themselves have no memory but the spider at the centre of the web functions to register and record sense data. An individual's identity thus resides in this perceptual history. This is also the place of man's consciousness. Dr Bordeu explains: 'It [consciousness] can only be at one place, at the common centre of all sensations, where memory resides and comparisons are made. Each individual thread is only capable of registering a certain number of impressions, that is to say sensations one after the other, isolated and not remembered. But the centre is sensitive to all of them; it is the register, it keeps them in mind or holds a sustained impression, and any animal is bound, from its embryonic stage, to relate itself to this centre, attached its whole life to it, exist in it.'[12] Louis Dupré notes: 'With this argument Diderot thinks he has accomplished his goal of uniting the mechanistic theories of Descartes and Newton with a sensationalism derived from Locke and thus of having eliminated the separation between material and mental principles of reality.'[13]

D'Alembert, albeit delirious at the time, rejects the ancient Platonic and Aristotelian concept of an immaterial essence: 'You poor philosophers, and you talk about essences! Drop your idea of essences … What is a being? The sum of a certain number of tendencies … Can I be anything more than a tendency? … No, I am moving towards a certain end.'[14] Likewise, Dr Bordeu rejects the idea of 'abstractions' (Platonic essences) as simply a by-product of language. He notes how, 'Every abstraction is merely a symbol devoid of particularized meaning. Every abstract science is simply juggling with symbols. The exact picture was dropped when the symbol was separated from the physical object, and it is only when the symbol and the physical object are brought together again that science once again becomes a matter of real things.'[15]

It is a small step to move from the idea of a biological record to a written one. It is no coincidence that Casanova titles his memoirs *History of My Life*. So important to him is this association between memory and the self that in his 1797 Preface he declares: 'My history, which must begin with the earliest fact that my memory can recall, will begin when I was eight years and four months old. Before that time, if it is true that *vivere cogitare est* [to live is to think], I was not living: I was vegetating.'[16] By collecting together in his memoirs data of every aspect of his life, good and bad, Casanova is simultaneously reflecting upon and shaping his identity, at least his identity in the sense of his self-awareness as an independent being (clearly others will perceive his identity differently). If we accept Diderot's argument, then without that historical record there is no 'me', for there is no immaterial essence, no immaterial soul. It is the history of your life which will tell you who you are, not some Rousseauian introspective search for divine properties bequeathed to you by the Almighty.

In the final dialogue, picking up another theme of interest to Casanova, Dr Bordeu and Mademoiselle Lespinasse raise the issue of morality and sexual pleasure, adopting a typically libertine position. They agree that chastity is of no benefit to the individual or to society, and Bordeu attacks those laws which restrict sex to the confines of marriage: 'They were made without regard for equity, without any clear object and without attention being paid to the nature of things or public usefulness.'[17] Such laws are crimes against nature. The main culprits in this state of affairs are religion and its 'fanatics'. He emphatically rejects the idea that 'chastity and absolute continence' are virtues but instead that they have negative effects, notably madness, especially for the young.[18] For radical *philosophes* such as Diderot and d'Holbach, desire and its satisfaction through pleasure were intrinsic to human nature and not in itself moral or immoral. Philipp Blom notes: 'To Diderot, erotic desire, the nonrational impulse to live and to seek pleasure, was fundamental to all consciousness, to all culture.'[19] It was part of what drove the human machine and was essential for its continued existence. Reason was the tool of passion, its slave, not its master. Rational pleasure-seeking which did not harm others was beneficial both to society and the individual. It was to be encouraged, not condemned or forbidden. It was this form of libertinism, one that took account of the needs of the other, which was advocated by Casanova.

Works such as *Philosophical Thoughts, Letter on the Blind* and *D'Alembert's Dream* expressed several principles which together enabled Diderot to provide a coherent account of creation from the formation of planets to the development of life to the emergence of consciousness. Most important, it was an account that dispensed with the need for God. As the editor of the *Encyclopedia* he had access to a huge repository of ideas as well as being at the hub of an intellectual network comprising the foremost thinkers of his day, including mathematicians, naturalists, biologists and doctors. Particularly influential for Diderot were Lucretius's description of Epicureanism, work on probability by Blaise Pascal and Pierre de

Fermat, the physician William Harvey, the aforementioned mathematician Pierre Louis Maupertuis, and the naturalist and mathematician George-Louis Leclerc, Comte de Buffon.

Diderot adopted the Epicurean proposition that we live in a material universe constructed out of the random collisions of indivisible atoms. Over time they produce increasingly elaborate forms. Drawing on probability theory, Diderot was able to point out that with a constant stream of events (or flux) and infinite time it was certain that every possible combination would occur. Via this mechanism order would form out of chaos, and likewise, return to chaos. He also allowed that the intrinsic qualities of each particle included motion and, as suggested by Maupertuis, consciousness, raising the spectre of Spinozan pantheism. All matter was, in some sense, alive, and as it acquired complexity so did its conscious state also become more complex. In this regard the difference between humans and other organisations of matter was simply degree.

Constant change was built into this system. Any perception that nature was fixed was an illusion based upon Christian theology and limited time frames. Neither could there be any clear distinctions between kingdoms (mineral, plant or animal) or species, a point underscored by Buffon who observed how characteristics of different species overlapped. There could be no chain of being, simply variation descended from prototypes. Indeed, Diderot's view was that there was one single prototype. He accepted the commonly held belief in spontaneous generation for small creatures such as flies, which arose from matter through some kind of process of fermentation. If every particle contained motion and consciousness, and had the potential to combine in any conceivable way, then why not? Many of these combinations, of course, could not survive and flourish in the environment in which they found themselves. Numerous variants, or monsters, would quickly appear and disappear. What we see about us are entities that are temporarily successful, suitable as they are to prevailing conditions.

Unsurprisingly, Diderot rejected preformationism. This was an established theory that offspring unfolded and grew from a perfectly formed miniature or homunculus which was pre-existent in either the egg or the sperm. Preformationism was consistent with the theological doctrine that all species were fixed by God at the time of creation. But it had difficulty in explaining birth defects and mutations. Instead, Diderot was persuaded by Harvey's epigenetic theory that different parts of an embryo bud out and develop successively from what is initially undifferentiated matter, another process that allowed for the possibility of variation and change.

Philosophy was only one aspect of Diderot's intellectual output. He was a novelist who created idiosyncratic masterpieces such as *Rameau's Nephew* and he was a playwright. In 1757 he published *The Natural Son, or the Trials of Virtue*, a sentimental play which explored the complications of love and friendship, and the following year *The Father of the Family* in which a young man falls in love with a woman from a much humbler background and wants to marry her, mirroring the circumstances of himself and Toinette. Inspired by the Venetian playwright Carlo Goldoni, he sought to shift French theatre towards more realistic dramas that were centred on the lives and moral concerns of ordinary people. He wrote essays on the theatre and was an influential art critic. He has sometimes been labelled the first great art critic because of his writings on the official art exhibitions of the Académie des Beaux-Arts in Paris, known as *The Salon*, which he produced for *The Literary Correspondence* from 1759 to 1781, most famously those on the Salons of 1765 and 1767.

Unsurprisingly, these works are influenced by the ideas that preoccupy his philosophy. Unlike more uncompromising materialists such as d'Holbach and Helvétius, Diderot struggled with some of the logical implications of materialism and sensationalism, and this is reflected in his analysis of art. Materialism describes a deterministic universe that would appear to rule out the possibility of free will, while sensationalism only offered the possibility of knowledge of the effects of objects on the senses, forever sealing man off from understanding objects as they truly are. Diderot was unwilling to accept either of these conclusions. Reality was too complex to be abandoned to such soulless reductivism. He was open to more abstract and intangible possibilities. He recognised in artists the ability to act with a certain degree of freedom to reveal the intrinsic qualities of nature. Art for Diderot could not simply be the transmission of ideas. Its prime function had to be aesthetic. It had to give pleasure, and for both the artist in its production and the spectator in its appreciation a creative process was required.

In his *Essay on Painting*, which he appended to his review of the salon of 1765, he brings out this dynamic connection between beauty, nature and art. Describing a sunset walk in a wood, he writes: 'Our steps cease involuntarily; our eyes stroll on the magic canvas, and we exclaim: "What a painting! Oh! How beautiful that is!" It seems that we consider nature the result of art; and, conversely, if it happens that the painter repeats the same enchantment on the canvas, that we look at the effect of art as that of nature. It is not at the Salon, it is in the depths of a forest, among the mountains that the sun shines and illuminates, that Loutherbourg and Vernet are great.'[20] For Diderot that which is good and true contains a beauty which the artist is capable of revealing to those who are sufficiently receptive and knowledgeable but 'Nature, or the art that copies it, says nothing to the stupid or cold man, little to the ignorant man.'[21]

It was when Diderot was released from Vincennes in 1749 that he was introduced by Rousseau to d'Holbach, whose salon was to become an intellectual powerhouse and a centre of materialist philosophy. According to historians such as Jonathan Israel, it was the work of such radical Enlightenment thinkers that facilitated an abrupt shift in the 1770s to a modern conception of human rights defined by equality, universality and inalienability. Previously rights had been tied to property and social status. Now they were to be grounded in individual and collective happiness, echoing the ideas of Epicureanism but going much further as they were folded in to a critique of established political and religious authority. Visitors to d'Holbach's salon included luminaries such as Buffon, Étienne Bonnot de Condillac, Condorcet, Ferdinando Galiani, Helvétius, Guillaume Thomas Raynal, Turgot as well as, of course, once close friends d'Alembert, Diderot, Grimm and Rousseau. Among occasional foreign guests were Cesare Beccaria, Benjamin Franklin, David Garrick, Edward Gibbon, David Hume and Adam Smith.

Paul-Henri Thiry, Baron d'Holbach was born in 1723 in Edesheim in the Rhenish Palatinate, the son of a prosperous winegrower. In 1728 his fortunes changed dramatically when his wealthy uncle took him under his wing and brought him to Paris. He had a love of learning and a particularly strong interest in nature, the sciences and experimentation. In his early 20s he went to study at Leiden, not only one of the greatest universities in Europe but one the freest and most tolerant. While there he became good friends with a 19-year-old John Wilkes. Upon his return to Paris in 1748, the young d'Holbach decided to recreate a similar sort of free-thinking, intellectual environment. Five years later his father and uncle died, and his inheritance made him a rich man.

D'Holbach and his circle supported Diderot's ambitious plans for the *Encyclopedia*, the baron himself contributing almost 400 articles as well as translating material from German. Meanwhile, Diderot was inserting his own ideas into the productions of others. One of the most controversial and widely read publications in the second half of the century was Abbé Raynal's ten-volume *History of the Two Indies* (1770), an encyclopedia on European commerce and colonisation in Africa, the Americas and the Far

East. It is estimated that Diderot may have written 20 per cent of the book. In it he made the moral case for American independence, condemned the evils of slavery, and predicted that oppressive rule would lead to popular uprisings and revolution both at home and in the colonies. For Diderot sovereignty ultimately resided with the people. Some of his analysis was prescient. He predicted the rise of a Black Spartacus who would lead slaves in rebellion against their masters. In Haiti, Toussaint Louverture did just that. So incendiary was the 1780 edition that Raynal had to flee to Prussia. Diderot, along with other friends, also had a hand in editing the works of d'Holbach whose style tended to be rather wordy. D'Holbach attacked the present social order, most notably in his influential text *The System of Nature* (1770). It is very probable that Diderot influenced d'Holbach's writings through the discussions that took place in his salon, and to which Diderot was a prominent contributor.

By 1772 the final volumes of the *Encyclopedia* were finished. Diderot was at last rid of a burden which had dominated much of his adult life. It had been one of his main sources of income and now, entering old age, he needed to shore up his finances. His solution was to try to find a buyer for the considerable library he had amassed as he worked on the *Encyclopedia*, not a straightforward task given his reputation as a notorious atheist. Diderot's saviour was Catherine II, and she proved to be exceptionally generous. She not only paid him up front but allowed him to hang on to his books and papers until his death and gave him an allowance to act as its librarian. But Diderot's relief was tempered by the fact that he was now indebted to an authoritarian ruler and under an obligation to visit her. Eventually Diderot did so in 1773. He got on well with the Empress but his hopes that he might be able to persuade her to initiate progressive government reforms proved to be naïve. After six months at the court he undertook the punishing return journey home, arriving back in Paris in October 1774, visibly aged. For the next almost ten years he continued to work on a range of projects such as a rebuttal of Helvétius's *On Mind,* his novel *Jacques the Fatalist,* and an essay on the life of Seneca. He died in July 1784.

Diderot's reputation languished relative to those revolutionary heroes Voltaire and Rousseau. The bodies of Voltaire and Rousseau were ceremoniously interred in the Panthéon while Diderot's was to end up in a mass grave after his remains in the Church of Saint-Roch were desecrated by burglars. There were several reasons for this lack of recognition. Following upon his imprisonment in Vincennes much of what he wrote was produced in secrecy and often anonymously, unknown to many of his contemporaries, while those of his works which did circulate after his death tended to be mangled pirated editions. Neither had Diderot constructed a clearly defined, systematic philosophy. And unlike Voltaire and Rousseau, he carried the enormous social stigma of having been an atheist. Even the French revolutionaries concocted a Supreme Being to replace the deposed God of the Christians. Not until the late 1940s was the scope and genius of his achievement fully uncovered with the discovery of the Vandeul archives – a collection of manuscripts which had been suppressed by his daughter.

The *Encyclopedia*

In a letter to Sophie Volland dated 26 September 1762, Diderot writes of the *Encyclopedia*: 'This work will surely produce in time a revolution in the minds of men, and I hope that the tyrants, the oppressors, the fanatics and the bigots will not win.'[22] The *Encyclopedia* or, to give it its full name, the *Encyclopedia, or a Rational Dictionary of the Sciences, Arts and Trades*, was one of the towering achievements of the Enlightenment. A quarter of a century in the making, comprising 28 volumes (17 volumes of articles and 11 volumes of illustrations), 2,900 engravings, 18,000 pages of text, 74,000 entries supplied by more than 140 contributors and adding up to 20 million words, it was a huge undertaking the aim of which was to provide a thorough account of the branches of human knowledge.

But the numbers only convey part of the immensity of its ambition. The *Encyclopedia* was the culmination of the challenge of the Enlightenment, pitting reason and empirical knowledge in a democratised form against hierarchy and dogmatism. While by 1750 there was a growing acceptance of moderate Enlightenment thought even within religious circles, its more radical ideas continued to provoke disquiet. Consequently, along with the practical difficulties the *Encyclopedia* faced, it had to struggle against fierce opposition from conservative social forces, in particular elements of the Catholic Church. To its aid rallied many of the greatest minds of the time, a number of whom have already been mentioned. It also acquired surprising allies in the form of Louis XV's chief mistress, Madame de Pompadour, and Guillaime-Chrétien de Lamoignon de Malesherbes who, among other things, was in charge of supervising the state's censorship of printed texts.

For contemporaries the publication of the *Encyclopedia* was an event of tremendous significance. The first volume came out in June 1751, receiving applause or condemnation depending upon which side of the political and religious aisle commentators stood. Among its most vociferous critics were the Jesuits, while its most high-profile defender was Voltaire. Following upon the publication of the second volume in 1752 the Parlement of Paris decreed that the *Encyclopedia* should be burned, and Louis XV ordered its suppression. But the work continued in secret. A man such as Casanova, deeply fascinated by philosophy and intellectual debate, would have followed the furore surrounding the *Encyclopedia* with close interest, particularly as he was familiar with some of the main protagonists involved and lived in Paris for a chunk of the 1750s. He was 26 when the first volume was published and 47 when the project was completed. The *Encyclopedia* played its part in shaping his knowledge and understanding of important currents in Enlightenment attitudes as well as being a valuable warehouse of ideas and information. There are various occasions in Casanova's own writings where he directly references the *Encyclopedia*. In his *Critical Essay on Science, Morals and the Arts* he draws on the *Encyclopedia*'s organisation of knowledge as described in the *Preliminary Discourse to the Encyclopedia of Diderot* (1751) written by Casanova's friend d'Alembert.

To get a sense of the significance of the work to its editors, and how they conceived of its place both in terms of its relationship to the Enlightenment in particular, and in the flow of history more generally, it is worth having a look at Diderot's opening comments in his entry 'Encyclopedia':

> Encyclopedia. This word signifies chain of knowledge; it is composed of the Greek preposition ἐν, in, and the nouns κύκλος, circle, and παιδεία, knowledge.
>
> Indeed, the purpose of an encyclopedia is to collect knowledge disseminated around the globe; to set forth its general system to the men with whom we live, and transmit it to those who will come after us, so that the work of preceding centuries will not become useless to the centuries to come; and so that our offspring, becoming better instructed, will at the same time become more virtuous and happy, and that we should not die without having rendered a service to the human race.[23]

In the eighteenth century, this chain of knowledge could be traced back to the ancient Greeks and Romans. The transmission of that knowledge stretching across well over two millennia had been precarious. The vast bulk of what was written had been lost. The challenges which the chain of knowledge faced are well illustrated by the Great Library of Alexandria, founded during the Ptolemaic dynasty around the third century BCE. One of the greatest repositories of texts and centres for scholarship in the ancient world, even by the second century BCE the institution was being undermined by political and economic instability. In the first century BCE, during a civil war involving Julius Caesar, Cleopatra and her brother Ptolemy, tens of thousands of scrolls were destroyed in a fire. Under Roman control and neglect, its once peerless reputation for scholarship fell into decline. Its collections were used to stock other libraries. By the middle of the third century CE references to the Great Library began to dry up, while a war that engulfed the city in 272 CE is likely to have done considerable damage to whatever, if anything, of the Great Library remained.

If we continue on to look more broadly at the Roman Empire, for a considerable time wealthy Romans possessed their own private libraries and there was a flourishing industry in the production of texts. These libraries were costly and time consuming to maintain. As the empire in the west struggled from the third century CE onwards to contend with the growing threats of barbarian tribes from the north as well as homegrown disputes among leadership rivals, libraries became less of a priority. Religious antagonism did not help matters. Christianity, ascendant across the continent from the fourth century, treated pagan literature with a combination of suspicion and contempt. Where the ideas of writers such as Plato and Aristotle could be yoked to the Christian cause there was a certain amount of tolerance, but an unredeemably atheist-seeming tradition, such as Epicureanism, would be denounced and suppressed.

But the greatest challenge to the chain of knowledge was not political instability, religious conflict or the occasional bonfire. It was neglect. Few texts, unless carved in stone, survive across two millennia. Almost everything that was written in antiquity, apart from some rarities such as the Dead Sea scrolls, and a few charred remains thanks to Vesuvius, has now vanished. Papyrus and parchment can be long-lived but they do decay. Ultimately, overuse, accidents, mould and, above all, the notorious bookworm, would be too much. Then there was also the widespread practice of scraping off the ink from old parchment texts to make them ready to be written upon anew. What exists today is not merely a copy but the product of a chain of copies. And until the establishment of the printing press in the fifteenth century, that copying was carried out over the centuries by armies of scribes. *History, Medea, Metamorphoses, Odyssey, Plato's Republic*, none of these would have survived by default. A dynamic process that was labour and resource intensive was required. For ancient texts to disappear it was enough simply to leave them on the shelf and forget about them for a few hundred years.

For Diderot and the *philosophes* one text more than any other epitomised the fragility of knowledge, a text without which the Enlightenment may have looked very different. That text was the remarkable poem *On the Nature of Things*, written in the first century BCE by Lucretius. Rediscovered in 1417 by the dogged book hunter Poggio Bracciolini, this work of power and beauty sets out to explain the materialist metaphysics of Epicureanism, founded in the fourth century BCE but which by Bracciolini's time had been as good as lost. The advent of the printing press later in the century, of course, revolutionised the copying business and let the Epicurean genie well and truly out of its bottle. Had Bracciolini not found Lucretius in 1417, had the ink of that copy been scraped away or had it been devoured by bookworms, then perhaps what was arguably one of the most influential branches on the genealogy of modern thought may never have come to be.

Diderot's conception of the *Encyclopedia* as a mechanism through which knowledge could be passed on through the ages 'so that our offspring, becoming better instructed, will at the same time become more virtuous and happy' could not have had a better example than *On the Nature of Things*. In a fitting metaphor for Diderot's great Enlightenment project Lucretius himself wrote of 'Passing on life's torch, like relay runners in a race'.[24] Under the entry 'Epicureanism' Diderot dusted down a 2,000-year-old philosophy that was anathema to the dogmas promulgated by the Catholic Church and placed it full-square before the educated public of his day. His entry begins: 'The Eleatic school gave birth to the Epicurean school. No philosophy has ever been less understood and more slandered than that of Epicurus.'[25] He then goes on to expound the Epicurean atomic theory of the universe, the validity of seeking happiness and pleasure, and the irrelevance of the gods to human life except as a source of fear and superstition.

That the *Encyclopedia* was an explicitly Enlightenment project and a challenge to the old ways of thinking is made crystal clear at the outset of Volume 1 in d'Alembert's *Preliminary Discourse*. Drawing upon the ideas of Epicurus and John Locke while rejecting the Cartesian 'system of innate ideas', the *Preliminary Discourse* records that the consensus of opinion among contemporary scholars had moved in support of empiricism and the idea that there were only two sources of knowledge: information which is derived from the senses, and reflections upon that information. Communication and the invention of language, he goes on to argue, emerged from a desire on the part of individuals to benefit from the exchange of this knowledge.

The idea of beneficial knowledge, of course, went back to Bacon and, indeed, Epicurus. And the value of collaboration, another of the cornerstones of Bacon's scientific model, could not have been better exemplified than through a project such as the *Encyclopedia*. It was Bacon's formulation of the categories of human knowledge in his 1605 *Advancement of Learning* that served as the inspiration for the 'encyclopedic tree' adopted by the Encyclopedists. The *Preliminary Discourse* boils knowledge down to three interconnected areas that parallel the workings of the human mind: History (memory), Philosophy (reason) and Fine Arts (imagination). From these branches further sub-divisions extend outwards, defining areas of knowledge with increasing specificity. In this way, the diversity of knowledge could be united into a coherent whole. The consequence of this method was to remove the special status which had been enjoyed by religion. The 'Science of God' was now merely one aspect of Philosophy, alongside the 'Science of Man' and the 'Science of Nature', while Philosophy itself was only one of three branches. Throughout the *Preliminary Discourse* the demotion of religion is evident. Even concepts of good and evil are discussed not so much in religious terms but in terms of the context of history and social interaction. There could be no doubt upon reading the *Preliminary Discourse* that the *Encyclopedia* was a secular work. Its central figures are Bacon, Descartes, Newton and Locke not St Augustine or St Thomas. Although penned by d'Alembert, it was, like the *Encyclopedia* itself, a joint effort that called upon the insight and opinion of like-minded, progressive thinkers, notably Rousseau, Diderot and Condillac.

The story of the *Encyclopedia* begins with a project to produce a French translation of Ephraim Chambers's English *Cyclopedia, or An Universal Dictionary of Arts and Sciences* (1728). Control of the project ended up in the hands of the publisher André Le Breton, an official printer to the king who had been doing pretty good business from royal commissions. He was not a man you would expect to involve himself in the publication of something that might jeopardise his good name and his profits. At that time, a reference work such as this was unlikely to have rung any alarm bells. The man he hired as its editor in 1746 was mathematician Jean Paul de Gua de Malves who, in turn, hired d'Alembert and Diderot to assist him. D'Alembert was recognised as an accomplished mathematician who since his early 20s had been a member of the Academy of Sciences, and in 1743, at the age of 26, had published an important paper on dynamics. His name provided the enterprise with the intellectual star appeal that the unknown Diderot lacked. Both were gregarious men and witty conversationalists who took full advantage of the lively Parisian social scene.

Malves was fired after just over a year, to be replaced by d'Alembert and Diderot as joint editors, which is when the scope and nature of the enterprise changed. Rousseau introduced them to Condillac, a radical empiricist whose philosophical ideas were to have a strong influence upon the direction the *Encyclopedia* was to take. In 1750 Diderot revealed in a prospectus its new form and ambition, and the extent to which it was a huge collaborative exercise. As well as being an up-to-date storehouse of learning written by contributors, a number of whom were experts in their fields (although not as many as Diderot had implied), it would offer a means to explore the myriad ways knowledge could interconnect and enrich understanding. Its overarching alphabetical structure would be intrinsically anti-hierarchical and asynchronous as well as providing some future-proofing; new information would be easier to absorb in later editions.

Instead of footnotes, which were typical in equivalent works of the time, the *Encyclopedia* would adopt a system of cross-referencing. Such a system was far more efficient and flexible, akin to the use of hyperlinks, and could be used for several purposes. It could save unnecessary repetition of information, in particular with regards to contextualisation. It could be used to promote discussion by linking entries where the content or argument on a topic may have been in conflict. It could indicate to readers other potentially fruitful avenues of investigation that bypassed conventional subject categories and was less restricted in comparison to texts with more linear structures. It could also be used ironically and subversively. So, in the *Encyclopedia* we have an article on apricot jam that leads to an entry on sugar production which in turn eventually leads to an attack upon the practice of slavery. An entry on 'Cannibals' is cross-referenced to 'Communion' and 'Eucharist'.

A typical entry would include a term ('Epicureanism'), where that term was situated in the genealogical tree ('History of philosophy), cross-references ('see Brucker, Gassendi, Lucrece, etc'), and an initial or mark to indicate who was the author. A reader of the *Encyclopedia* would have a more dynamic and independent relationship with the text. They would not be shepherded along pre-ordained pathways with all the assumptions of prestige and authority that validated certain forms of knowledge at the expense of others.

Another radical dimension to the *Encyclopedia* was the attention it gave to trades and industrial processes. Subjects ranging from carpentry to glassmaking to metalworking to printing to textiles to wigmaking were described in detail, coupled with illustrations of unprecedented clarity and precision. This was useful knowledge of the sort that Bacon would have approved. It encouraged innovation and resulted in direct economic benefits that improved people's lives. In a world that was organised around hierarchy, status and privilege, it offered a re-evaluation of the importance of the mechanical arts relative to the liberal arts, and of the worth of ordinary people.

As already touched upon, the *Encyclopedia* offered endless opportunities to subvert established authority. For example, Abbé Edme-Francois Mallet wrote an entry on 'Noah's Ark'. A lengthy and pedantic piece, Mallet surveys scholarly debates on the numbers of animals contained, the amount of dung they would produce, the quantity of supplies needed, the ark's dimensions (some assumptions requiring it to be significantly larger than a modern supertanker), the time taken to build it, the kind of wood used and so on and so forth. The deadpan absurdity of it all could not help but undermine the Bible as a reliable historical source. In an entry on the 'Clergy', the same contributor spends a significant proportion of the article drawing attention to the tax exemptions and legal immunities enjoyed by the Church, and its determination to hang on to them (before ostensibly defending the system). On 'Nobility', Louis de Jaucourt remarks that democracies can happily do away with the nobility and that 'noble birth commonly stifles industry.'[26] In an entry on 'Intolerance', Diderot writes: 'Ecclesiastic intolerance consists of considering as false all religions other than one's own; proclaiming it from the rooftops without being held back by terror, respect for humanity, or fear for the loss of one's life. This article will not address such heroism that has generated so many martyrs across the church's centuries.'[27]

But although the *Encyclopedia* enjoyed the support of Pompadour and Malesherbes, the editors were cautious not to go too far. This was largely because they did not want to exacerbate further the hostile forces lined up against them but also partly because they did not want to undermine the fundamental seriousness of the enterprise. To appease the censors, they made sure to include orthodox opinions and arguments as counterweights to more radical ideas. The reader could then decide for themselves which was the more persuasive. This was not an uncommon strategy for writers of the time. Particularly sensitive topics, such as materialism, they approached gingerly.

How perilous for Diderot and d'Alembert the situation could be was illustrated in the second half of the 1750s. In 1752 growing pressure by various religious groups led to the first two volumes being banned. It was looking as though the project might be over, at least in the form envisioned by the *philosophes*. At this point Malesherbes intervened to negotiate a compromise which enabled work to be discretely resumed so that between 1753 and 1756 volumes III to VI were released. But in January 1757 the mood in Paris darkened considerably with the attempted assassination of Louis XV. The enemies of the *philosophes* looked to redirect popular anger against the *Encyclopedia*. It was publicly denounced by the Archbishop of Paris while Parlement decreed severe punishments, including the death penalty, for any author or publisher who produced seditious literature. Increasing numbers of tracts and pamphlets appeared attacking the Encyclopedists. One such was authored by Jacob-Nicolas Moreau, royal historiographer and staunch defender of absolute monarchy. He satirised the Encyclopedists as members of a tribe whose purpose was to take advantage of a credulous public in order to undermine religion and the government. D'Alembert himself did not help matters. In volume VII, published the same year, he had written a rather unflattering portrait of Geneva, causing a diplomatic outcry. Pressure upon the publisher and editors increased. The Jansenists in Parlement wanted them thrown out of Paris or imprisoned, and the whole thing shut down, while the Jesuits wanted to take over the venture for themselves. Voltaire became concerned that he might get caught up in the backlash and demanded that his manuscripts, evidence of his involvement, be returned to him.

The crisis deepened with the publication of *On Mind* by Helvétius, a friend of Diderot's and a prominent figure in radical Enlightenment circles. This work of Epicurean materialism and utilitarian calculus had been nodded through by an overburdened censor who had not read it properly. Helvétius's wealth, courtly influence and several humiliating retractions enabled him to survive but only just. As pressure against the *Encyclopedia* continued to mount, in March 1759 its production and distribution was banned. D'Alembert, who had come close to leaving the year before, now definitively jumped ship. The dangers were becoming too great. But Diderot persevered despite all his fears of arrest and the terrible consequences that might ensue. He had been the *Encyclopedia*'s driving force. For over a decade it had consumed his life but now it looked as though it was all going to be over.

It was Malesherbes who saved the day. Getting wind of a plan by the authorities to raid Diderot's office, he tipped Diderot off and spirited away to safe keeping all his manuscripts and notes. He then lobbied at court. Always in the *Encyclopedia*'s favour was its commercial importance to Paris. Even in its early days this had been substantial and was one of the levers used to release Diderot from Vincennes. It was a monumental undertaking that required a pretty monumental workforce. It had thousands of subscribers and employed hundreds upon hundreds of workers, including printers, binders, illustrators, paper merchants, typesetters and so on. A lot of people had a great deal to lose. This was not something to be lightly brushed aside by a government as cash-strapped as that of Louis XV's, mired as it was in the Seven Years War. It also garnered enormous prestige for France: as an advertisement of French genius the *Encyclopedia* could not be bettered. Given the vanity and egos of the European princely class, this was another weighty consideration. An agreement was reached that work could continue but without any guarantee that future volumes would be published.

Attacks carried on but the worst was over. In 1764 the Jesuit order was expelled from France and with it some of the *Encyclopedia*'s most implacable opponents. But there were still a number of bumps along the road. At the same time that the Jesuits were being expelled, Diderot discovered to his horror that for at least two years Le Breton had been editing and censoring articles written by himself and others, while in 1766 Le Breton himself was imprisoned in the Bastille for eight days for a breach of regulations governing the *Encyclopedia*'s distribution. It was also the year when the poor, 20-year-old nobleman Francois-Jean de la Barre was tortured and beheaded on charges of blasphemy, with Voltaire's *Philosophical Dictionary* used as evidence against him. It was a salutary reminder of the penalties awaiting those deemed to be impious. Diderot persevered with his editorial duties, relentlessly demanding though they were. Ultimately, the workload and anxiety wore him down and left him disillusioned. He had sacrificed an enormous amount, including his ambitions to be a great dramatist. The seventeen volumes of articles were finished in 1765 but it was not until 1772 that the project was complete. That was the year when the eleventh and final volume of illustrations was published.

Chapter 8

Jean-Jacques Rousseau: 1712–1778

> 'At that time, Madame d'Urfé wanting to know J-J Rousseau, we went to Montmorency to pay him a visit, bringing him music that he copied marvellously well. He was paid double the money that would have been paid to another; but he vouched that no fault would be found with it.'
>
> Giacomo Casanova, *History of My Life*

Notwithstanding Casanova's claims to have had 'three interviews' with Rousseau, there is a debate over whether he did ever meet him.[1] Possibly the account he gives in his memoirs was constructed from anecdotes that he had come across from others. It would not have been the first time that he had made himself an eyewitness to an event at which he was never present. Whether true or not that he had met the man, it is likely he would have wanted to. Rousseau was one of the great figures of the eighteenth century and was to be a major influence upon the direction of the French Revolution.

The Genevan was very different to Voltaire and Diderot, both of whom were highly educated, possessed quicksilver minds and relished society. Rousseau, by contrast, lamented his 'slow thoughts': 'Ideas take shape in my head with the most incredible difficulty.'[2] Conversely, he was an extremely emotional man: 'It is as if my heart and my brain did not belong to the same person. Feelings come quicker than lightning and fill my soul, but they bring me no illumination; they burn me and dazzle me.'[3] He never attended school, gained little from any sort of formal tuition, and tended to be awkward and withdrawn in elevated company, although perhaps not to the degree that he liked to make out. He enjoyed solitary pursuits, especially walking and wandering in the countryside when he got the opportunity, and one of his favourite pastimes was botany. It was during such walks he did much of his thinking. Throughout his life he had tremendous stamina and a degree of fitness that made his frequent claims of debilitating ill health rather questionable, suggesting a psychological cause as much as a physical one. He did indeed recognise that at times he used illness to manipulate others.

Rousseau was self-taught and driven by what appealed to him, devising his own somewhat hit-and-miss strategies for learning. He developed a love of music but was not particularly gifted, acquiring some mastery of the discipline by dint of years of perseverance. Keen to examine the works of various philosophers, Rousseau gave up trying to analyse and reconcile their arguments and instead built up 'a store of ideas, true and false but all of them clear'. He continues: 'After I spent some years never thinking independently, but always following the thoughts of others unreflectively, so to speak, and almost without reasoning, I found myself equipped with a great enough fund of learning to be self-sufficient and to think without the help of another.'[4] In addition to this store of ideas, Rousseau reflected deeply about his own feelings and experience of life, and applied his conclusions not only to himself but to society at large. In the process he produced original and important works across a range of genres.

Rousseau was an outsider in many ways, in his adulthood often by choice, and the perspective this gave him may have helped nurture his originality, less constrained as he was by the social and intellectual assumptions either of the traditional conservative kind or of the progressive Enlightenment. He defended himself tenaciously from any form of imposition that might compromise his liberty to act, to a degree that at times left even his closest allies bewildered and alienated. This concern became more pronounced as Rousseau sought to protect his reputation as a philosopher who had exposed the intrinsically corrupting nature of society. He would routinely reject gifts and offers of support in order to avoid becoming entangled in obligations to others or to be perceived as a hypocrite who was willing to profit from a society that he so excoriated. This wariness of others fed into a paranoia which was to blight his later life. It was partly for this desire to achieve independence from others that he chose to earn his living as a music copyist even at the height of his fame.

Women found him attractive but his passionate and turbulent interior was belied by a timid and passive exterior that could only confuse any potential love interest. He idealised women to the extent that he could not abide the thought of imposing himself upon them:

> I have loved with too much sincerity – too perfectly I might even say – to attain easy success. No passions were ever at once

> so pure and so strong as mine. Never was love more tender, genuine, and disinterested. On countless occasions I would have sacrificed my happiness to that of the woman I loved. Her reputation has been dearer to me than my life, and never for all the joys of gratification have I been willing to risk her peace of mind for a single moment. Therefore I have brought so much care, so much secrecy, and so many precautions to my affairs that not one of them has ever been successful.[5]

On the few occasions he did have a sexual relationship his tender conscience was salved by the fact that it was the woman who took control, possibly with the exception of his long-term partner Thérèse Levasseur but perhaps not even then. There are suggestions that she herself was sexually assertive although portrayed by Rousseau as modest and docile. The prospect of physical intimacy was a source of immense anxiety for him. It was something he both yearned for and feared; a promise of gratification but accompanied by shame and guilt. It may have been this dissonant cocktail that led to his tendency to fetishize women's accoutrements such as ribbons or items of clothing.

Rousseau had a distinctly non-reciprocal conception of friendship as he makes clear in his correspondence with his friend and royal censor Malesherbes: 'intimate friendship is precious, because with it there are no longer any obligations. One follows one's heart and all is done.'[6] Rousseau's introspective quest to discover his true self (not in order to change who he was but to demonstrate his fundamental goodness), his difficulty in empathising with others, his reference to himself at times in the third person, his humblebragging and regular claims to being exceptional in this or that regard, and his preoccupation with his own freedom and needs, smack of narcissism. Combined with his paranoia it was a temperament which was not suited to maintaining stable relationships, and it is not surprising that except for Thérèse most of them broke down. To be a friend of Rousseau required patience and no small measure of diplomatic skill.

He was born a citizen of Calvinist Geneva, a city-state bordered by Catholic France and with its fair share of internal political friction. His father Isaac was a watchmaker, his mother Suzanne from a more affluent family background, raised by her uncle Samuel Bernard (who Rousseau believed was her father). He also had a brother François who was seven years older. Rousseau's mother died shortly after his birth, bequeathing her son a legacy of guilt. He recounts a history of passion, romance and enduring love between his parents but it was one which owed as much to wishful thinking and family invention as it did to reality. He imagined that his first years had been happy ones, although he could not really remember them, and he tended generally to view his childhood until the age of 10 rather nostalgically. His earliest memory, and one of his fondest, was practising his reading with his father after supper when he was around 6. The pair took turns to read together novels that his mother had owned, sometimes reading into the early morning: 'I acquired by this method, not only an extreme facility in reading and expressing myself, but a singular insight for my age into the passions.'[7] The following year they moved on to a collection of books left by Samuel. It consisted of histories and works by classic authors such as Ovid and Plutarch. This stimulated discussion with his father 'that created in me that proud and intractable spirit, that impatience with the yoke of servitude, which has afflicted me throughout my life.'[8] From a young age Rousseau was becoming politically aware.

Life for Jean-Jacques changed abruptly when he was 10 years old. His father was involved in a dispute which resulted in him fleeing Geneva. Jean-Jacques was left in the care of a maternal uncle, Gabriel Bernard, who sent him along with his own son to the nearby village of Bossey to board with pastor Lambercier, who was a Calvinist minister, and Lambercier's sister Gabrielle. From Lambercier he received tuition in Latin and religion. One moment of note was Rousseau's discovery when he was 11 that he enjoyed being spanked by Gabrielle when she punished him for some misdemeanour or other. On another occasion he was accused of breaking a comb, incurring several harsh beatings from his uncle Gabriel. After two years Rousseau returned to Geneva for six months prior to being employed briefly in the office of the City Registrar and then beginning an apprenticeship with an engraver, Abel Ducommun.

The apprenticeship was meant to last five years and Rousseau was to board with his master, as was usual. Initially he liked the work but Ducommun was unpleasant, and the young apprentice found his new circumstances oppressive. Rousseau had access to a lending library and threw himself into reading to alleviate his unhappiness. Less constructively, he also responded by neglecting his work and resorting to small acts of rebellion: 'My master's tyranny … drove me to vices.' Rousseau's innocence and good nature were corrupted: 'So it was that I learnt to covet in silence, to conceal, to dissimulate, to lie and finally to steal.'[10] More beatings ensued.

When he was 15, he ran away. His action was triggered after a Sunday trip with friends outside the walls of the fortified city. The gates were locked on their return so they waited together until the morning when they were opened again. But Rousseau had had enough; he resolved to flee. He ended up in Annecy in neighbouring Savoy where he found refuge with Françoise-Louise de Warens. She was to be a major influence in his life, taking on the roles of patron, mother and, when he was 20, lover. He had been sent in her direction by a priest who was interested in converting him to Catholicism. It turned out that Madame de Warens was young, attractive and well educated. Rousseau was smitten. He duly converted after a brief stint at a Catholic hospice in Turin where he remained for a little while taking on a couple of mundane jobs before eventually returning to Annecy the following year. With the exception of a one-year break during which he attempted unsuccessfully to forge a career as a music tutor, Rousseau was to stay with de Warens for ten years, she supporting him financially. She was an ideal mentor for the adolescent Rousseau, engaging him through her warmth and generosity rather than resorting to the brute force of authority. His intellectual maturity gathered pace. De Warens' encouragement and resources allowed him to take the opportunity to study history, politics, philosophy, mathematics and, above all, music, which he began teaching again. Rousseau also began writing. As well as poetry, he wrote an early draft of his play *Narcissus, or the Self-Lover*. He had a song published in the *French Mercury*, a newspaper and literary journal to which he subscribed.

At one point during this time Rousseau considered becoming a priest. There were not many other career paths open to him. Rousseau was a firm believer in God but relaxed on matters of doctrine, mirroring the attitude of de Warens. There was a pietist influence in her upbringing which prioritised inner spirituality. Likewise, Rousseau's relationship with the Almighty was a personal one rooted in conscience. Not for Rousseau the idea that the Heavenly Father was a distant and abstract being. God offered hope, and a universe without God, or with a type of God who may as well not be there, was too bleak and terrifying for him to contemplate. But Rousseau was also critical of established religions with their various ceremonies and trappings and claims to uniqueness. He was sceptical that God would ever reveal himself in these ways. How would any individual be able to sift through all this evidence and argument and evaluate which was the true faith? If you wanted proof of God it could be found in motion, both the ordered motions of the world and the spontaneous motion of living creatures, not in superficial externalities. Rousseau's lack of theological dogmatism made him sympathetic to pleas for religious toleration, although not with regards to atheists whom he felt jeopardised social harmony and for whom he was willing to contemplate the severest punishment. For Rousseau, in the model of society he describes in *The Social Contract* (1762), all citizens need to commit themselves to a basic civil religion. Those who are not prepared to recognise it should be banished, 'not as impious, but as unsociable, as incapable of sincerely loving law and justice and of sacrificing at need his life to his duty'.[10] In the last resort, if someone reneges on their public declaration of faith, and acts like an unbeliever, then they should be executed.

In 1740 Rousseau finally moved on. Thanks to de Warens he was able to obtain a post in Lyons as tutor to the two oldest sons of the nobleman Jean Bonnot de Mably. De Mably was a provost general of police and older brother of Gabriel, a well-known writer. The youngest of the three brothers was Étienne Bonnot de Condillac (Mably and Condillac were family properties). Condillac was in his mid-20s and was to become an important Enlightenment thinker. This was a promising opportunity for Rousseau to make his own way in the world. In addition, it enabled him to keep company with a range of well-educated and scholarly men. The family were welcoming but Rousseau lacked the skills and personality to be an effective tutor, the boys successfully resisting his efforts to teach them. After a year he threw in the towel. Rousseau made an abortive attempt to reconnect with de Warens but already prior to Lyons the relationship had cooled. A new estate manager had become a rival for her affections, on top of which, financial difficulties were making it difficult for her to support him. In 1742 he made his way to Paris with various letters of recommendation.

The year Rousseau arrived he befriended Diderot. They met at the Café de la Régence, a centre for chess that attracted some of the greatest European players. They were both keen on the game, Rousseau the stronger of the two. But they had many other interests in common: music, theatre, literature and an unquenchable thirst for learning. And their circumstances were similar: they were from artisanal families, had no clear career path and were scratching around to make ends meet. It was Diderot who Rousseau was later to blame for him becoming a philosopher.

Like others who aspired to kick-start their careers, Rousseau was drawn to the world of salons but his social awkwardness and lack of anything about him that was singularly entertaining made him poor salon material. In turn he regarded the culture as superficial and insincere. Rousseau did manage to find another tutoring post, for the wealthy Dupin family, but his tenure was short. On this occasion it was not so much Rousseau's teaching skills but his pupil that was the issue. His charge turned out to be uncooperative and impossible to work with. A different opportunity now arose. He was offered the position of secretary to the French ambassador in Venice. It was not well paid but it was something.

Rousseau was to be in Venice from September 1743 to August 1744. His boss was Pierre-Francois, Comte de Montaigu, according to Leo Damrosch 'a virtual parody of a parasitic aristocrat, incredibly stupid, irascible, and swollen with self-importance'.[11] The Venice ambassadorship was not regarded as important, and Montaigu had been given the posting largely to get him out of the way. The alternative was the army where he would have been a more serious liability. Because of Montaigu's laziness and incompetence much of the embassy's work was left increasingly to Rousseau. He seems to have carried out his responsibilities with a reasonable degree of diligence and effectiveness, perhaps for the first time in his life. He took particular satisfaction from the fact that he was able to act successfully on his own initiative. He records how on one occasion 'I got the captain of a merchant vessel out of trouble by my own almost unaided efforts.'[12] Rousseau regularly visited the theatre and acquired a great fondness for Venetian music. But his relationship with the ambassador was poor, and the pair would quarrel. Montaigu was irritated by what he saw as his official's overblown pretensions and lack of deference. In August their already rocky relationship broke down irredeemably. Rousseau found himself on the way back to Paris nursing a rich vein of grievances about how he had been mistreated, including Montaigu's failure to pay him his salary. Rousseau's inability to obtain redress despite his complaints was to be a personal lesson in how authority allied with the strong to oppress the weak. Apparently much later Montaigu did settle up.

While he had been away Diderot had married, and now it was Rousseau's turn to settle into a life-long partnership. Thérèse Levasseur was a laundress and was to have five children by Rousseau, all of whom he persuaded her to give away to the Paris Foundling Hospital. That this was the man who went on to write *Emile* (1762), a book on how to bring up and educate a child, was an irony not lost on Rousseau's critics. It is worth pointing out that a baby consigned to the Paris Foundling Hospital had only a one in three chance of reaching its first birthday and a one in twenty chance of reaching maturity. It was to be another source of guilt. Despite that, and despite Rousseau suggesting to his friends that his relationship with Thérèse was a matter of domestic and sexual convenience, there does seem to have been a strong bond between them.

After Venice he was in debt and looked to see if he could earn money through writing. In the process of composing and trying to stage his masque *The Gallant Muses* he made some useful contacts, notably the wealthy tax farmer Alexandre Le Riche de La Pouplinière, but the masque itself was unsuccessful, damned by a critical assessment from the famous court composer Jean-Phillipe Rameau. Eventually he found employment once more with the Dupins, this time as a secretary. He stayed with them for five years, helping members of the family with various scholarly writing projects, and broadening his own knowledge of history and politics in the process. His friendships with Diderot and Condillac continued to flourish, later to be joined by d'Alembert. It would be difficult to imagine a more intellectually stimulating group. It was to this group that Diderot revealed his project to create an encyclopedia for which Rousseau was to contribute 344 articles on music and politics.

This was the period when Diderot was imprisoned in Vincennes, and an event took place that was to be a major turning point in Rousseau's life. On one of his journeys to visit his friend, which he did so on foot, he took with him the *French Mercury* where he came across an essay competition on the theme of science and the arts which he decided to enter. He discussed it with Diderot who encouraged him to take a critical, contrarian position. Rousseau was to go on to win the competition with what was to be his first major work, and finding a receptive audience, he experienced also his first taste of fame. His treatise *Discourse on the Arts and Sciences* (1750) (or the *First Discourse*) was to become central in the development of his later thought. Drawing on the histories of ancient civilisations such as Egypt and Rome, he argued that cultural progress bred decadence and immorality. Simpler societies such as Sparta were happier and more virtuous than their sophisticated Athenian cousins. Art and science engendered vanity, pride and a desire for luxury. It was an argument that flew in the face of ideas of Enlightenment progress.

In 1751 Rousseau ended his employment with the Dupins, resolving to live as independently and inexpensively as possible. It was now he decided to earn his livelihood by copying music, much to people's astonishment, especially the Dupins who initially thought he had gone mad. So determined was he to follow this course that when his 1752 opera *The Village Soothsayer* turned out to be a success, he declined the opportunity to receive a royal pension. He was uncomfortable that it might place some sort of restriction upon him: 'I should have to flatter or be silent.'[13] Nonetheless, he still did well out of the venture, earning over 5,000 livres, more money than he had ever had in his life.

In 1754 he wrote his *Discourse on the Origin and Basis of Inequality Among Men*, to be published in 1755. It was his next major work. Having lived so much of his life on the margins of society, at least relative to those educated and affluent groups who dominated scholarly debate, it was a topic for which he was able to draw upon his own personal experience. In this *Second Discourse*, Rousseau traces the problems of civilisation back to ownership. It was ownership that led to the division of labour, social inequality and the domination of society by those who possess wealth and inhabit positions of power. What is arbitrary and artificial comes to be seen not as an expression of culture but as something which is natural and inevitable. The notion that inequality is natural was a view that had been previously adopted by most thinkers and was embedded in Christian ideology. Instead, for Rousseau, the fact of social injustice is being rationalised away. The drive to satisfy needs that are bogus creates selfishness, undermining our conscience and compassion. Rousseau distinguishes between that love of self which is healthy in that it is necessary for self-preservation, and the love of self which is unhealthy in that it seeks to obtain the esteem of others. It is through this process that people become separated from their true nature, a nature bestowed upon them by God; man is innately good, it is society, by its very existence, that corrupts and oppresses. Interestingly, although Rousseau was heavily influenced by Plato, here they disagree. For Plato, human desires that extend beyond basic needs and complicate men's behaviour in society may lead to corruption but they are a condition of growth towards greater perfection.

Once he had finished the *Second Discourse,* but before it was published, Rousseau visited the city of his birth, converting back to Calvinism. This son of Geneva, now a well-known philosopher and composer, received an enthusiastic welcome. The return to the fold of such a celebrity was quite a coup for the local authorities. After a pleasant four months he returned to Paris where he resumed the company of Diderot and Baron d'Holbach.

Rousseau had been an early visitor to the baron's salon, probably since 1748, but his serious and reserved temperament was never going to be an easy fit in such sparkling company. In addition, the currents of radical materialism and hostility towards religion that were so prevalent among other members of the circle, notably d'Holbach himself, made Rousseau a maverick figure. Highlighting the importance of Plato on Rousseau's philosophy, David Lay Williams notes the Genevan's 'commitment to the central doctrines of modern Platonic metaphysics – the existence of God, free will, an immaterial soul and transcendent ideas'.[14] The *Second*

Treatise had been coolly received by the *philosophe* community, including Diderot. Voltaire had been particularly scathing, pointing out the benefits of civilisation, deliberately misreading Rousseau's core argument all the better to ridicule it. By the time he wrote the second part of his memoirs, *The Confessions* (1782, 1789), his mistrust and paranoia had convinced him that his 'so-called' friends had become jealous of his genius: 'as soon as I had a name, I ceased to have friends.'[15] Worse, he was to come to the conclusion that the d'Holbach circle had been behind elaborate plots to destroy him although Rousseau remained vague about their precise nature. That may have been somewhat far-fetched but it was true that his relations with his old friends eventually became so embittered that there was some attempt to discredit him, particularly on the part of Friedrich Grimm with whom he had once been close.

To escape the moral depravity of this environment, at least as Rousseau saw it, in 1756 he took up an offer from Madame d'Épinay to live in a cottage on her estate a few miles north of Paris. During his relatively brief time here, he worked on his *Dictionary of Music*, composed his *Letter to Voltaire on Providence* (in response to Voltaire's *Poem about the Disaster in Lisbon*) as well as working on *Emile* and the *Social Contract.* But being away from Paris brought its own worries. He felt marginalised and ignored. To make matters worse, Diderot was making a name for himself as the primary editor of the *Encyclopedia.* Following a couple of episodes of spectacular ingratitude towards his hostess Madame d'Epinay, in 1757 Rousseau moved to the estate of the Duke and Duchess of Luxembourg in Montmorency (where Casanova claims to have visited Rousseau). Charles François Frédéric de Montmorency-Luxembourg was one of the most powerful men in France, and his patronage of Rousseau was in part a snub aimed at the court of Louis XV and Madame de Pompadour. Here Rousseau wrote his enormously successful 800-page epistolary novel *Julie, or the New Héloïse,* which was published in 1761, and completed *The Social Contract* and *Emile, or On Education.*

Published in 1762, *The Social Contract* (or to give it its full title, *On the Social Contract, Principles of Political Right*) was Rousseau's third major philosophical work. He was well-versed in classical philosophy, and in echoes of Plato's *Republic* he addresses the relationship between the interests of the individual and that of the community as a whole. He asserts that an individual's true happiness is tied to the well-being of all, as directed by the General Will. Unlike a Hobbesian contract in which the individual surrenders their freedom to an all-powerful sovereign in exchange for security, Rousseau's contract requires that individuals surrender their sovereignty to each other as a collective group. The General Will is not to be confused with the will of the majority or even the will of all citizens. It is what a just citizen would desire for the good of their community as opposed to their own private good and is, in this sense, a collective moral conscience. It was rooted in a concept of justice that transcended material reality and, in this way, avoided the dangers of moral relativism that dogged the Hobbesian materialist metaphysics of *philosophes* such as d'Holbach, La Mettrie and Helvétius. The existence of factions, anti-meritocratic prejudices, rich and poor and a society that is too large for democratic government, all features typical of cities and civilisation, would work against this Platonic, abstract ideal. It would render any ruling authority less legitimate because it would have diverged from the General Will. For Rousseau, the legitimate political authority that resides in the moral force of the General Will manifests itself through the rule of law (and a rule of law that is the same for everyone). The state, the body that applies the law, becomes the means by which to overcome selfishness and enable people to exist in civilised society as moral beings. By being subject to the General Will, people, paradoxically, 'shall be forced to be free' by forcing them to be their best (moral) selves.[16] But in reality the individual can never be entirely free from society's negative influence. To some extent they will always be enslaved. *The Social Contract* offers an unrealisable ideal. The best hope to maximise freedom and happiness is for the state and society's laws to facilitate the General Will as far as possible, even if it can never be entirely successful.

In the same year of 1762 Rousseau published *Emile, or On Education*, which he considered to be his most important work. He uses its eponymous hero to explore possible solutions to the problem he raised in his earlier works. Through appropriate education he hopes to show how it is possible to ameliorate society's malign effects. Reason and nature, two gifts from God, are to be Emile's tutors. Direct education by nature and experience would avoid the pernicious influence of culture. He should not be constrained by conventional assumptions, beliefs and objectives but have the freedom to flourish according to his own individual character, a remarkable suggestion for the time. People were neither blank slates, as the supporters of Locke believed, nor cursed by original sin. In particular, fear of authority should have no place in the curriculum either as an aim or a pedagogical tool. Moral development, mediated by Emile's conscience, and understanding the natural world were both to be derived from the consequences of direct interaction with the environment without the detrimental interference of men or books. According to Rousseau, boys should not be taught religion until their teens and should learn a useful trade. His educational prescription for females, however, was far less radical to put it mildly. Emile's future partner, Sophie, is taught domestic skills and prepared for the role of long-suffering, uncomplaining wife. After all, Rousseau concludes, 'woman is made specially to please man.'[17]

Rousseau's portrayal of religion in *Emile* led to condemnation from both the Catholic and Calvinist churches. The public outrage that accompanied its publication was such that not even friends of the influence and stature of Malesherbes, Prince de Conti and the Luxembourgs, who were supportive of his writings, were able to protect him. *Emile* and its author were denounced by the Jansenists, and the Parlement of Paris followed their lead. On 9 June 1762 a warrant was issued for Rousseau's arrest. He had been warned of the storm that was coming his way but remained confident that his allies would be able to protect him. Not until the last moment did the desperate entreaties of the Luxembourgs and de Conti's mistress, de Boufflers, prevail upon him to flee Montmorency and seek asylum beyond the reach of French authorities. From 1762 to 1765 he settled down in Môtiers, a village in the principality of Neuchâtel. The territory was under the control of Frederick II, a man who as we know had a soft spot for refugees and Enlightenment intellectuals. In Môtiers Rousseau became close friends with its governor, the Scottish Earl Marshal George Keith, exiled from Britain for his part in the Jacobite Rebellion of 1715. But this blasphemous and outlandish foreigner (Rousseau walked about in a rather exotic robe) was never accepted by the community and, worse, found himself entangled in local politics. An attack upon his home after a Calvinist minister had agitated people against him eventually forced him out.

Rousseau now accepted an invitation to stay with David Hume in England, where Rousseau was to work on *The Confessions*. He arrived in January 1766, and Hume's initial impressions were favourable despite prior warnings. Rousseau had by now fallen out with many of his oldest and closest friends, including Diderot. Friedrich Grimm, one of those who had fêted Hume on his stay in Paris in the early 1760s, cautioned, 'I will tell you plainly, you're warming a viper in your bosom.'[18] The famously good-natured Hume took no notice and shortly found himself enmeshed in a dispute that was to resound across Europe, Rousseau complaining at length that Hume was plotting against him. Given Rousseau's fame, authority and rhetorical skill Hume was horrified at the turn of events and the danger that his social standing could be seriously damaged. In May 1767, amidst the controversy, and hastened along by a belief that someone wanted to poison him, Rousseau and Thérèse left England to go back to France.

The Genevan received warm support and shelter from his many and influential admirers despite being a fugitive with an arrest warrant in place against him. Initially, Rousseau appeared in public quite openly until de Conti persuaded him to keep his head down and seclude himself in one of his properties, a château at Trye, forty miles from Paris. This was not an altruistic act. Di Conti had encouraged Rousseau to publish *The Social Contract* and *Emile*, and he was concerned that it would put him in jeopardy if his connection became known. Isolated, treated with disrespect by servants and consumed by paranoia, he decided to leave Trye, staying briefly first at Lyon, then Grenoble, then Bourgoin, then Lyon again, pursued by his fears all the while. Eventually in 1770 he returned to Paris expecting to be arrested. In fact, he was left alone to go about his business, earning his living copying music, seeing friends, playing chess, visiting the theatre and carrying on with his writing. In 1771 he completed *The Confessions* although he remained dissatisfied with it. These last years were tranquil ones compared to what had gone before. Then on 24 October 1776 an accident in the street left him concussed. Afterwards his health began to decline and on 1 July 1778 he died, five days after he turned 66.

Rousseau was to have a major effect upon the French Revolution. The National Assembly's *Declaration of the Rights of Man* explicitly states that, 'The law is an expression of the General Will.' Deism, egalitarian republicanism in which sovereignty was invested in the people, and the concept of the 'common good', to which the individual was subordinate, were all expounded by Rousseau. At times he even seems to endorse violence and the overthrow of the established order whereby a state 'springs forth so to speak from its ashes and regains the vigour of youth.'[19] In *Emile* he declares, 'we are approaching a state of crisis and the age of revolutions … All that men have made, men can destroy.'[20] This was not Rousseau's intention but it was how he could be read. For a revolutionary politician to be taken seriously he had to align himself to some degree at least with the ideas of Rousseau. Robespierre was strongly influenced by him.

In 1794, Rousseau's remains were transported to the Pantheon, a copy of *The Social Contract* carried on a velvet cushion. Beyond the French Revolution, Rousseau's ideas have had an impact on a wide range of theorists and intellectual thought, notably that of Immanuel Kant who drew on Rousseau in his moral psychology (in his formulation of the idea of the categorical imperative) and in his writings on international justice. He was a major inspiration behind nineteenth-century Romanticism. His analysis of how cultural behaviours can become accepted as natural and inevitable can be seen in the work of Marx and Foucault. And the thinking of many educators has been influenced by *Emile*.

Along with Voltaire, Rousseau was the most widely read and popular of the Enlightenment *philosophes*. The astonishing success of *Julie, or the New Héloïse* cemented his celebrity as did the controversy that surrounded him and his status of persecuted intellectual. In an age of priests and pulpits his readers were open to the kind of moral authority that he conveyed. His ideas may have contained paradoxes, as he admitted himself, but the originality of his vision, his deeply personal religious conviction and the rhetorical force of his prose captured people's attention.

Chapter 9
Threads of Recollection

> 'I have done many foolish things in my life; I confess it with as much candour as Rousseau, and with less pride than that unhappy great man.'
>
> Giacomo Casanova, *History of My Life*

Casanova and Rousseau can claim to have written among the most important autobiographical accounts in modern history, accounts of two lives that encompassed a critical period in the moral and intellectual development of the West. The word 'autobiography' itself was not coined until 1797. The term memoirs was used. It was an aristocratic genre that usually referred to a person's public rather than private life, and this is the term used both by Casanova and Rousseau. *The Confessions of Jean-Jacques Rousseau* and *History of My Life* are linked by the authors' close involvement in the fierce debates that were taking place at the time. The positions they adopted reflected contrasting ways of understanding the world, and this shaped both how they went about living in it and their report of the experience. While Rousseau did not have as direct an impact upon Casanova as Voltaire, the Venetian did engage with his writings and ideas, and Rousseau's memoirs influenced his own. *The Confessions* was published posthumously in two parts, in 1782 and 1789, and runs to around 275,000 words, less than a quarter of *History of My Life* but substantial nonetheless. Rousseau wrote Books 1 to 6 from 1765 to 1767, and Books 7 to 12 from 1769 to 1770. *The Confessions* may well have influenced Casanova's decision to get on and write his own memoirs, although it had been on his mind for a while, certainly since 1780. Casanova's attempt to emulate the work of this titan of the Enlightenment would be typical of him.

European societies remained highly religious but the new intellectual climate spurred a re-evaluation of the source and character of knowledge and meaning. This had important implications for the place of individual experience. Were knowledge and meaning obtained directly from God through revelation? Were they to be found in nature, the product of divine will, of which mankind was a part? Had God supplied humans a priori with innate ideas? Was reality perceived according to the ideas the mind imposed upon it? Or was understanding constructed by an internal creative process tied to sensory input, perhaps unrelated to God at all? To what extent was the mind's ability to grasp reality shaped by that very reality itself? And how much of reality, at the end of the day, could ever be accessible?

In this environment the self became a legitimate object of empirical enquiry: material, spiritual and moral. In several works, notably his *Treatise on Human Nature* (1739–1740), David Hume conducted insightful explorations of the 'passions', including scrutiny of his own emotional states, and the role they played in thinking, behaviour and our interactions with others. For Hume, it is our emotions that drive us to act. The eighteenth century grew introspective. The subjective experience and inner life of the individual acquired increasing significance not just for philosophers but novelists, poets, biographers, historians, the religious, and society in general, including, of course, Rousseau and Casanova.

When we read *History of My Life* and *The Confessions* we experience two different perspectives. We find the world of the extrovert juxtaposed against the world of the introvert. Casanova's attention focusses more on what is happening outside himself whereas Rousseau is concerned more with his inner reflections and emotions. Of course, binary comparisons should not be pushed too far but when you read the two sets of memoirs such differences shout out at the reader from almost every page. The importance of personal freedom is apparent to both men but while Casanova wanted freedom to, Rousseau wanted freedom from. There were exceptions, such as when Rousseau was a secretary at France's embassy in Venice, but on the whole he sought to minimise, avoid and explain away obligations to others. In contrast, Casanova actively looked to engage with the world and the people who lived in it. He recognised that the duties which typically attached themselves to friendship, love, kinship and common humanity were the price of that engagement. Rousseau seeks shelter and certainty under the skirts of God and his own powers of deductive reasoning. Casanova embraces ambiguity, chance and doubt.

The Confessions

Rousseau is regarded as the founder of modern autobiography. His memoirs were very different to those of a de Bernis, a Horace Walpole or a Voltaire. They were highly personal, psychological and intimate, and, unusually, focused upon the importance of childhood in the shaping of who he was to become. *The Confessions* chimed with a growing interest in people's private and domestic lives, no better illustrated than in the proliferation of moral weeklies, erotic literature and the rising popularity of the novel. The purpose of an autobiography is for the writer to reveal who they are as truthfully as possible although truth is not simply a matter of presenting facts. It is to be found in the writer's personal and emotional experience. The truth, or truths, may relate to themselves as an individual, to their society, to their time or they may believe it to be an absolute truth that is good for all times such as in the nature of God, as exemplified by St Augustine's *Confessions in Thirteen Books* (c 400 CE). In an autobiography, emotional truth trumps factual accuracy. That does not mean the writer can get away with deliberate falsification but that the reader is liable to be forgiving of unintentional errors, particularly given how unreliable human memory can be. They are likely to be less forgiving if a writer makes claims to sentiments or emotional responses that run against what they have come to learn about the writer's character or what seems believable in any particular set of circumstances.

The relationship of the reader to the author, more than is the case with other genres, is one of trust, and this is intensified through the operation of writing itself. Experiences that are numerous, fragmentary and disparate have to be corralled and selected. This process of sifting information and impressions militates against the chances of faithful representation. But more than that, the writer will be attempting to recreate in some sense the feelings that they experienced in order to share them. The emotional and psychological, after all, is central to much of what the writer is trying to convey. In other non-fiction genres, such as history, the audience would be able to draw upon sources external to the text to evaluate its credibility. If you wanted to reassure yourself about what is in this book there are a plethora of other books, documents, sites and expert opinion that you can consult. But in a text whose truth claims lack even the possibility of such checking then you are left dependent upon your faith in the writer. The social dynamic between the writer and their audience becomes more sensitised to issues of reputation and face.

Rousseau titled his book of memoirs *The Confessions* after that of St Augustine, a central figure of Western Christianity. The term 'confession' refers to one of the seven sacraments of the Catholic Church in which a worshipper reveals their sins to their priest and God in order to regain God's grace and heal their soul. The attitude of the penitent is expected to be one of humility, sincerity and acceptance. It is not difficult to see parallels here between the writer and their audience, a relationship rooted in self-examination and trust. *Confessions in Thirteen Books* (Rousseau restricts himself to twelve) was written between 397 CE and 400 CE outlining the journey of Augustine of Hippo's conversion to Christianity in the form of prayers addressed to God. He charts his life from infancy to the age of 32, just after his conversion to Christianity, recounting episodes of immoral behaviour and internal struggles, reflecting upon their personal and spiritual significance. The books were used as texts to encourage and guide the conversion of others. They are meant to be read aloud which, along with their prayer style, explains the speaking qualities of the prose, filled as it is with imperatives, exclamatories, interjections, vocatives, discourse markers and in employing first and second person address. The result is tremendous energy and directness:

> Oh! that I might repose on Thee! Oh! that Thou wouldest enter into my heart, and inebriate it, that I may forget my ills, and embrace Thee, my sole good! What art Thou to me? In Thy pity, teach me to utter it. Or what am I to Thee that Thou demandest my love, and, if I give it not, art wroth with me, and threatenest me with grievous woes? Is it then a slight woe to love Thee not? Oh! for Thy mercies' sake, tell me, O Lord my God, what Thou art unto me.[1]

Rousseau began writing his memoirs in his 50s, by which time he was famous throughout Europe. However, he had turned against him many of those who had been his closest allies. His increasing social isolation only served to stoke his fears that enemies were conspiring to destroy him and his reputation, and these fears seemed to be confirmed by the publication in 1764 of an anonymous pamphlet called the *Sentiment of the Citizens*. In a devastating attack upon him, the writer (who was Voltaire) revealed how the celebrated author of *Emile* had abandoned his own five children:

> We confess with pain and embarrassment that this is a man who still bears the nefarious marks of his debauchery, and

> who, dressed up like a clown, drags around with him from village to village, and from mountain to mountain, the unfortunate woman [Thérèse Levasseur] whose mother he killed, and whose children he abandoned at the door of a hospital, rejecting the care of a charitable person who wanted to look after them, abjuring all natural feelings. … This is the one who dares to give advice to our fellow citizens…! This is the one who talks about the duties of society![2]

Rousseau had previously contemplated writing an autobiographical work but it was Voltaire's criticism that triggered him to act. His defiance is palpable:

> Let the last trumpet sound when it will, I shall come forward with this work in my hand, to present myself before my Sovereign Judge, and proclaim aloud: 'Here is what I have done, and if by chance I have used some immaterial embellishment it has been only to fill a void due to a defect of memory. I may have taken for fact that which was no more than probability, but I have never put down as true what I knew to be false. I have displayed myself as I was, as vile and despicable when my behaviour was such, as good, generous, and noble when it was so. I have bared my secret soul as Thou thyself hast seen it, Eternal Being! So let the numberless legion of my fellow men gather round me, and hear my confessions. Let them groan at my depravities, and blush for my misdeed. But let each one of them reveal his heart at the foot of Thy throne with equal sincerity, and may any man who dares, say "I was a better man than he."'[3]

It is a resounding statement of intent. Rousseau vows to reveal his private self to the public, warts and all. The religious framing and the fact that he appears to address God can be treated as a literary device rather than a practice of confession: Rousseau is addressing his fellow man for the purpose of defending his character more than he is God for the purpose of healing his soul. Like the prose of St Augustine, Rousseau's is passionate and intense, again employing first and second person address, and filled with imperatives along with other devices such as listing, parallelism, contrasting pairs, abstract nouns and so on. And he does not speak to his audience in the spirit of humility you might expect of a confession. His tone is assertive and demanding, even of God. Simultaneously he builds upon and diverges from St Augustine's autobiographical model. Like Augustine, he traces out his life from infancy to adulthood to draw conclusions about his fundamental nature. But unlike Augustine's *Confessions*, his is to be a secular work not a religious one.

As outlined in the previous chapter, in 1750 Rousseau won a prestigious essay competition in which he argued that art and science corrupted society. He wrote a second treatise in 1755 which traced the problems of civilisation to ownership and inequality. In 1762, in *The Social Contract*, he explored the political relationship between the individual and the community and formulated his concept of the General Will. In the same year he published *Emile* on how to educate children. It is worth pausing for a moment to recap on the ideas contained in these texts before examining *The Confessions* further.

Together these works formed a consistent and coherent vision of the world. Private ownership leads to a division of labour, social inequality and the creation of rich and poor, the politically powerful and the politically weak. The cultural progress borne onwards by art and science breeds vanity, decadence and immorality, particularly among the rich and powerful who compete with each other for status. These processes generate selfishness, erode human conscience and separate people from their intrinsically good, God-given nature. To achieve true happiness, individuals need to align their wants with the happiness of the community as a whole by means of guidance from the General Will. To give a child the opportunity to develop according to their true nature, unpolluted by the perversities of culture, they should derive their education, including their moral understanding, directly from the natural world, unmediated by books or the preconceptions of others.

In Rousseau's *Confessions* these ideas were confirmed by personal experience. Despite the death of his mother, he describes his early childhood as one of happiness: 'No royal child could be more scrupulously cared for than I was in my early years.'[4] But when he grows older he becomes corrupted. Society changes him - a society defined by ownership, division of labour, inequality and the misuse of status and power. He was apprenticed to an engraver who was abusive towards him and 'who managed in a very short time to quench all the fire of my childhood', leading him down a path of 'falsehood, idleness, and theft'.[5,6] His memoirs contrast the beauty, simplicity and virtues of the country with the negative effects of the city. It was the city, above all, where people competed against each other, and cruelly exploited their fellow man in the process. Rousseau describes his disillusionment with Paris as he enters the city for the first time: 'I saw nothing but dirty, stinking little streets, ugly black houses, a general air of squalor and poverty, beggars, carters, menders of clothes, sellers of herb drinks and old hats. All this so affected me at the outset that all the real magnificence I have seen in Paris has not been sufficient to efface my first impression, and I have always retained a secret aversion against living in the capital.'[7] Elsewhere in his memoirs he writes: 'It is in the country that one learns to love and serve humanity; in the cities all one learns is to despise it.'[8]

Nonetheless, despite instances of poor behaviour, Rousseau's reflections assured him that he was fundamentally a good person. In a letter from Diderot included by Rousseau in the *Confessions*, Diderot pointedly observes: 'I know that, whatever you do, the testimony of your conscience will always speak in your favour.'[9] Rousseau's virtuous nature may have been overborne by pernicious cultural forces, by mistakes, by weaknesses of character or reason; it may at times have been lost from view but it was still there and could be uncovered by careful introspection. He records that he is able to think of himself, 'on the whole the best of men'.[10] 'He would acknowledge his sins,' writes Leo Damrosch, 'but unlike Augustine he would also prove his essential goodness.'[11] Rousseau's meticulous examination of his conscience informed him that, despite any appearances to the contrary, at the core of who he was there existed an intrinsic moral force. This was the same moral force that constituted the General Will, and the same moral force that needed to be protected from cultural decadence by means of a careful education such as that he prescribed for Emile.

By opening up to inspection every nook and cranny of his life with all its faults, merits and formative experiences, Rousseau hoped to have fireproofed himself against attacks. He revealed a wide range of imperfections and vices. There was his exhibitionism. There was the erotic pleasure he derived from being smacked, which he traced back to childhood punishment he received at the hands of a female guardian. There was his betrayal of a domestic servant whom he had accused of stealing a ribbon that he himself had stolen, and which led to her being sacked. There was the abandonment of his children. There was his use of prostitutes. There was his pretence to be a music teacher despite, at that time, having little understanding of music. There was the selling of a theatre ticket he had been gifted by a friend. And so on.

But Rousseau's radical and unprecedented solution to defending himself against the attacks of his enemies was ultimately flawed. The facts he recounted may have been true but the conclusions he drew frequently lacked psychological credibility, most damningly in the case of the abandonment of his five children:

> If I were one of those low-born men, deaf to the gentle voice of Nature, a man in whose breast no real feeling of justice and humanity ever arose, this hardness of heart would have been quite easy to explain. But my warm-heartedness, my acute sensibility, the ease with which I formed friendships, the hold they exercised over me, and the cruel wrench when they had to be broken; my innate goodwill towards my fellow men; my burning love for the great, the true, the beautiful, and the just; my horror of evil in every form, my inability to hate, to hurt, or even to wish to; that softening, that sharp and sweet emotion I feel at the sight of all that is virtuous, generous and lovable: is it possible that all these can ever dwell in the same soul along with depravity which, quite unscrupulously, tramples the dearest obligation underfoot? No, I feel, and boldly declare – it is impossible. Never for a moment in his life could Jean-Jacques have been a man without feelings or compassion, an unnatural father. I may have been mistaken, but I could never be callous. If I were to state my reasons, I should say too much. For since they were strong enough to seduce me, they would seduce many others; and I do not wish to expose any young people who may read me to the risk of being misled by the same error. I will be content with a general statement that in handing my children over for the State to educate, for lack of means to bring them up myself, by destining them to become workers and peasants instead of adventurers and fortune-hunters, I thought I was acting as a citizen and father.[12]

To decide that giving away his children, repeatedly, against the wishes of their mother, to a foundling hospital where even their chances of survival, never mind their chances of having a happy and productive life, were slim, could be anything other than callous, was little short of delusional. Yet Rousseau duly interrogated his soul and found nothing with which to reprimand himself apart from having made an 'error'. When he stole the ribbon: 'Never was deliberate wickedness further from my intention than at that cruel moment.'[13] Indeed, on reflection he realised that the culpability lay with those who inquired into the incident. He would have confessed, 'But all they did was to frighten me, when what I needed was encouragement.'[14] On selling the theatre ticket: 'there are moments of a kind of delirium, in which men cannot be judged by what they do.'[15] During a period of sexual infatuation, he refers to 'the follies which the memory of my dear Mamma [Madam de Warens] caused me to commit.'[16]

He makes errors, he is overcome by madness, his emotions get the better of him. None of these things, he would have his audience believe, are sufficient to cast doubt upon his core moral goodness. Indeed, at times this fundamental goodness was such that his 'free and open nature' and his 'too loving and tender heart' exacerbated his 'torments'.[17,18] On his romantic relationships he observes, 'My lack of success with women has always come from loving them too much.'[19] He was virtuous to a fault, it would seem. Ironically, one of the themes pursued by St Augustine is individual moral responsibility, a responsibility that Rousseau's *Confessions* seems designed to rationalise away. Compounded by the regular intervention of destiny, free will for the Genevan assumes a rather hypothetical quality. 'Grim fate,' Damrosch notes, 'was his customary way of explaining why he so often found himself doing things he didn't intend or understand … Rousseau argued fervently for free will, but he needed the notion of a cruel destiny to explain why he so often felt unfree.'[20] Of course, in diminishing his responsibility for the bad, he undermines his claims to possess an essential moral goodness in any sense that is meaningful.

Rousseau's expectations of his readers are contradictory. On the surface he sets them up as impartial arbiters of his character. He has nothing to hide. He will provide them with exhaustive evidence, and they will make their judgement. The facts will speak for themselves: 'I must remain incessantly beneath his [the reader's] gaze, so that he may follow me in all the extravagances of my heart and into every least corner of my life'; 'Intelligent reader, consider and decide. For my part I say no more.'[21,22] Yet he wants his audience to treat him with tolerance and to recognise that he is likely their superior: 'Anyone reading this will not fail to laugh at my amorous adventures, and observe, that after lengthy preliminaries, my most advanced of them concluded with a kiss of the hand. Make no mistake my readers. I probably had more pleasure from this affair which ended with a kiss than you will ever have from yours which, at the very least, begin there.'[23] In a similar vein he boasts how Sophie d'Houdetot inspired in him 'a passion perhaps stronger than any man has ever felt before.'[24] In Book 12 the cat is well and truly let out of the bag: 'Here is one more of these confessions which I am certain in advance will meet with the incredulity of those readers who always persist in judging me by their own standards.'[25] Further on he declares: 'I have told the truth. If anyone knows anything to the contrary to what I have here recorded, though he prove it a thousand times, his knowledge is a lie and an imposture.'[26]

His attempt to sway his audience is reinforced by how he shapes his narrative. He is, of course, a highly accomplished prose writer who deploys a wide range of literary devices to immerse the reader in his world as he claims to have experienced it. He regularly uses second person and rhetorical questions to engage his readers directly and to strengthen their relationship with him. DG Wright has drawn attention to a repeating pattern in which Rousseau identifies a key event that signals the end of some period of happiness and pitches him decisively forward towards some future adversity: 'that fatal moment that was to bring the long procession of my misfortunes'; 'In the midst of this temporary prosperity a catastrophe was preparing afar off'; 'Here begins the work of darkness.'[27,28,29] These events might be instances of bad behaviour (when he stole some asparagus), bad luck (when he ran away from Geneva) or coincidence (coming across an essay competition in the *Mercury*).

The Confessions and *History of My Life*

It was inevitable that Rousseau should loom large in Casanova's mind when he wrote his own memoirs; the Genevan loomed large in the minds of all the educated men and women of Europe. In 1788, six years after the publication of the first part of *The Confessions,* Casanova published his autobiographical work entitled *The History of My Escape from the Prisons of the Republic of Venice*. In the opening to his foreword, he writes: 'JJ Rousseau, famous relapser, very eloquent writer and visionary philosopher, playing the misanthrope and striving for persecution, wrote a foreword to his novel *Héloïse* which is unique: it both insults the reader and yet does not indispose him.' And a little later he continues: 'you will see, I hope, that I make no claims either by my style or through any new and surprising moral discoveries, like the author I just named, who does not write as we speak and who, instead of reasoning by means of a system, pronounces aphorisms resulting from the casual linking of his warm circumlocutions, and not from cold logic; his axioms are paradoxes made to make the mind sneeze.'[30] In *History of My Life* Casanova records a similar criticism of Rousseau made to him by the distinguished scholar Albrecht von Haller who disliked Rousseau's eloquence 'because he only made it brilliant by means of antithesis and paradox.'[31]

At the point Casanova began to compose his memoirs we have someone who for a long time had not only actively engaged in debating ideas but someone whose life had been substantially influenced by them: Epicurean materialism; the association of pleasure with the good, and suffering with the bad; the sensationalism of Locke; the importance and limitations of reason; empirical inquiry; libertinism and the rejection of 'prejudices'; questions of morality, consciousness, free will and the soul; the place of religion; courtly ideals of honour and love. Now, before him, he had *The Confessions* where Rousseau, through the filter of his own beliefs, reflected upon the forces that had made him who he was, in the process exposing himself to public scrutiny to a degree which was unprecedented. *History of My Life* gave Casanova an opportunity to do something similar: examine his own life in the context of his intellectual interests and beliefs. But as a historian who in this domain could reasonably claim to be a superior scholar to both Voltaire and Rousseau, Casanova uses his life experience as primary evidence to demonstrate how people behave in fact, not how they ought to behave or how they would like to think they behave. If not as extreme as Enlightenment radicals such as d'Holbach, Casanova had materialist leanings and valued objective rationality even if he did believe that human understanding had its limits. Hence his swipe at Rousseau for his 'warm circumlocutions' and love of paradoxes. Casanova regarded his memoirs as a contribution to history and moral philosophy and, indeed, science. They provided case studies that could be used for empirical investigation by moral philosophers such as himself.

Casanova's decision to approach his memoirs as history may have been inspired by Diderot. As discussed in Chapter 7, Diderot was dissatisfied with the subjectivety which was the foundational basis of Cartesian knowledge, and from a materialist perspective explored the problem of knowing who we are and how our perception of self changes. How can we be sure of our existence and our sense of ourselves if, at any point in time, we are different from whom we were at some previous point? Our senses cannot help us directly as they are tied to the immediate. He suggests that the key to our identity is our memory, which preserves our sense impressions through time. Ivo Cerman writes: 'Inspired by this sensualist conception, Casanova endeavoured to write down this histoire de sa vie [history of his life] and become the historian of his own existence.'[32] Consistent with Diderot's argument, Casanova himself endorses the centrality of memory to human consciousness and rejects the possibility that human reason might ever be able to resolve claims that an immaterial soul or mind (and Descartes treated those entities as more or less equivalent) could interact with a material body. When Casanova refers to the mind, he is describing an object whose operation is dependent upon biology and maturation: 'my mind and my matter are one substance.'[33]

It is hard to read the preface to *History of My Life* without detecting references to *The Confessions*. Casanova would have expected his reader, at least the sort of sophisticated reader he had in mind, to be able to read between the lines. This style of writing came naturally to a man for whom indirectness and allusion had played such a large part in the strategies of seduction and dissimulation in which he had engaged for so much of his life, simultaneously enabling deniability and promoting complicit knowingness. Indirectness was a strategy employed by Socrates, with whom Casanova was well familiar. Like Rousseau, in his preface Casanova asserts the truthfulness of what he writes. But while Rousseau declares, 'I shall come forward with this work in my hand, to present myself before my Sovereign Judge,' Casanova's reference is secular rather than religious and notably less pretentious, perhaps satirically so: 'I imagine myself giving an account of my management, as a butler renders it to his lord before disappearing.'[34,35] On another occasion, he notes: 'I put my reasonings down on paper without needing either paradoxes or intertwining sophisms with sophisms designed more to deceive myself than my readers, for I could never bring myself to give them counterfeit money if I knew it to be false.'[36] It is hard to avoid the impression, given his previous criticism of Rousseau's use of paradox, that he is questioning the sincerity (and hence truthfulness) of Rousseau's account. In the opening line of his 1797 Preface, he writes: 'I begin by declaring to my reader that in all that I have done, good or bad, in all my life, I am sure that I have deserved merit or blame, and therefore I must believe myself free.'[37] Here he is taking full responsibility for his actions, or at least his actions as he describes them in his memoirs, a stark contrast to Rousseau's 'confession'; only if you are an independent moral being can you deserve merit or blame. A little later there is another reference to confession and another apparent swipe at Rousseau: 'I hope, dear reader, that far from finding in my history the character of impudent boasting, you will find there that which is appropriate for a general confession, although in the style of my narrations you will find in me neither the air of a penitent, nor the constraint of someone who blushes to give an account of his adventures.'[38]

In Casanova's earlier autobiographical work, *The History of My Escape from the Prisons of the Republic of Venice,* we find similar expressions of commitment to truth: 'I declare that I have written nothing but according to the maxim of telling only the pure truth'; 'I prefer a judgement based on the truth and condemns me, to one that could be favourable but based on falsehood.'[39,40] When he referred to truth Casanova did not intend to mean that every reference and verbal exchange he recorded was factually accurate. Rousseau had made that point himself in relation to *The Confessions*. Casanova was writing about events that had occurred decades earlier. There were going to be gaps in his records and recall. To smooth out the potholes of his narrative he filled them with best guesses, and where sections of the road were completely missing he constructed them from scratch. Cerman has pointed out that in so doing Casanova was following the practice of Classical and Renaissance historians: 'They invented descriptions of battles, and inserted direct speeches which gave moral lessons to the reader and many other things which are unacceptable in modern critical history … When he [Casanova] encountered lacunae in his memory, he simply invented a story.'[41]

As already mentioned, it is impossible for any writer to be objective in an absolute sense when constructing a text. By necessity there will be, consciously or unconsciously, some preconceived outcome which will shape the presentation of information, and pressure to imbue a narrative with a degree of coherence that is unlikely to reflect actuality. For Casanova, as long as he was faithful to the essential truth of his history and was not being intentionally deceptive about who he was and how he behaved, then this was acceptable. And it has to be said, in the context of the values of his time, the various transgressive and morally disreputable acts he describes himself as committing suggests he was not trying to shield himself from disapproval. Like Rousseau, his relationship with the reader is founded on claims of openness, sincerity and truth telling. But whereas Rousseau sets himself above his reader, chiding them and intervening to head off any incorrect impressions they may make about his character, Casanova addresses his audience as he would a friend. Indeed, the audience for his memoirs as he was writing them was comprised of acquaintances and friends such as the Prince de Ligne.

A central philosophical divide between Casanova and Rousseau was materialism. Rousseau did not completely reject materialism, after all it did play a part in the educational programme he devised for Emile. But while Casanova was willing to conceive of selfhood as a phenomenon based on past sensory experience collected in memory, Rousseau rejected claims that reduced the self to no more than an interaction of matter, denying its intrinsic spirituality. Such a mechanical explanation may have been adequate for animals but not for mankind. Man possessed free will, enabling him to resist the deterministic processes of nature: 'No material creature is active by itself, and I am. One may very well argue with me about this; but I sense it, and this sentiment that speaks to me is stronger than the reason combatting it. I have a body on which other bodies act and which acts on them. This reciprocal action is not doubtful. But my will is independent of my senses.'[42]

These contrasting perspectives of reality may offer at least a partial explanation of one of the significant differences between *The Confessions* and *History of My Life*. Thomas Kavanagh has drawn attention to the extent to which in the *History of My Life* chance is a dominant theme: 'Casanova's autobiography is unique within the genre. Chance has presided, it would seem, over every aspect of this work's production and dissemination.'[43] The *History of My Life* is filled with countless examples. Sometimes his quick wits allowed him take advantage of the unexpected but on other occasions events could spiral out of his control. This was the case when he was being held under arrest in Pesaro in 1744 while awaiting the arrival of a new passport. It was the Pesaro misadventure which led to his separation from Bellino and the end of one of his first great loves. The incident is worth recounting in full:

> In the nine to ten days I was waiting for my passport, which could not be long in coming, I came to be known and liked by the whole army. I would go for a walk even out of sight of the sentry; and they were right not to fear me escaping, for I would have been very mistaken to consider it; but here is one of the most singular accidents that has happened to me in my entire life.
>
> Walking at six o'clock in the morning a hundred paces from the guardhouse, I observe an officer, who gets off his horse, puts the reins on its neck, and goes somewhere. Reflecting on the tranquillity of this horse who stood there like a faithful

> servant whose master has ordered it to wait for him, I approach it, and without any intention, I take the reins, I put my foot in the stirrup, and I mount it. It was the first time in my life that I had been on a horse. I don't know if I touched it with my cane, or with my heels; the horse sets off like lightning, and flat out when it feels my heels pressing against it, which I pressed only to stay on, even having my right foot out of the stirrup. The last advanced post orders me to stop: it was an order that I did not know how to carry out. The horse keeps going. I hear gunshots, which miss me. At the first advanced post of the Austrians they stop my horse, and I thank God for being able to get down.[44]

If we consider reality through the filter of materialism, we have a world that is built bottom up. Indivisible units of matter collide and cohere into larger units taking on more complex properties which in turn interact with other units. It is a process of improvisation, vastly complex and unpredictable, at least at the human scale. It may be intelligible to a divine understanding, it may have a purpose, it may be predetermined, and this divine understanding may even be communicable through revelation but the power of human reason by itself is too limited to make sense of it beyond abstract scientific laws such as those uncovered by Newton. The individual's experience is of a life buffeted by random events that can no more be understood by them than an ant caught up in the battle of Marathon would be able to understand the strategies of Darius and Miltiades.

Casanova did not rule out providence and he was quite superstitious. But for Casanova the historian, a rational, empirical scholar, explanations couched in terms of supernatural intention, and which did not recognise the limitations of human understanding, would be wholly unsatisfactory. Had not Newton famously declared '*hypotheses non fingo*' ('I will not pretend an explanation') when he refused to speculate on what caused gravity? It is true that the *History of My Life* frequently refers to fate but it carries little explanatory power. Casanova would have been aware of those figures of antiquity who were led to disaster by their misinterpretation of fate. For the ancients, the gods and fate were both as capricious as the British weather. At the level of what was meaningful to human experience, the workings of fate would be as unfathomable as the workings of the mind of God and the complexity of material interaction. Two rather idiosyncratic exceptions to this were Casanova's belief in a personal daemon and the effect of debilitating illness. He deemed that both existed largely to prevent him from getting up to mischief.

Rousseau, by contrast, did believe that it was possible to understand God, at least to some degree, and to understand God's presence in the world. He knew that God did not intend people to live in cities. He knew that God had made people intrinsically good and had provided each person with an inner moral force to guide them. He knew that evil in the world was a consequence of people's own actions, and he had uncovered the social mechanisms at the root of this corruption of the good. Rousseau's world was not random but comprehensible and, as we have seen, this is reflected in *The Confessions* where he writes of catastrophes 'preparing afar off'.[45] *The Confessions* is far less a narrative of haphazard events and much more an unfolding of explicable forces, both material and immaterial.

On the topic of love, Casanova and Rousseau were not so far apart. Federico de Trocchio compares attitudes towards erotic love expressed in *History of My Life* with those conveyed through immensely successful eighteenth-century libertine novels such as *Thérèse the Philosopher* which would have been familiar to Casanova.[46] Indeed the Venetian paid a visit to its reputed author, Boyer d'Argens, whom he described as 'a determined Epicurean'.[47] In line with libertine philosophy, the protagonists of these pornographic novels are uninhibited sexual beings who recognise that pleasure is natural. They reject traditional religious and social norms such as marriage and procreation as illegitimate restraints upon the rational exercise of their desire. But the portrayal of such a hedonistic lifestyle was an idealised one that glossed over its flaws. In particular, women faced the costs of childbirth, abortion and ostracism as a consequence of casual sex.

In contrast to such novels, *History of My Life* exposes the reality of libertinism, especially for those who are unprotected by wealth and privilege. Several times Casanova was involved in helping women to deal with unwanted pregnancies, and he frequently contracted venereal disease which he treated with a combination of mercury and diet. Perhaps more pertinently, *History of My Life* reveals the unsatisfactory shallowness of relationships based on an individual's search for their own selfish physical pleasure. While libertinism rejected sentimental love and its matrimonial trappings as an unnatural obstacle in the way of maximising pleasure, it is this sentimental love that Casanova values so highly: 'Those who believe that a woman is incapable of making a man equally happy all the twenty-four hours of a day have never known a Henriette. The joy that flooded my soul was much greater when I talked with her during the day than when I held her in my arms at night.'[48]

This focus on mutual love and a recognition of responsibility for the needs of the other perhaps indicates a dissatisfaction with libertinism in its cruder and more self-centred forms. When Casanova the libertine is examined by Casanova the historian, we discover that he achieves happiness as much by deviating from strict libertine principles as he does by adhering to them. Di Trocchio comments: 'Casanova has distanced himself not only from the pornographic trivialisations of libertine morality, but also from Voltaire, in order to place himself within the same perspective as Rousseau and Goethe.'[49]

From a literary perspective a key difference between *The Confessions* and *History of My Life* is the extent to which the writer's standpoint dominates. In *The Confessions*, the world is seen overwhelmingly through the eyes of Rousseau whereas *History of My Life* is populated by a much wider variety of points of view. The latter frequently includes long stretches of dialogue between different individuals expressing their own observations and opinions, often in opposition to Casanova's. More significantly, there are sections when an individual recounts a personal story of their own at considerable length. Casanova also includes the text of letters he has received, offering the reader the voice of another which is entirely unmediated apart from its contextual framing. Rousseau describes and explains the world to his audience whereas Casanova enables his audience to experience it. Concerned that the reader does not misunderstand what is going on or what kind of person he is, Rousseau inserts himself between the reader and the events of his life. Casanova, by contrast, invites the reader to roam around and come to their own conclusions.

Consistent with this aim to recreate the past (and relive it for himself) Casanova often goes into detail about the places he visits and the scenes where action takes place. His world is far more visceral than that of Rousseau's. The reader of *The Confessions* is reduced either to the role of the passive recipient or the sceptic, left to accept or reject the judgement of the narrator: 'To crown all, there arrived from the Val d'Aosta a young organist the abbé Palais, a good musician, a good man, and an excellent accompanist upon the clavichord. I made his acquaintance, and we became inseparable. He was the pupil of an Italian monk, who was a fine organist. He talked to me of his theories and I compared them with my Rameau's.'[50] Rousseau here describes this relationship entirely from his perspective. Neither then nor later do we hear the voice of Abbé Palais or have a chance of judging his personality or the nature of their friendship for ourselves. It is enough that Rousseau has told us.

By contrast *History of My Life* is filled with exchanges such as this one:

> Madame Quinson comes upstairs and enters my room furious. She throws herself on an armchair, recovers her breath, relieves her anger by insulting me, and ends up telling me that I should prepare to marry her daughter. With this notification I realise what it is all about, and I answer that I am married in Italy.
>
> 'And why therefore did you go and give my daughter a baby?'
>
> 'I assure you that I did not have that intention, and anyway, who told you that it was me?'
>
> 'She, sir, herself. She is sure of it.'
>
> 'I compliment her. For me, I'm willing to swear that I'm not at all sure.'
>
> 'So?'
>
> 'So nothing. If she is pregnant, she will give birth.'[51]

History of My Life reads like a blend of autobiography and picaresque, libertine novel, the latter manifest in not only its erotic content but its libertine philosophical discourse. Scenes are constructed to generate tension, speculation, interest and surprise – qualities that are consistent with an unpredictable, materialist world where, if God exists, They keep Their distance. But unlike a novel, events are not driven by relevance to the internal logic of an overarching, preplanned schema. Instead, there is an uncoordinated and shifting landscape of people and places. Events and complications spring up out of the ground, isolated, anecdotal, unforeseen, resolved through improvisation or yet more manifestations of chance. Sometimes these events occur alongside other ongoing narratives but without any relevance to them and with no causal impact upon them. Sometimes they bring those other narratives to a shuddering halt, like 'The End' sign dropping into what the audience believes is the middle of the film.

Casanova and Rousseau's lifelong and profound engagement with the Enlightenment has meant that their memoirs are deeply influenced by the movement's ideas and intellectual and personal conflicts. Typical of Enlightenment scholars, both Casanova and Rousseau were searching for a more satisfactory relationship between God, religion, society and the individual, one which recognised the importance of God but which was more tolerant of individual conscience, and which sought to place reason rather than superstition or institutional bigotry at the centre of human affairs. This transition from the religious to the secular is most striking in *The Confessions*. Rousseau draws upon the ancient Christian practice of confession stretching back to the Old Testament prophets, whose aim was to awaken people to the true nature of the sinful lives they were leading, and he takes St Augustine for his literary model. Yet, as mentioned, *The Confessions* is directed not at God but squarely at his fellow man. It was a response to what he perceived to be an urgent need to protect his reputation and his ideas from his enemies, most notably fellow Enlightenment scholars such as Voltaire, both in the present while he was alive, and for posterity. It is unsurprising that his beliefs should appear to be endorsed in his account of his life: that he, like all mankind, possesses an innate moral goodness (fundamental to his concept of the General Will); that civilisation is a corrupting force, especially the city; and that sentimental love is not a social artifice but expresses a transcendent quality that is intrinsic to love, as demonstrated in *The Confessions* through his portrayal of the love between his mother and father.

Like *The Confessions*, *History of My life* is intimately linked to the author's scholarly interests and philosophical beliefs as well as a desire to be respected as an accomplished writer and intellectual: the historian, the libertine, the philosopher and the theist are all in different ways represented. And in the same way that *The Confessions* is in part a response to the *Sentiment of the Citizens* so *History of My Life* is in part a response to *The Confessions*. There can be little doubt that in charting so many aspects of his life, so many moments of vice and virtue, at such length and with such extraordinary openness, that Casanova has taken his cue from Rousseau. It is hard not to imagine a mischievous glint in Casanova's eye as he reads Rousseau's opening sentence: 'I have resolved on an enterprise which has no precedent, and which, once complete, will have no imitator.'[52]

Chapter 10

A Philosopher and a Christian

> 'Man is free; but he is not if he does not believe that he is, for the more influence he ascribes to Destiny the more he deprives himself of that power which God gave him when He granted him reason.'
>
> Giacomo Casanova, *History of My Life*

> 'Casanova was intensively preoccupied with philosophical and political questions throughout his life.'
>
> Ivo Cerman, *Casanova: Enlightenment Philosopher*

We tend to associate philosophy with names such as Aristotle, Descartes, Kant, Leibniz, Marx and Rousseau – people whose works are characterised by carefully reasoned and systematic thought, on occasion culminating in grand metaphysical edifices. Sometimes their ideas attract disciples and engender entire schools of thought or set off political movements. Today, the typical habitat of the philosopher is the college and the classroom. They are mainly professional academics, often producing work that is so specialist that much of it will be incomprehensible to anyone who is not a specialist themselves. But while these are important traditions within philosophy, they are not the whole story. We must be wary of making unhelpful assumptions about what can legitimately be regarded as the practice of philosophy and who can legitimately be regarded as a philosopher.

Much philosophy in the past was expressed in a range of forms including drama, letters and poetry. Plato's dialogues, as mentioned in the introduction, were a frequently emulated form of philosophical discourse. To make his own work accessible, the influential third Earl of Shaftesbury exploited a wide variety of genres, so much so, writes Michael Gill, that 'this diversity of forms, styles, tones, and personae makes it difficult to attribute to Shaftesbury a single philosophical system of thought.'[1] Voltaire's masterpiece *Candide* was a philosophical tale that attacked Leibniz's theory of optimism. Voltaire was perhaps the greatest of the French *philosophes* but was a brilliant polemicist rather than a creator of philosophical systems. Isaac Newton was a natural philosopher, and science was natural philosophy. Friedrich Nietzsche's *Thus Spoke Zarathustra* (1883–1892) comprises prose and poetry in a fictional philosophical narrative. Samuel Johnson's 1755 dictionary definition of 'philosopher' is 'A man deep in knowledge, either moral or natural'.

Within this historical and cultural context, if we consider philosophy as broadly understood to be an active engagement with questions of knowledge and what can be known then Casanova was unquestionably a serious philosopher and viewed himself as such. For almost 200 years researchers have investigated Casanova's writings but for much of that time their interest lay in discovering and verifying the facts of his life rather than getting to grips with his ideas and their development. Serious work on his philosophical beliefs and his place in the Enlightenment has really only been undertaken in the last thirty years or so, notably by scholars such as Gérard Lahouati and Federico di Trocchio and, more recently, through publications such as *Casanova: Enlightenment Philosopher* (2016).

Casanova is not usually described as a *philosophe* but the similarities between him and that renowned category of French intellectuals are striking. Casanova was steeped in learning, a man of letters, and a skilful and versatile author who could be pugnacious and witty. He was a sociable urbanite who engaged with some of the foremost Enlightenment minds and influencers of the time, along with many lesser lights. He met the likes of d'Alembert, Fontenelle, Albrecht von Haller, Voltaire – of course – Winckelmann, possibly Diderot and possibly Rousseau.[3] His intellectual interests mapped closely on to those of the *philosophe* tradition. There was his attraction to pagan writers and ideas, his eclecticism, and his high regard for reason and education. He advocated tolerance and moderation. He questioned prevailing moral norms and was critical of the Church and religious doctrine. His own philosophical and historical writing is infused with a spirit of critical enquiry, coupled with a preference for knowledge founded upon empirical investigation and human experience rather than abstract systems that were tortuously deductive. Casanova was politically conservative, but this was not untypical either. Most Enlightenment figures of any stature, although progressive in some ways, were closely aligned to the established social order. Their allies, friends, families and they themselves were often drawn from the most affluent and privileged strata of society. They wanted reform from within. They did not want to burn everything down.

Philosophical Pursuit

Casanova recounts an exchange in his memoirs in which a Mademoiselle Vesian quizzes him on the nature of philosophy. Casanova would have been 26 at the time and it underlines the extent to which philosophy was an ever-present interest in his life. The exchange is, in effect, a short philosophical dialogue in which Casanova is taking on the role of tutor and Mademoiselle Vesian that of a curious and receptive student. The dialogue form was one of Casanova's favourite ways of expressing and exploring ideas, most of which he wrote during his time at Dux. Ivo Cerman has identified over a score of mainly unpublished Casanovan dialogues on philosophy and religion alone.[4]

Mademoiselle Vesian was a young Italian woman from a respectable family who had been orphaned, and now found herself in Paris with her brother trying to repair their fortunes. Taking her under his wing, Casanova hatched a plan for her to snare a nobleman by putting her on the stage and having her feign to be virtuous for a little while in order to make her all the more alluring. Addressing the issues of virtue, tolerance, pleasure and happiness, Casanova berates the 'prejudices' of people who adopt more conventional moral behaviours. He endorses ideas commonly associated with sensationalism, natural religion, deism, libertinism and Neo-Epicureanism. Unlike classical Epicureanism, seventeenth- and eighteenth-century Neo-Epicureanism placed more emphasis, among other things, upon the principle of self-preservation and the positive importance of pleasure, not pleasure simply in the form of tranquillity and the absence of pain.

Late one evening Casanova returns to the Hotel de Bourgogne where the two are staying. He notices that the door to Vesian's room is open, and so he goes in to visit her where he finds that she is in bed. She informs him that she wants to talk to him a bit more about the strategy he has concocted:

> [Mademoiselle Vesian] 'I will exercise virtue to find he who loves it only to destroy it.'

> [Casanova] 'Precisely; and believe me, that is what life is about. We relate everything to ourselves, and each of us is a tyrant. This is why the best person is the one who is tolerant. I'm pleased to see you becoming a philosopher.'
>
> 'How do you become one?'
>
> 'One thinks.'
>
> 'For how long?'
>
> 'For one's whole life.'
>
> 'So one never finishes?'
>
> 'Never. But one gains what one can, and one procures all the portion of happiness of which one is susceptible.'
>
> 'And this happiness, how does it make itself felt?'
>
> 'It makes itself felt in all the pleasures that the philosopher procures for himself, and when he thinks that he has procured them by his care and by the means of trampling all prejudices under foot.'
>
> 'What is pleasure? And what is prejudice?'
>
> 'Pleasure is an enjoyment of the senses in the present. It is an entire satisfaction that one grants them in all that they desire. And when the exhausted or weary senses want rest, or to catch their breath, or to be reborn, pleasure becomes imagination, which delights in reflecting on the happiness that its tranquillity brings it. The philosopher is he who does not deny himself any pleasure which does not produce greater pains, and who knows how to create that pleasure.'
>
> 'And you say it depends upon trampling on prejudice. What is prejudice, and how do we trample it underfoot, and find the strength to do so?'
>
> 'You ask me a question, my dear friend, a more important one than which is not known to moral philosophy. That is why it is a practice which lasts a lifetime. But I will tell you briefly that prejudice means any so-called duty whose reason cannot be found in nature.'[5]

Casanova next comments about Socrates, ethics and metaphysics, declaring that 'morality is the metaphysics of physics, for everything is nature.'[6] As the dialogue reaches its end, he confesses that their conversation has inspired in him a desire to kiss her, from which Vesian deduces, concordant with Casanova's lesson and much to his satisfaction, that 'our soul can only be happy by being in tune with our senses.'[7] Fittingly, they go on to enjoy each other's company in love-making and conversation until the following dawn.

Another example of an embedded philosophical dialogue can be found elsewhere in Casanova's memoirs. One of his lovers, Hedwig, is learned in theology and on occasion holds question and answer sessions that are something of a social event, astonishing people by her religious insights and depth of understanding. In one such event that is described by Casanova, it is evident that he uses Hedwig as a means to express his own ideas.

> M Tronchin asked her if, simply by reading the Old Testament, one could establish the immortality of the soul.
>
> 'The Old Testament,' she replied, 'does not teach this doctrine; but without its being spoken about, reason establishes it; for what exists must necessarily be immortal, since the destruction of a real substance is repugnant to nature and to thought.'
>
> 'I will therefore ask you,' continued the banker, 'if the existence of the soul is established in the Bible?'
>
> 'The idea is unavoidable. Smoke always indicates the fire that produces it.'
>
> 'Tell me if matter can think.'
>
> 'That is something I won't tell you, because that is not within my expertise; but I will tell you that, believing God almighty, I cannot find sufficient reason to infer his inability to give matter the faculty of thought.
>
> 'But what do you believe about yourself?'
>
> 'I believe that I have a soul by means of which I think; but I don't know if after my death I will remember with my soul that I had the honour of dining with you today.'
>
> 'So you believe that your memory may not belong to your soul? But in that case you would no longer be a theologian.'
>
> 'One can be a theologian and a philosopher, because philosophy spoils nothing, and saying "I don't know" does not mean "I know".'

> Three quarters of the guests uttered cries of admiration, and the beautiful philosopher enjoyed seeing me laugh with pleasure at hearing the applause.[8]

As the dialogue continues, Hedwig reiterates that matter is co-eternal with God, highlights the problem of reasoning on the basis of 'empty ideas' (that is, ideas unsupported by sensory experience), illustrates the importance of faith, and recognises that reason has its limits – all beliefs held by Casanova, which we will take a look at below.

Casanova studied philosophy at the University of Padua where he is likely to have discovered eudemonism, a theory that identifies personal happiness as man's primary goal, a central theme of Aristotle's *Nicomachean Ethics*. Ancient culture and philosophy is a pervasive feature of Casanova's writing. He knew Latin, Greek and Hebrew, and his works abound with classical learning. He had a particular fondness for Socrates, whom he rated as the best philosopher because, according to the Venetian, he made the fewest mistakes. In the spirit of Socrates, Casanova was to observe that a true philosopher is aware of how little they know, and that a fool makes pretentions to knowledge that they do not possess, a criticism he directed in particular at members of the Church.

While Casanova makes plenty of explicit references to the ancients, there are other times when their presence is not always clearly signposted. Casanova was familiar with the works of Plato and in one dialogue he pits a Jesuit theologian against a cook in an exchange which would seem to draw from Plato's *Republic*.[9] In the *Republic*, a crucial turning point occurs when the city that Socrates has been constructing shifts from one that satisfies people's basic needs to one that seeks to serve more sophisticated desires. In the new city people are no longer satisfied with meeting their minimum bodily needs but seek higher things that accord with the needs of the soul. This dissatisfaction is a blessing and a curse: it motivates people to strive for greater perfection but it leads to selfishness, immoderation and corruption. The same dichotomy is highlighted in Casanova's dialogue. The Jesuit argues that primitive peoples (equivalent to those in Socrates' first city) existed on a simple diet and were healthier than present-day people as a result. But the cook credits fine dining for acting as a catalyst for scientific curiosity, and hence human progress. It is a defence not only of sensationalist philosophy but a response to Rousseau's one-sided claim that civilisation, based as it was upon science, innovation and luxury, promoted not progress but corruption and degeneracy.

Despite Casanova's fondness for Socrates as a model of what a philosopher should be, it was philosophy derived from the materialism of Epicurus rather than the essentialism of Socrates, Plato and Aristotle that appealed to him, allied as it was in the eighteenth century to sensationalism and libertinism. But such a materialist bent did not necessarily exclude the metaphysical in a transcendental sense. It was quite possible to posit a dualist reality that comprised both a material and an immaterial dimension, and one in which matter could think, as was the case with the late eighteenth-century Christian philosophers, Christoph Meiners and Michael Hißmann.[10] One section of Voltaire's *Encyclopedia* entry on the soul gives a materialist account of its nature that appears similar to ideas expressed by Casanova, including his description of his own awakening into consciousness as an 8-year-old, before which time he claims that he 'vegetated'. Likewise, Voltaire's entry notes that initially the soul 'is only vegetative & similar to that of a plant; that afterwards it becomes sensitive by perfecting itself; & that finally it is made reasonable [rational] by the cooperation of God.'[11] Casanova is also clear that it is God who has given mankind the power to reason, which he describes as 'a particle of the Creator's divinity'.[12] While Casanova was willing to recognise the close interdependence of the material and the immaterial, he was ultimately reluctant to argue that the soul itself could be material.

The materialist ideas of Epicurus fed into the seventeenth-century philosophical debate between the rationalist supporters of Descartes and empiricists such as Gassendi, Hobbes, Locke and Newton. In contrast to the Cartesian doctrine of innate ideas, Lockean sensationalism laid out the case for the blank slate. For Locke, man possessed no innate ideas but did possess a desire for happiness. Beyond the self-contained, logical constructions of a discipline such as mathematics, sensationalism disqualified the possibility of knowing that which was inaccessible to our senses. This left a large hole in man's rational understanding of reality, based as it traditionally had been upon a belief in an immaterial, creator God. It was a hole which Epicurean atomism could fill. As mentioned, this sensationalist (or sensualist) philosophy was picked up and developed by French thinkers such as Condillac, Helvétius, Voltaire and Diderot.

After John Locke and his notion of a blank slate, relativistic perspectives about not only societies, cultures and moral norms but human character became more widespread. People's characters were believed to be more malleable given that their personality was a product of sensory experience. Previously, an individual was generally regarded as having been stamped by fate with a fixed set of qualities. In the world of Shakespeare's bastards, leopards rarely changed their spots. But a conception of the mind as a blank slate led to a different understanding. A person's nature was no longer an invariable product of the stars under which they were born but shaped by their environment. It was a development which was to have a major influence upon conceptions of psychology, education, art and literature as well as philosophy and science. In a more nuanced and, in some ways, a more modern understanding, however, Casanova concludes that individual psychology is comprised of qualities some of which are mutable and others immutable: 'Defects of temperament are irredeemable, because temperament itself is independent of our powers; but character is something else. What constitutes it is the heart, and the mind; and it follows that, with temperament having very little influence, character depends on education, and that it is susceptible to correction, and of reform.'[13]

Casanova's view of human character is, on the whole, rather negative. He spends considerable time deliberating upon people's moral weaknesses, particularly on what leads them to act foolishly. In his *Soliloquy of a Thinker* (1786) he provides insightful analysis into the personality flaws that makes someone a dupe. Paradoxically it is not the 'big fool' who is most vulnerable. Such a person is usually suspicious by nature and so they tend to avoid any traps set for them. Those who are most vulnerable are those who are most credulous, and those with exaggerated self-esteem: 'A man of intelligence, cultivated, full of confidence in his enlightenment, believes in himself and gives into it [the deception] headlong.'[14] Once caught, the victim rarely escapes. The prospect of humiliation prevents them from acknowledging even to themselves that they have been tricked. For this reason, he argues that 'the goal of all good education is to set limits to the self-esteem of the student.'[15]

Casanova saw education as a way to help alleviate the problem of foolishness and was in favour of government by enlightened philosopher princes. A number of his own unpublished Socratic dialogues were written with this in mind, such as *Thirteen dialogues between philosopher K and young Alcibiades* and *Dialogue between the old philosopher Pandolphe and the young Alexis*.[16] The character names were pseudonyms for aristocrats known to Casanova. But despite this hypothetical remedy, the old librarian was not hopeful. Those in an ideal position to advise others, philosophers such as himself who could draw from their observations of human behaviour over many years, tended not to be taken seriously. Casanova believed that it was in people's character to want to discover things for themselves, and as a result each generation made the same mistakes. He found little ground for optimism that mankind would ever be able to progress, morally at any rate.

Two central philosophical concerns of the Enlightenment generally, and of Casanova in particular, were religion and the Church: Casanova's most extensive overtly philosophical text, made up of eighteen dialogues, was *The Philosopher and the Theologian* (1789–1790).[17] If the Enlightenment represented freedom of thought and the operation of reason, for many the Church represented dogmatism and superstition. Such criticisms of the Church led English thinkers towards deism and natural religion. They accepted that there was a creator God – evidence of this could be found through reason and the discovery of laws that governed nature – but they rejected traditional Christian doctrine. While such a position was taken up by some French thinkers there was also among the French a more radical materialist stance that denied the existence of God altogether. The Italian debate went in a different direction and appears to have had a stronger influence upon Casanova despite his familiarity with the more dominant philosophical traditions of the north.

The Italian Enlightenment focused on Church reform and the relationship between the Church and the state rather than an outright rejection of God or Christian doctrine. Some thinkers such as Dalmazzo Vasco (1732–1794) looked to accommodate Christian doctrine, accepting Christianity as the true religion. But he believed that the state should allow individuals to be able to choose the religion they wished to follow as well as regulate the Church in such a way as to maximise the well-being of its citizens. Men such as Cosimi Amidei (1722–1784), writer of *The Church and the State within their Limits* (1768), argued for the ecclesiastical power of the Church to be subject to the secular power of the state. He drew on the Bible to point out that such a separation of Church and state would not contradict fundamental Christian principles. Drawing on social contract theory, Amidei maintained that it was the body of the people that legitimised the authority of the state. Its authority was not derived from God, and therefore the state was not subordinate to the Church. Nonetheless, he recognised the importance of religion as a social good.

Other common criticisms of the Church were directed against special privileges such as tax exemptions, legal immunities and Church asylum, as well as celibacy and the large numbers of clerics who were frequently ill-disciplined and a drain on economic resources. More radical reformers, such as Carlo Pilati (1733–1802), called for monasteries and religious orders to be disbanded. Among the most influential Italian Enlightenment figures of the time were Cesare Beccaria and the Verri brothers, Pietro and Alessandro (Casanova met Alessandro in 1770). Beccaria condemned the cruel punishments meted out by the Inquisition and drew attention to the contradiction between the barbaric practices of the Church and the principles of love and forgiveness that underpinned the Christian faith. Meanwhile Pietro Verri castigated the papacy for being a self-interested political and economic entity that exploited religion for its own ends.

Embracing materialism, at least to a significant degree, while simultaneously asserting his Christian faith, made Casanova rather anomalous as far as the English or French Enlightenment traditions were concerned. Similarly, some of his criticisms of doctrines central to Catholicism contrast with the more religiously orthodox opinions of Italian thinkers. He was able to point to inconsistencies in Church dogma relative to early Christianity such as the doctrine of the Trinity and the influence of non-Biblical sources such as Platonism. His concern was not so much with Christianity itself but the theologians and other agents who purported to speak and act on God's behalf. But he did share common ground with his compatriots in their criticisms of the institution of the Church and the clergy. Wolfgang Rother writes: 'Casanova blames the indecent life of the cardinals in Rome; he casts doubt on the Church's claim of infallibility; he criticises celibacy and in particular monasticism.'[18] Casanova also attacks the crimes of the Inquisition.

While the criticisms referred to by Rother are expressed by the character of the philosopher in Casanova's dialogue *The Philosopher and the Theologian*, there can be little doubt that in this case the opinions of the character reflected the author's own views. Casanova repeatedly draws attention in his memoirs to the ignorance, malice, venality, superstition and general immorality of priests. In one encounter rich with irony, the Venetian has a conversation with the nun MM. They agree that the claims of priests are an obstacle to a true understanding of the nature of God. MM remarks, 'I can say that I only began to love God after I was disabused of the idea of Him that religion had given me.'[19] Like Italian thinkers such as Cosimo Amidei (1722–1784), and going back earlier, Pietro Pomponazzi (1462–1525), Casanova does not question the importance of religion as a source of social stability. Debating face-to-face with Voltaire he argued that effective governance required a monarch buttressed by religion: 'superstition is necessary, since without it the people will never obey the monarch.'[20] One of Casanova's objections to the polemics of Voltaire was that he felt the great man's criticism of the deficiencies of the Church spilled over into criticism of religion itself, and that this prepared the ground for atheism. In agreement with Rousseau's *Social Contract*, Casanova believed that a well-ordered society required some sort of basic religion, such as the one he creates for his philosophical science-fiction novel, *Icosameron* (1788).

A related and highly controversial topic that was also closely tied to questions of morality, religion, authority and the law was that of suicide. For centuries it had been prohibited by the Christian Church. St Augustine asserted that the commandment 'Thou shalt not kill' applied to the taking of one's own life as much as it did to the taking of another's. St Thomas Aquinas later added that it was God's right to decide how long we should live, not ours, that suicide went against our natural self-love – the object of which was to preserve our lives – and that it damaged the community. In the Middle Ages the property of a suicide was forfeit and they were denied Christian burial.

In the ancient world there was not such a clear consensus although self-slaughter had been widely criminalised. For Plato it was an act of cowardice or laziness in the face of life's difficulties. The only occasions when committing suicide was not immoral was when an individual was not in their right mind, when it was a consequence of a judicial punishment (as in the case of Socrates), due to shame at having committed a terrible and unjust act, or in the face of the most extreme personal circumstances. The well-being of the individual was secondary to their obligations to society. But for Stoics such as Seneca suicide was excusable if the conditions of an individual's life compromised their private good. For Seneca a person 'lives as long as he ought, not as long as he can.' For Epicureans the implication of death was the obviation of possible future pleasures. It should be an act of last resort occasioned when the pain that an individual suffered was bearable no longer.

From the seventeenth century the doctrinal certainty on suicide was being questioned and entwined with issues such as individual autonomy. In his essay *Biathanatos* (1607–1608), John Donne argues that there are circumstances when suicide can be justified, most notably for the glory of God. He points out that the Bible itself does not overtly condemn suicide. Nonetheless, throughout the seventeenth century the broad consensus against suicide persisted. But attitudes did begin to change in the eighteenth century. The breakdown of religious authority, and the influence of alternative systems of thought, such as empiricism, materialism and libertinism, created a space for dissident voices. Bernard de Mandeville, in his infamous *The Fable of the Bees* (1714), defended suicide by describing it as a consequence of self-love that acts in order to avoid something more dreaded than death. Alberto Radicati di Passerano's *A Philosophical Dissertation upon Death* (1732) mounted a defence based on materialism. He argued that nature gave individuals an inalienable right to suicide and euthanasia. For Passerano, fear of death was due to religious superstitions peddled by imposters who claimed to know God's will in order to acquire power over their more credulous fellows. Philosopher Johannes Robeck argued that suicide was not a sin as according to Christian theology life was a gift from God and as such the receiver could do with it what they wished. Beccaria, in his *On Crimes and Punishments* (1764), asserted that suicide could not be a crime, whatever the morality of it, as the individual could not be punished and it would be unjust to punish the family as they were not responsible for the act. Montesquieu and Voltaire both argued in favour of decriminalisation while David Hume's essay *Of Suicide* (1777) attacked the theological foundations that underpinned the Christian prohibition, arguing instead in favour of personal liberty. Other authors drew on the Stoic tradition to defend suicide or to argue in favour of exceptions.

The question of suicide was a subject that Casanova addressed a number of times, including in his *Discourse on Suicide* (1769), *Nine Dialogues* (1782) and *The Philosopher and the Theologian* (1789–1790).[21] Casanova himself had felt the urge to take his own life on more than one occasion, in particular during his stay in London. He was about to fling himself off Westminster Bridge, lead weights in his pockets, when a chance encounter with a friend prevented him. But he takes a conservative approach in his *Discourse on Suicide*, influenced as he was by a desire to ingratiate himself with the Venetian authorities. Casanova was an exile from Venice at this point in his life and hoping to obtain permission to return. He marshalled various arguments to buttress his case against suicide. These ranged from the generally hostile attitudes of the ancients, to the flaws in English culture and character – the English having a reputation for being the suicides of Europe – to claims that self-slaughter could never be beneficial whether you were a theist, deist or atheist. He also reasoned that such an act was unnatural given that man's primary instinct was for self-preservation.

Over a decade later, now back in Venice but with health and financial problems, Casanova's attitude towards suicide had become less clear-cut. In his *Nine Dialogues*, a philosopher who is a materialist and atheist debates with a theist. Casanova considers a range of philosophical themes. The utilitarian case that suicide is justified when the pains of life outweigh the benefits is met by the claim that suffering will be rewarded in the afterlife, although that, in turn, is rebutted by the point that it would entail believing that a loving God could permit his creatures to suffer unnecessarily. The argument that self-destruction goes against nature rears its head again but this time is countered by the assertion that God has provided man with reason to be able make rational decisions which can override instinct. What's more, the rational person does not succumb to the superstitions and delusions of the religious, or the machinations of rulers and priests who use religion to keep people cowed. Instead, reason helps man to attain peace and tranquillity, unassailed by false fears – the Epicurean ideal. Other topics covered include determinism and free will, the existence and cause of evil, and whether the source of the cosmos is material or divine. Paolo Bernardini and Diego Lucci, commenting on *Nine Dialogues*, observe: 'What is sure is that this writing gives the reader the impression that its author was a torn man, stretched between the voice of reason, which disposed him to suicide, and the natural instinct to survive.'[22]

In *The Philosopher and the Theologian* Casanova reiterates the view that suicide can be justified, while cautioning that it ought not be an act of despair but a clearsighted judgement as to what the future holds, untrammelled by religious superstition. Such honest individuals should not be condemned. Casanova adds that, ironically, the Church itself tempts people to take their own lives by its claims that an immortal and reasoning soul will be liberated from the body and all its vicissitudes through death.

Casanova's preoccupation with the competing forces of reason and nature also surfaces in his memoirs, notably in his 1797 Preface which he wrote the year before he died, and fifteen years after *Nine Dialogues*. Unlike *Nine Dialogues* we are listening to the voice of Casanova himself, and there is a sense of a man who is making his peace with God. In this context he is not the philosopher who champions the merit of suicide, although he appears to accept that it is a right that people possess because of the faculty of reason with which God has endowed them, 'if, after a true or faulty reckoning, we have the misfortune to find it beneficial for us. This is the strongest proof of our moral freedom, which sophism has fought against so hard. It is, however, justly abhorred by nature; and all religions must proscribe it.'[23]

For Casanova, death should be avoided for as long as possible and certainly not precipitated. Here the philosopher takes over and faith takes a back seat. Reason tells him that the annihilation of his material self will be the annihilation of his memory, his senses and the person he is, whatever the nature of his soul may be. The possibility of future pleasures and happiness will be destroyed. Casanova the Christian believes this will not be the case, but Casanova the philosopher is in no hurry to find out:

> I am far from consoling myself by hoping that when my memoirs appear I will be no more. I cannot imagine without horror contracting some obligation to death, which I detest. Happy, or unhappy, life is the only treasure that man possesses, and those who do not love it are not worthy of it. Honour is preferred to it, because infamy stigmatizes it. If, forced to choose, we kill ourselves, philosophy must be silent. O death! Cruel law of nature, which reason must condemn because it works to destroy reason. Cicero says that it delivers us from sorrows. This great philosopher records the expense, and does not take into account the receipts. I don't remember if when he was writing his Tusculanes, his Tulliole was dead. Death is a monster that chases an attentive spectator from the great theatre before the play that profoundly interests him has finished. This reason alone should be enough to hate it.[24]

Casanova the Eclectic

Casanova did not attempt to develop his own self-contained philosophical system, nor did he buy into one. In fact, he was typical of many Enlightenment protagonists who were scornful of rarefied system building. As we saw in Chapter 2 on Horace, he dismissed such efforts by early Christian scholars as 'ingenious and chimerical'.[25] Voltaire employed ridicule not logical refutation to debunk Leibniz's explanation of why a benevolent God could create a world with so much evil in it. Philosophers and theologians had gone about constructing their air-borne castles since antiquity. As often as not these were abstract affairs, inflated by deduction and analogy. Christian theology in particular was tethered precariously to the earth by little more than intricate word play, reverence for authority and biblical say-so. But generations of speculation and squabbling had left mankind little the wiser. The incontestable triumph of Newton demonstrated that the best route to meaningful knowledge was through empirical investigation based ultimately in human experience and what was measurable. The Enlightenment mind was more magpie than grand designer, happy to build its nest from ideas, insights and evidence gathered from a range of different sources whether they be pagan philosophy, humanist history, renaissance voyages of discovery or contemporary science. Enlightenment thinkers were intellectual eclectics interested in what worked, what could be subject to proof and disproof, and what was rational and reasonable to believe. For Casanova, moral philosophy was a deeply personal affair that required close observation of, and engagement with, the world, not detachment from it. As he said to Mademoiselle Vesian, it was the work of a lifetime.

This eclectic and empirical mindset is liable to lead at some level to paradoxes, logical inconsistencies and fudges, and Casanova was aware of this, his views shifting and evolving over time in his attempt to reconcile different perspectives on subjects such as free will, suicide and his relationship to God. One way of making sense of some of the apparent contradictions we find in Casanova's writings is to consider his ideas as reflecting different preoccupations and frames of reference. We have Casanova the philosopher, Casanova the Christian, Casanova the libertine and Casanova the historian. It is worth reiterating that when he writes a philosophical dialogue, it does not necessarily represent his settled opinions on a matter. It may just as well be a way for him to work through issues from that point of view.

In several places Casanova seems to have accepted the Epicurean vision of a cosmos constructed from indivisible atoms whose nature is coeternal with that of God's. In an *Essay on Created or Uncreated Matter* (1795?) he writes that 'the eternal existence of matter is of physical necessity, just as that of God is of metaphysical necessity.'[26] By seemingly placing a restriction upon the power to create, preserve or destroy as the Almighty sees fit, Casanova looks to have undermined the idea of an omnipotent creator. But it is a charge that he defends himself against vigorously: 'if He has found nothingness coeternal with Himself, and if in spite of that He finds Himself the master of destroying it, why would he not have the same power over matter if it were coeternal to Him? Believe me, sir theologian, that matter coeternal to the author of nature in no way prejudices His omnipotence and all His divine qualities.'[27] Elsewhere he seems to be drawing on something like the idea of ordained power to support his position. Ordained power is the notion that although God does indeed possess absolute power, that it is conceivable there are circumstances when They could never avail themselves of it and remain consistent to Their nature. If God can only create that which is good, for instance, then it would make no sense for Them ever to destroy it. In *Freedom of Will* (1769?) Casanova writes, 'but God, who can do whatever He wants, must not do whatever He can, and it is not up to us to question divine reasons and to scrutinize divine impenetrable judgements.'[28]

Unlike other Enlightenment thinkers who were willing to embrace deism and, a few, even atheism, Casanova's ingrained conservatism made him reluctant to question key tenets of classical theism: 'The greatest philosophers have gone into disparities when they wanted to reason too much about His nature. Immaterial, infinite, and almighty. All is said.'[29] Casanova would take reason as far as he could but ultimately accepted that some things were beyond human understanding. It may be that, as Casanova the Christian, his faith enables him to accept Christian doctrine even if, as Casanova the philosopher, reason directs him to question some aspects of it. In the end, he appears to reject attempts to fully reconcile the two perspectives. The danger is that you would just end up with bad philosophy. As a philosopher, he sees himself as putting forward the best case that reason can provide but he acknowledges the limits of reason and defers to faith, using his own subjective experience of God's benevolence to reinforce that faith. This is perhaps one of the reasons for his criticism of Rousseau, who he felt resorted to deceptively profound sounding paradoxes to support his claims about the nature of the world rather than clear and systematic logic. 'With regards to my future, as a philosopher I never wanted to trouble myself about it, because I know nothing about it; and as a Christian, faith must believe without reasoning, and the purest faith maintains a deep silence.'[30]

Casanova's Epicurean materialism helps to underpin his rejection of 'prejudice' and his unabashed pursuit of pleasure but it does not explain the fact, much to the surprise of many no doubt, that he subordinates the pleasure of his senses to the virtue of duty, another route to pleasure, as it turns out. It is a point he makes on a number of occasions in *History of My Life*: 'The happiest of men is he who best knows the art of making himself such without encroaching on his duties'; 'the strength of my senses never drew me from my duties, when I had any'; 'Feelings of love must give way to those of honour.'[31, 32, 33] Torn between his love for the widowed Madame Dubois and the offer of marriage from another man that would make her financially secure, he chooses to let her marry. To see what's going on here, we need to make a Stoic and sociability adjustment to our Epicurean lens. Considering the relationship between pleasure and the Enlightenment, Thomas Kavanagh has highlighted a fusion that took place between Epicureanism and Stoicism that might in part explain the Venetian's willingness to prioritise duty. Kavanagh describes it as 'a merging of the

Epicurean's pleasure with the Stoic's distance and control'.[34] In Casanova's case, when norms of duty were present to act as a corrective, and reinforced by a natural impulse in man for sociability, reason could escape passion's thrall. This is most apparent in the guardian role that Casanova frequently adopted towards women. For eighteenth-century French *philosophes*, Stoicism, like Epicureanism, offered an alternative material intellectual tradition that challenged the metaphysical abstractions of Christianity, Platonism and Descartes.

A philosophical framework

In the absence of a clear description from Casanova himself, one question worth exploring is whether his thinking is characterised by disconnected generalisations and personal idiosyncrasies or whether there is a unifying framework underlying his ideas. What might it look like if such a framework does exist? This is what I will attempt to construct. Any solution is bound to be speculative to some degree, of course, not least because Casanova's position shifted on a number of topics. On the whole, I will give more weight to the opinions he expresses in his memoirs than elsewhere. The memoirs were, after all, a product of a lifetime of engagement with these issues, and subject to careful revision over several years. Neither, unlike some of his other work, did he have any obvious ulterior motives behind his arguments, such as currying favour with the Venetian government or sabotaging the reputation of Voltaire (and on at least one occasion, with *Refutation*, doing both at the same time). What I present will be what strikes me as the best fit in terms of his own writing, guided by past and contemporaneous religio-philosophical traditions. It will inevitably be flawed but, even so, hopefully it will give some insight into his philosophical outlook and how he may have arrived at it.

In his 1797 Preface Casanova makes clear that he believes in an immaterial God. But he goes further. He describes God as the 'great principle of all principles' and 'master of all forms'.[35, 36] This terminology is redolent of Neo-Platonism, a reworking of the ideas of Plato that stretches back to Plotinus (204/5–270 CE). Neo-Platonist concepts were assimilated into Christianity and, to a certain degree, the Jewish mystical tradition of cabbala. Interestingly, although Casanova calls himself a Christian, he does not call himself a Catholic, an indication of his rejection to some extent at least of Catholic doctrines. He specifically rejects Spinoza's idea of

God as nature, regarding Spinoza as an atheist, as did many of Casanova's contemporaries.[37] Unlike Spinoza, Casanova's God was very much the anthropomorphic God of the Bible. Casanova trained as a priest, was immersed in classical learning, including Plato, and was deeply attached to cabbala. On top of this, he demonstrates his awareness of the interaction of philosophy and early Christian scholars in writings such as *Of Philosophy and Philosophers*, which he wrote around 1780, and *The Philosopher and the Theologian*, which he wrote around 1789. However they may have influenced Casanova's thinking, it would be reasonable to assume that he was knowledgeable about these various strands of theology and philosophy.

Casanova's belief that God was coeternal with matter, of course, was contrary to orthodox Christianity. Ivo Cerman refers to the opening of Casanova's *Icosameron* and the Hebrew text of Genesis: 'the original Hebrew text does not say that there was nothing at the beginning but that there was *Tohu-Bohu*, or chaos. In Casanova's view this word denotes unformed matter which was floating in the Universe until God formed it into our world.'[38] In one letter to a friend, Casanova repeats this idea: 'matter, never perishing, only changes form.'[39] Also there is Casanova's careful wording in his memoirs when he refers to God as the 'master of all forms'.[40] This is not the orthodox Christian God who is the creator of all things, including matter in its raw state. Casanova was here adopting the position of the Stoics and Epicureans, although for Epicureans the gods were entirely passive and did not interact with the world. But whether this is sufficient to label Casanova a deist, as some have done, is questionable in the light of Casanova's acceptance of most other aspects of classical theism, and his anthropomorphising of God.[41]

Unlike Epicureanism, and consistent with an interventionist Christian God, Casanova believed in revelation. He accepted the notion of general revelation as espoused by natural religion – the idea that proof of God's existence could be found in the rational organisation of nature. He also believed that revelation could take other forms:

> If we don't doubt it [revelation] in physics, why wouldn't we admit it in religion? It's just the form it takes. The spirit speaks to the spirit, not to the ears. The principles of all that we know can only have been revealed to those who communicated them to us by the great and supreme principle which contains them all. The bee that makes its hive, the swallow that builds its nest, the ant that makes its cellar, and the spider that weaves its

> web would never have done anything without a prior eternal revelation. Either we must believe it to be so, or agree that matter thinks. Why not, Locke would say, if God had willed it? But we dare not do so much honour to matter. So let's stick to revelation.[42]

These other forms of revelation included ones that were more direct and personal. 'I have always counted on His providence,' he writes, 'having recourse to Him by means of prayer in all my misfortunes; and always finding my prayer answered.'[43] There was Casanova's interest in cabbala. There was his daemon who possessed an intermediate and intermediary status between man and God. And there was his belief in innate moral ideas. In one of Casanova's philosophical dialogues, between a pupil and a teacher, Casanova once again seems implicitly to reject Locke, this time Locke's claim that the mind was essentially a blank slate. The teacher asserts that God's moral laws, rather like Rousseau's conscience, were 'imprinted by God in your soul'.[44] Similarly, in his 1797 Preface he writes of 'divine moral principles' that were 'rooted in my heart'.[45] For Casanova, there is an intimate connection between the soul, reason and morality, to the extent that he seems to suggest that the primary, or divine, purpose of reason is to read, and act in accordance to, these embedded moral principles that God has provided for our well-being: 'Every aphorism [sic] in morals, if it is new, can be reputed to be a discovery in metaphysics, since morality is none other than the metaphysics of reason.'[46] Perhaps reinforcing this idea of, or wish for, a direct relationship with God, Casanova wrote two dialogues with God as a character.

Along with his Neo-Platonist description of God as 'the great principle' there are references by Casanova to a world-soul. In his earlier 1791 Preface to his memoirs, he writes: 'Life in general is nothing but the soul of the universe. This general life is an immense mass of particular lives of a hundred thousand million beings, which do nothing but die, and are reborn in a continual uninterrupted succession.'[47] For Casanova the nature of man mirrored that of the universe: 'the globe on the surface of which we live is, so to speak, a living animal … man is like a micro cosmos composed of matter and endowed with the spirit which is the rational soul.'[48] Among many ancient philosophers the universe was conceived as a living being and the soul as a suffusing animating force that was the basis of life. Different philosophical traditions had their own explanations as to the particularities of its nature and cause. For Plato the world-soul was the creation of a deity that wrought the material world. For Neo-Platonists the world-soul was the product of Intellect or pure Consciousness, itself derived from the One – that which was the ultimate source of all things and beyond being. For the Stoics it was the organising principle both at the level of the universe and that of the individual entity, animate and inanimate. It was termed *pneuma*, or breath of life, an eternal, material substance composed of air and fire and that existed in different states. The concept of *pneuma* also featured in Epicureanism although not the idea of a world-soul. The aspect of a soul's rebirth in Casanova's description would seem to most resemble Neo-Platonism. For some Neo-Platonist traditions this was a method of purification which ended when an individual's soul was finally re-united with the world-soul. This scheme also featured intermediary spiritual entities that existed between the individual and the One (or the Principle, the Being of Beings), a notion which would seem to correspond with Casanova's (and Socrates') daemon.

For many thinkers the existence and nature of the soul played a part in the devising of their moral philosophies, and Casanova was no different. For Voltaire, it was necessary for people to believe that they possessed a soul that could be subject to rewards or punishments in the afterlife. Without that, what would motivate people to behave well? Casanova's opinions on the soul varied over time but ultimately, he did believe that people possessed a soul, that it was the site of man's reason, that it was eternal, and that it was probably a non-material entity (as we have seen, he was resistant to the opinion that matter could think). For Casanova, belief in a material soul was a road that might lead to atheism, a possibility he entirely rejected.[49] By the time of his memoirs he was settled on the view that, irrespective of whether it was material or non-material, the soul was dependent upon a material body. As a consequence, when the body perished, the stored memories and sensual information of the body perished with it. In that case, having been stripped of all identity and individuality, the idea that divine judgement awaited people's souls after death made little sense to him.

If Casanova was not convinced by the existence of some form of heaven and hell, and that it could serve as a basis to motivate rational people to behave morally, neither was he persuaded by the Stoic idea that virtuous behaviour was its own reward: 'It is not true,' he writes, 'that a desire for reward conflicts with true virtue, and that it undermines its purity, because, on the contrary, it serves to support virtue, man being too weak to want to be virtuous only for his own contentment.'[50] For Casanova, drawing on personal experience, what motivated people to behave well and to achieve great things, was the good opinion of their peers. If consideration of the afterlife was a factor in people's thinking, then it was, or ought to be, as far as he was concerned, for their posthumous reputation.

Casanova believed that he possessed free will and took responsibility for the results of his actions, while at the same time acknowledging that it was often difficult to judge whether in any particular circumstance something you did would be good or bad: 'But always do good, says the moralist. All right; but what do I know? I challenge the most profound of men to do the slightest good, certain that it will not produce the greatest evil. We cannot see utility in what we do not like, nor prefer the pleasure of others to our own.'[51] Throughout his memoirs when things go wrong typically he blames himself: 'Everything unfortunate that happened to me in Stuttgart was entirely due to my bad behaviour.'[52] He also alludes to a tension between individual agency and the existence of an omnipresent, omniscient, omnipotent deity – that is, the attributes of God as conceived according to classical theism, which Casanova seems to have accepted. 'I can never have done anything other than what God wanted,' Casanova writes in his 1791 Preface. 'God being present in everything, always acting and never indifferent, is it possible for man to do something contrary to his divine will? I don't think so, but in spite of that I have always believed myself to be free in action, and consequently I am sure that if I have been at fault for the bad, I must have been deserving for the good.'[53] Once again we can see how Casanova's taking of responsibility stands in stark contrast to Rousseau's fudging. Thinkers of the Middle Ages had disentangled divine destiny from free will by positing two different kinds of causality – primary, or divine, causality, and secondary causality – with the one not compromising the operation of the other. Casanova may have accepted this solution, or he may have adopted a compatibilist version of free will similar to that proposed by Aristotle in his *Nicomachean Ethics* (c 340 BCE). Free will for Aristotle was a voluntary act over which you have control relative to the kind of person you are, in contrast to an involuntary act, such as yelling out after having been jabbed by a needle. Either way, the credit or blame Casanova takes for his behaviour can be read as consequentialist. He seems to suggest that his actions ought to be judged by their consequences whatever his intentions, presumably because those consequences reflect God's inevitable will. A person may intend to do harm but inadvertently do the opposite. If so, it is in some way to their credit because they are being used by God as a vehicle for good.

In agreement with Neo-Epicurean materialism, for Casanova pleasure was an indicator of the good. He rejected Christian notions that denigrated the body and bodily functions as impure relative to the immaterial and spiritual. The allegorical medieval logic of Christian theology deemed that which was non-bodily – intellect, the soul, spiritual beings – as morally superior, approaching more nearly as it did the absolute perfection and purity of God. For this reason, celibacy was to be preferred over sexual congress. Traditionally, only sexual relations sanctified by marriage for the purpose of procreation could be justified. By contrast, Casanova regarded the attainment of physical pleasures, as well as mental pleasures, as integral to achieving what he accepted as man's ultimate goal – happiness. Rather than adopting the allegorical logic of the Church founders, of which Casanova was highly critical, Casanova inferred that a benevolent God would not want people to abstain from pleasure: 'Happy are those who, without harming anyone, know how to obtain it [pleasure], and foolish are they who imagine that the Great Being can enjoy the pains, sorrows, and abstinences that they offer him in sacrifice, and that He cherishes only the fanatics who procure them.'[54, 55]

The essential form of man's nature, for Casanova, was inscribed by God – a Cartesian, rationalist position. In his 1791 Preface he writes: 'He engraved natural religion on our hearts: those who violate it are damned; those who follow her are sure to be happy.'[56] And in his 1797 Preface: 'God can only require of his creatures the exercise of those virtues the seeds of which he places in their souls, and he has given us nothing except for the purpose of making us happy: self-esteem, ambition for praise, desire to emulate, strength, courage.'[57] It is clear from the first three items on this list that Casanova believed that man from inception was intended to exist as a member of society. Unlike Rousseau, he did not believe that mankind was inherently good or bad but, as mentioned, that they were born with some sort of moral understanding. In contrast to Rousseau's claim that man was intrinsically good but became corrupted by civilisation, Casanova was predisposed to the view that people were free agents who ought to take responsibility for their own actions.

If Casanova did not believe that man was inherently good or bad, neither did he believe that man was driven by self-interest narrowly understood, unlike Hobbes. Instead, he favoured the notion of innate sociability. In his 1791 Preface he writes: 'man can neither adore, nor pray, nor thank the being of beings except by making himself loved by all his creatures. Such is the division of justice, and the philosopher who seeks happiness elsewhere is mistaken.'[58] A little further on he writes: 'The human race hates the wicked; he loves the righteous. Man can be happy only through the exercise of virtue.'[59] Later in his memoirs he observes: 'in this world, to be happy you must be loved.'[60] Innate sociability was not necessarily a moral good (as the unsociable sociability of mob behaviour can testify) but it did incline people towards organisation and cooperation at some level. This principle of taking into account the perspectives, concerns and priorities of others, entailed for Casanova 'being entirely submissive and obedient to the princes, of whom we are born, or have become, subjects.' He adds that such obedience to the princes (presumably by which he includes the institutions of government and the law) 'produces in us the satisfaction of pleasing them.'[61] This satisfaction is very much apparent in Casanova's memoirs when he himself is called upon in some capacity to serve a court, prince, king or important government minister.

This last observation helps to tie together sociability, reason, free will, pleasure, and the good. A God-given desire to be sociable is mediated by reason and free will to elicit virtuous behaviours in order to inspire the friendliness, or love, of others. This friendliness produces pleasure, an indicator of what is morally good. It is a utilitarian formula consistent both with Epicurean hedonistic calculus, and with Casanova's experience that people are, by and large, too weak and imperfect to behave virtuously if left to their own devices. It provides a moral incentive that does not rely on the existence of heaven and hell, a possibility negated by Casanova's claim that the soul is materially dependent. Extending the operation of sociability to encompass political authority and social hierarchy allows Casanova a mechanism with which to underpin good social order, the basis for the proper exercise of all other rights and moral goods. It is a philosophical narrative that enables Casanova to integrate aspects of Epicureanism with his Neo-Platonic Christianity.

To rise to the challenge imposed by sociability Casanova adopts moral precepts that are rather conventional for the most part. Some, directly or indirectly, he takes from Aristotle's *Nicomachean Ethics*, notably the four cardinal virtues of prudence, justice, moderation and courage. Casanova particularly stresses the importance of moderation, or the mean between the extremes, which is a key feature of Aristotle's moral scheme. Courage would be an example – the mean between the extremes of cowardice and recklessness. Other precepts Casanova advocates include, as we have seen, the prioritising of duty over pleasure – implicitly preferencing the needs of the other (an individual, a group or a society) over the needs of oneself – and the golden rule: 'The pious pastor must preach that love of the neighbour which consists of doing to others what we would like to be done to us.'[62]

Attempting to make others happy was central to Casanova's ethics: 'He [God] will show us that if we succeed in making people happy, we will never be unhappy, because we will at least enjoy our conscience. We will descend with pleasure into ourselves, and in the bottom of our hearts we will find the consoling imprints of the love of the creator.'[63] In the same spirit, Casanova expresses a deep-rooted antipathy to intolerance or any form of what he regarded as fanaticism: 'the horrible man is the intolerant, as the tolerant is always amiable, and everywhere. But who is the truly tolerant man? It is the tranquil man. This man in my opinion is certainly neither Voltaire nor a J.J. Rousseau. He is a Haller, a Hume, a d'Alembert, a philosopher who has never worried anyone, a scientist who bene vixit si bene latuit ['He who has kept himself well hidden, has lived well' – from Ovid].'[64]

Casanova derives some moral precepts from God's assumed providential benevolence and concern for human well-being. One example is self-preservation, which was generally understood by contemporaries to be a natural right. For Casanova, self-preservation involved three primary needs – sustenance, procreation and revenge.[65] He asserts that the urge to satisfy those needs has been built into man's animal nature. But unlike brute animals, man has also been gifted the faculty of reason, which man employs to make the gratification of needs as pleasurable and enticing as possible. Given that the source of these needs is of divine origin, as well as reason and the ability to experience pleasurable fulfilment from them, then it can be inferred that their enjoyment is not, in itself, immoral. It follows that the natural right of self-preservation can be used as a counterweight to moral judgements established by the theology of the Middle Ages, such as the claim that celibacy is superior to sexual intercourse.

On the surface, at least, it does seem to be arguable that Casanova's philosophical vision was a tolerably unified one, and one that was able to synthesise quite successfully ideas from a range of different intellectual traditions. What is more, it would be fair to say that his memoirs – a carefully documented personal moral history – lend empirical weight to his moral claims and observations.

Chapter 11

An Experimental Moral Philosopher

> [Casanova] 'I read as much as I can, and I enjoy studying man while travelling.'
>
> [Voltaire] 'This is the way to know him; but the book is too big. It is best achieved by reading history.'
>
> [Casanova] 'History lies.'
>
> Giacomo Casanova, *History of My Life*

A conspicuous theme in Casanova's writing is the importance of acquiring knowledge through direct experience. Casanova rejects Descartes' claim that animals cannot feel pain by reference to the distress he had witnessed of a dolphin stranded on a beach: 'If the cries of this fish did not come from genuine sensitivity and great pain, it was the cleverest charlatan of all the fish in the sea.'[1] He uses his inability to remember anything of his childhood before he was 8 years old to prove that the soul is dependent upon the body. This in turn allows him to cast doubt upon the notion of any kind of divine reward or punishment after death once the body and all sensory record of its existence has perished. In his account of his escape from the Leads he observes: 'I had read and learned from the great book of experience that great enterprises should not be discussed but executed, while recognising the role that chance plays in everything that men undertake.'[2] As mentioned in Chapter 2 on Horace, he also uses his experience of imprisonment in the Leads to cast doubt on claims made by Epicureans and Stoics that it was possible through training to possess 'perfect tranquillity' in all circumstances. Exploring the veracity of a rumour about a cardinal's impiety, Casanova writes: 'woe to all those who love the truth, and who do not know how to draw it from its source.'[3] And elsewhere in his memoirs, recalling his disappointment at what he saw on a visit to a famous monument, he notes that 'the wise man who wants to learn must read, and travel afterwards to rectify his learning.'[4] Bearing this in mind, if we wanted to identify Casanova with a more specific philosophical tradition beyond his resemblance to the *philosophes*, one promising candidate might be experimental philosophy. This was a movement that emerged around the late seventeenth century, with university courses in the method becoming established by the early eighteenth century.[5, 6]

Experimental philosophy

Prior to the Renaissance, it had long been accepted that only deductive reasoning offered the possibility of certain knowledge. Consequently, evidence that was acquired by the senses was often relegated to the role of providing supporting examples for conclusions that had been derived from logical theorising alone. But from the late Renaissance, humanist scholars increasingly emphasised the importance of experience, notably in astronomy, medicine and natural philosophy. They questioned whether the authority of texts and abstract speculation was a sufficient basis on their own to obtain a secure understanding of the world. The change was partly mediated by theological considerations and a move away from Aristotelianism. Peter Anstey and Alberto Vanzo note: 'many of Aristotle's principles, such as the eternity of the world, were contrary to biblical teaching, which, of course, had the status of revelation.'[7] This new emphasis led to an increased interest in gathering empirical evidence. Observations were collected from craftsmen, navigators, peasants, sailors and travellers. Catalogues of animals and plants were compiled. Botanical gardens were established such as those in Bologna, Oxford and Padua. And classical texts were read more critically than previously, with a closer eye on what was likely to be factually true or false.

Natural philosophers like Pietro Pomponazzi (1462–1525), an Aristotelian who taught at the universities of Padua and Bologna, used experiments and empirical evidence to challenge the truth claims of rival academics. Other Italian experimentalists included Girolamo Fracastoro (1478–1553), Gerolamo Cardano (1501–1576) and, particularly influential, later natural philosophers such as Galileo (1564–1642), Niccolò Cabeo (1586–1650) and Gassendi. But unlike their future Enlightenment counterparts, their aim was not to challenge religion or theological legitimacy. If anything, especially as far as the earlier scholars of the Middle Ages were concerned, they hoped that their investigations would help to confirm religious truths. For Pomponazzi and his ilk, where there was a conflict between truths derived from natural philosophy and those derived from theology, the latter took primacy over the former.

This development of interest in experiential inquiry was taking hold not just in Italy but across Europe. In the Dutch Republic you had Franciscus Sylvius (1614–1672) and Johannes de Wale (1604–1649), among others. In France you had Marin Mersenne (1588–1648). As mentioned in Chapter 4 on Gassendi, Mersenne was the scholarly priest and experimentalist at the heart of a European network of academics that included Descartes, Galileo, Gassendi, Hobbes and Christiaan Huygens (1629–1695). Also in France, experimental chemistry was flourishing. In England you had Francis Bacon (1561–1626), and moving into the Enlightenment you had Robert Boyle (1627–1691), John Locke (1632–1704) Newton (1643–1727) and members of the Oxford Philosophical Club and the Royal Society of London. Indeed, it is argued by Anstey and Vanzo that the specific philosophical movement described as experimental philosophy was decisively shaped in England in the mid- to late seventeenth century, before making its way to the Continent.[8]

Medicine was particularly significant in driving this shift towards experience-based understanding and a scepticism of theory, partly through its own practice – as evidenced by an increased interest in case histories – partly by its presence within universities, and partly by its close relationship with philosophy. Students who studied medicine would also study philosophy as part of their training. 'This new emphasis on observation in medicine,' Dmitri Levitin notes, 'thus effected both a "philosophisation" of experiential medicine and a "experienciation" of natural philosophy.'[9]

As well as medicine, natural history also pushed in that empirical direction. From the sixteenth century the importance of practical observation was emphasised by natural historians such as the botanist Luigi Anguillara (1512–1570), and from the late sixteenth and into the seventeenth century this became a systematised, classificatory practice. Figures such as Huygens, and organisations such as the Royal Society, recognised the value of natural histories as a way of facilitating progress in natural philosophy. In England, under the influence of the ideas of Bacon, the remit of natural history was expanded to include not simply the classification of animals and plants but descriptions of phenomena such as air, fluidity and heat. Additionally, to enable more sophisticated descriptions, an experimental dimension was incorporated into this new conception of natural history, although this development seems to have been relatively short-lived.

By the end of the seventeenth century a self-conscious distinction between experiential and speculative philosophy was becoming established, at least polemically. Anstey and Vanzo observe: 'The new experimental philosophers championed experiment and observation as the primary means of obtaining knowledge of nature, a necessary preparation for any theorizing, and the source of justification for any substantive claims or theories about the natural world.'[10] But in reality, the lines between the practitioners of these different methods of enquiry were not tightly drawn. Proponents might advocate the primacy of one method over the other in their pursuit of truth but nonetheless utilise both. Even Newton, who declared that he would not make truth claims on the basis of speculation alone, employed theories and hypotheses. Kirsten Walsh explains that 'Newton describes two permissible roles for hypotheses: (1) to explicate abstract theories with concrete metaphysics, thus providing a "possibility proof" for the theory; and (2) to suggest experiments, thus offering new avenues for empirical support.'[11] Hobbes, who privileged deductive reasoning, draws upon human experience in constructing his political philosophy.[12]

In the eighteenth century, Voltaire was significant in promoting experimental philosophy in France with the help of Madame du Châtelet, and the two themselves were actively engaged in their own experimental projects. But as was pointed out in Chapter 6 on Voltaire, the ground in France had already been prepared in advance of his *Philosophical Letters* and the *philosophes*' lionising of Newton, Bacon and experimental philosophy. Through scholars and educators like Fontenelle, Pierre Polinière (1671–1734) and Jean-Baptiste du Hamel (1624–1706) there had already been a growing, if not uncritical, awareness of this new method of philosophical enquiry. Hot on the heels of the publication of the *Letters* were Abbé Jean-Antoine Nollet's highly successful programme of lectures and public demonstrations on experimental philosophy. Nollet himself was to be made Professor of Experimental Natural Philosophy at the College of Navarre in 1753. And, of course, there was the acknowledgement by the editors d'Alembert and Diderot, through the *Preliminary Discourse* of 1751, of the influence of Bacon upon the organisation of the *Encyclopedia* as well as an endorsement of the ethos of experimental philosophy.

In German-speaking states of central Europe could also be found currents of intellectual thought that favoured experimental and observational forms of enquiry either over, or alongside, speculative philosophy. One of the preeminent philosophers of his time was Christian Wolff (1679–1754). He was influential and widely read, especially in German universities. Wolff was familiar with Bacon and British experimental philosophers such as Boyle, Newton and Locke, and his views on the experimental method aligned with theirs, although he was more conciliatory towards the use of hypotheses and theories. Another important influence was the Royal Prussian Academy of Science. Under Frederick II it specifically included experimental philosophy in its curriculum and employed, as we know, that renowned French mathematician and experimental philosopher Maupertuis to be its president. In the second half of the century, experimental psychology became popular among German scholars. The data for such study was to be gathered from observation and introspection, with recognised sources including histories, biographies and even novels and dramas. The practical value of such investigations for educators, judges, preachers and other professionals was emphasised. Inevitably such study was regarded as providing a basis for the examination of morality and ethics.

A philosopher of particular relevance to Casanova is John Locke. Locke's *An Essay Concerning Human Understanding* (1689) took the idea of experiential inquiry and applied it to an analysis of the nature of the mind – or soul – as Hume was also to do half a century later. This was a domain which had previously been the preserve of abstract speculation. Emphasising the difference between the speculative and the experiential method, he describes this enterprise, or at least its key conceptual foundations, as 'history': 'a … true history of the first beginnings of human knowledge.'[13] Locke's *Essay* opened up an avenue of empirical investigation into man as a moral being. Casanova observes that 'we have seen the experimental physics of the soul in the metaphysics of Locke.'[14] There is a suggestion that although the *Essay* covered far more ground than simply morality, it was the issue of moral knowledge that triggered Locke's interest.[15] What was the foundation of such knowledge? Was it possible to obtain certainty, or at least a high degree of probability, in questions of ethics? Supporting his case against the existence of innate moral principles, Locke draws evidence from people's social behaviour and practices, both generally, as well as those of particular societies.[16] In the first book of his *Essay*, Locke suggests that if such innate moral principles exist then one of them must be for parents to 'preserve and cherish' their children, but goes on to point out that 'it was a familiar, and uncondemned practice among the Greeks and Romans, to expose, without pity or remorse, their innocent infants.'[17]

For Locke, morality should be treated as mathematics or science, with moral principles, like natural laws, discoverable through reason and empirical evidence. In book 3 of the *Essay*, he declares: 'I am bold to think that morality is capable of demonstration as well as mathematics.'[18] It is a point he repeats several times. In book 4 he writes: 'from self-evident propositions, by necessary consequences, as incontestable as those in mathematics, the measures of right and wrong might be made out;' 'moral knowledge is as capable of real certainty as mathematics;' 'I doubt not, but if a right method were taken, a great part of morality might be made out with that clearness that could leave to a considering man no more reason to doubt than he could have to doubt of the truth of propositions in mathematics which have been demonstrated to him.'[19, 20, 21] Now Casanova, of course, rejects Locke's contention that, apart from man's desire to embrace pleasure and avoid pain, the human mind is a blank slate. This means, strictly speaking, that Casanova cannot be labelled an empiricist. But this does not alter the legitimacy of human nature, and morality in particular, being an object of study that can be explored using experience and observation.

How deeply Casanova engaged with Locke is difficult to judge. Casanova certainly had some familiarity with the Englishman's ideas, but this would not be surprising given the extent to which Locke set the intellectual agenda of the post-Renaissance world. Nonetheless, it is perhaps worth pointing out that Casanova does address several issues that Locke examines, sometimes in opposition to Locke, at other times in agreement. Both men acknowledge revelation as a legitimate source of knowledge. For Locke reason itself could be regarded as a form of divine revelation alongside other forms: 'Reason is natural revelation whereby the eternal Father of light and fountain of all knowledge communicates to mankind that portion of truth which he has laid within the reach of their natural faculties.'[22] They are both in agreement on the woeful inadequacy of speculative philosophy – Locke's *Essay* is filled with barbs directed at the 'schoolmen'. They both agree on the fundamental importance of pain, pleasure and sociability, but in Casanova's case sociability can be regarded as an innate quality that motivates moral behaviour through external social mechanisms even if it contains no intrinsic moral principles in itself. On the other hand, Casanova disagrees with Locke's rejection of the possibility of the eternal co-existence of matter and God, and provides a defence against the imputation that it circumscribes God's omnipotence. Likewise, Casanova disputes the idea of heavenly punishments and rewards, which Locke endorses. Again, as already discussed, Casanova is able to provide a convincing refutation.

Where Locke led, many others across Europe followed, for example Claude Helvétius who asserts in *On Mind* that moral philosophy should use the experimental method. It was a view taken by others, including Newton, Adam Smith and Hume, and the influence upon them of experimental philosophy was evident. As with natural philosophy, it was argued that substantial evidence needed to be collected before any attempts could be made at constructing theories or systems, reiterating suspicions of speculative inquiry. Given that gathering proof by means of active and planned experimentation was not really practical with regards to morality, the notion of experiment was understood more broadly to include observation, including introspection, and the construction of natural histories. There was a tendency to associate together physical and natural laws: the former being knowledge of that which is – derived from natural philosophy; the latter being knowledge of that which ought to be – derived from moral philosophy. For some, the connection was not simply a matter of parallel methods of enquiry. The relationship between physical laws, morality, natural religion, the works and intentions of a benevolent Creator, reason, the soul, pain and pleasure, good and evil, were all questions which inevitably arose. For a philosopher and theologian such as George Turnbull (1698–1748), general laws of nature incorporated that which was morally good.

Casanova

Turning to Casanova and experimental moral philosophy, let us first try to gauge the extent to which he was likely to have been familiar with the ideas of experimental philosophy itself. Experimental natural philosophy had been taking place in Venice since the second half of the seventeenth century, notably at the Sarotti Academy, and in November 1738 a chair of experimental philosophy was established at the University of Padua – probably the first in Europe. Fanny Marcon, Giulio Peruzzi and Sofia Talas write: 'The goal was to set up a totally new course – new content, new structure – with a totally new methodology: for the first time, the professor was not expected to simply read and comment on a text, but he had to present scientific theories and carry out demonstrations at the same time.'[23] It was to be led by the highly regarded Venetian scholar Giovanni Poleni. The Venetian government was supportive and invested significant funds to make it a success.

In 1737, just the year before, Casanova had been enrolled as a student in Padua to study law. He was 12 years old. Intellectual curiosity was always a hallmark of his character, and it is likely that this new chair of experimental philosophy would have sparked his interest. On top of that, experimental demonstrations typically attracted a lot of public attention. In fact, they were often designed specifically to do so. While Casanova was studying law, he also took additional classes in chemistry, physics and medicine, all subjects that were heavily engaged in the development of experimental philosophy, especially medicine. Indeed, Casanova's true ambition had been to study and practise medicine, a subject about which he remained fascinated and particularly knowledgeable throughout his life. In his memoirs he specifically states that he studied 'experimental' physics at the monastery of La Salute.[24] He would have been about 16.

Casanova's time in Paris during the 1750s, which he first visited in 1750 when he was 25, would have reinforced his early exposure to experimental philosophy in Padua. His presence in Paris coincided with a period in which experimental philosophy had become particularly prominent, championed as it was by the Encyclopedists. It can be imagined that this was only likely to have further spurred his interest in the movement. When the 34-year-old left Paris in December 1759 under something of a cloud, he took with him to read Helvétius's incendiary *On Mind*. Casanova's response is revealing. It tells us that not only was this an area of interest for him but it was one about which he felt he possessed a certain expertise: 'After reading it I was even more surprised at all the noise it had made than at the *parlement* which had condemned it, and which did everything it could to ruin the author who was a very amiable man, and who had much more intelligence than his book. I found nothing new there, neither in the historical part with regard to the customs of nations, where I found some tall tales, nor in that morality is dependent on reason. These were things that had been said over and over, and Blaise Pascal had said much more, although with more care.'[25]

Since his teens Casanova had been a devotee of Voltaire until he fell out with him after their meeting in 1760. There can be little doubt that Casanova would have read *Philosophical Letters* and been familiar both with Voltaire's advocacy of experimentation, and his criticism of philosophical systems and speculation. Similarly, he was friends with d'Alembert whom he admired and with whom he corresponded. It was d'Alembert, of course, who was one of the authors of the *Preliminary Discourse* that set out the Baconian foundations of the *Enyclopedia* along with his co-editor Diderot, someone else of whom Casanova thought very highly. On a couple of occasions in his memoirs he refers approvingly to the philosopher Christian Wolff, and on one of those occasions, when he was incarcerated in the Leads, he records reading his work, possibly the first two volumes of *Moral or ethical philosophy, treated by the scientific method* (1750).

As discussed previously, Jean-Jacques Rousseau became famous as a philosopher following his work *A Discourse on the Arts and Sciences.* It was based upon a spiritual-like moment of revelation. In that moment, Rousseau had come to understand that men were intrinsically good but that their virtue had been corrupted by the arts and the sciences. It was this so-called progress that was at the heart of much of the evil and unhappiness in the world if not, in fact, all of it (even that arising from earthquakes). From that insight everything else followed, to be put down in his subsequent works *The Discourse on the Origin of Inequality*, *The Social Contract* and *Emile*. It was classic speculative philosophy: the theory came first, and any experiential evidence that was provided was illustrative, not foundational. Now let's compare this to Casanova.

Consistent with his consequentialist notion of free will, for Casanova human misfortune is not the result of ineluctable social forces but, for the most part, due to individual human fallibility, or foolishness. In one quite substantial work, *Philocalies on the Foolishness of Mortals* (1784), it is evident that the approach he takes in his investigation of this question is that of experimental philosophy. He declares that 'Reason does not recognise a more absolute empire than that of demonstration.'[26] And a little later he adds: 'Our reason begins with doubt, goes slowly to probability, and stops at evidence.'[27]

In *Philocalies* Casanova addresses the issue of human misfortune and foolishness first by attempting to classify different types of fools. Casanova divides society into three categories – the slave, the free man and the sovereign. He then explores how each category – and sub-categories in the case of the free man – is afflicted by foolishness in their various ways. It is a descriptive approach rather than a speculative one. Apart from ascribing foolishness in a rather generalised way to human nature and a lack of prudence, he constructs no overarching explanatory theory, hypothesis or system. Instead, he explores how individuals in different social contexts are liable to fall prey to bad habits and poor decision-making. In one example, he points out how poor parents often choose trades for their children to which their children are not suited. But interestingly, he does not absolve the children themselves from responsibility because their acquiescence to undertake a trade 'to which his secret inclination is repugnant' is based on 'a spirit of misunderstood obedience'.[28] There is, then, a double foolishness at play here for which both the parent and the child are to blame. This instance clearly draws on Casanova's own experience when he enrolled to study law, which he disliked, instead of medicine, which he much preferred. Unlike Rousseau, Casanova's starting point is direct observation, often ones to which he can personally attest. *Philocalies* is filled with such references and anecdotes, either from his own experience or taken from history and literature, especially from Horace. In fact, he explicitly likens the examples he uses to 'a cabinet of natural history, which puts nature to shame.'[29]

In a section that very much brings to mind Rousseau the man, Casanova explains that 'the greater part of the unfortunate are so by their own fault, and I am going to make fun of all those who too easily find the causes of their misfortunes in fate, or in the malice of wicked men' or, he might have added, in the arts and the sciences. 'The real fool is he who, through boundless self-love, never wants to admit fault.'[30] Again, it is hard not to think of Rousseau here (as we know, the first part of the *Confessions* had been published just two years earlier, in 1782).

Once he has dealt with different kinds of fools, Casanova moves on to demonstrate how foolishness affects all disciplines of knowledge – as a result, among other things, of intellectual vanity, imposters, lies and credulity. He takes each discipline in turn. He points out, for example, how chemistry is filled with chemists engaged in alchemy and the search for the philosophers' stone, a substance which can change all metals into gold and extend human life by centuries. He observes how they also dabble in the occult, notably through the then fashionable mystical tradition of cabbala in which Casanova himself was an expert. Following this particular section on the occult he notes: 'Everything I have written is believed to the letter by men whom I know,' once again, emphasising the value of anchoring knowledge to direct experience and observation.[31] Casanova writes how foolishness has even crept into mathematics, that source of wonderful discoveries and absolute deductive truth, its work distorted and misused by others, especially medical doctors 'who treat the body like a very simple machine whereas there is nothing so complicated' (possibly a swipe at La Mettrie and his controversial 1747 work *Man a Machine*).[32]

Casanova redrafted *Philocalies* to produce his *Critical essay on morals, sciences, and the arts* (composed between October 1785 and August 1786). In an analysis of the latter, Severine Denieul has drawn attention to the influence of Bacon, and d'Alembert and Diderot's *Encyclopedia*. Denieul notes how the essay 'imitates the system of knowledge as it is exhibited in the *Preliminary Discourse* of the *Encyclopedia*' and how 'Casanova establishes a constant dialogue with the *Encyclopedia*.'[33] Denieul points out that several times in the *Essay* Casanova praises Bacon and draws on the philosopher to highlight the fallibility of human judgement, especially how it is subject to various undermining biases that Bacon labels 'idols'.[34] Casanova is particularly alert to the problem of self-deception, which can result from errors of our senses, our reasoning or both together, and which can contrive to mask reality with fiction, such as through the creation of superstitions. It is a theme that he explores elsewhere, notably in his *Soliloquy of a Thinker.*

Significantly, in his *Philocalies* and *Critical essay*, Casanova does not exclude himself from the category of fools, with all the human fallibility that entails, in contrast to the certainties of Rousseau. Questioning, doubt, scepticism and satirical hedging is typical of Casanova's intellectual outlook and is evident in his philosophical dialogues, his balancing of faith and reason, and his re-evaluation over the years of particular philosophical positions: 'What must one do in the world to know something? You have to distrust the accuracy of your own mind, always examine, never have any certainty, and manage to be able to say after a mature examination, this object seems to me such, but I am not sure, since it may look different to everyone who has looked at it for as long as I have.'[35] Casanova had been a habitual gambler for much of his life, and was a talented mathematician with some understanding of probability. He conceived of society not so much as a site of invariable constants but more as a complex of shifting relationships to be contemplated in terms of what was likely or unlikely, with due recognition of the ever-present possibility of chance.

An important dimension to Casanova's interest in moral philosophy was history. The study of history and the study of morality had long been intimate bedfellows. To investigate the past was to investigate and understand human ethics, both at the level of the individual and the level of society as a whole. Not only was Casanova an avid student of the subject but an historian in his own right. His *History of the Polish Troubles* (1774) is recognised as an important piece of historical scholarship. Unlike many other writers who drew on unreliable secondary sources, and often their imaginations, to construct interpretations of the past that were sympathetic to their religious and ideological tastes, Casanova's approach was more rigorous. He drew as far as he could upon original sources, to the extent that he interviewed those who were participants in, or had direct knowledge of, the events he was investigating, such as King Stanislas II of Poland. Maciej Forycki writes: 'What distinguishes Casanova from the host of those who wrote about Poland is precisely that he knew the country from his own experience.'[36] Casanova's aim was to gather material that as far as possible described events accurately, unmediated by the false reports and ideological bias of others. This included his own direct observations about the country, its people and its institutions. It was experiential knowledge, free of theories, systems and textual authority. The resemblance of his methodology to experimental philosophy is clear.

Part of the ethos of the experimental philosophy movement, which can be traced back to Bacon and which was embraced by the Encyclopedists, was utility. In contrast to scholasticism, Bacon argued that the pursuit of greater knowledge and understanding should be coupled with an intention to benefit mankind in tangible ways. For Casanova, the importance of his own philosophical investigations lay primarily in their educative value: to help people avoid foolishness, thereby giving them a better chance to attain happiness and generally improve the well-being of society. Of course, Casanova's most important work in this regard is *History of My Life*, which was to act as a moral guide by means of experience and example. 'My story is a school of morality, and it will give food for thought to those who know how little prudence has to do with the vicissitudes of life, and how independent the chain of events is of methods, and of what is called good behaviour.'[37]

History of My Life is recognised today as a literary masterpiece and provides us with most of what we know about Casanova. Like many people who have encountered this mammoth text of one and a quarter million words, the first question I asked myself was how could he have written in such detail about events that stretched back over four decades? It turned out that since his teens he had been keeping notes, correspondence and official papers, and over the years had collected a large amount of material that he was able to draw upon for his memoirs. Before he was enrolled in the seminary at San Cipriano in his late teens, he records leaving papers with his friend Signora Catterina Manzoni. He also mentions carting notebooks about with him on his travels. He writes that when he was arrested in Barcelona by the police and his possessions were confiscated, 'I open my trunk, and this man is surprised to see that it was at least two-thirds full of notebooks.'[38]

Well, that may have helped to answer one question, but it raised another. Why? The most straightforward answer is that he did so in anticipation that at some point in the future he was going to write about his life. But how plausible is that? How plausible is it that a teenager would set in motion a project that would not come to fruition for another thirty or forty years, one which involved considerable sacrifice in terms of time and effort, and one which he might not even live to complete? What's more, on at least one occasion in his memoirs he records that he had grave doubts about the wisdom of writing about his life and allowing others to pass judgement upon it. In the end he seems to have begun composing *History of My Life* at the instigation of his doctor to combat melancholy.

What if then, he had in mind a different purpose for his note-taking? What if this intellectually precocious teenager had been inspired by a new philosophical movement that had recently acquired elevated prestige at the very time and in the very university in which he was studying? Perhaps his note-taking habit and document collecting was the behaviour not of a budding memoirist but a budding experimental philosopher. In one escapade that Casanova records, he plays the hero to rescue the reputation of a young countess. She had been abandoned after having been seduced by the promise of marriage and was on the verge of suicide. In assuming the role of her rescuer, he was 21 at the time, Casanova writes: 'I was conducting an experiment on myself convinced that I didn't know myself well enough.'[39] Elsewhere in his memoirs he describes an occasion when he rented a small casino in Murano to be close to his lover, the nun MM, who was in a nearby convent and dangerously ill. His only companion was an attractive 15-year-old female servant called Tonina who also slept at the casino. During the seven or so weeks MM was ill, Casanova remained entirely faithful and, knowing what his character was like, he was very pleased at his restraint. He observes: 'I had just performed an experiment on myself which greatly flattered my self-esteem.'[40]

All in all, it would seem that a solid case can be made to support the claim that Casanova was an experimental moral philosopher, and that *History of My Life* can be regarded as a significant achievement within this philosophical tradition. In his memoirs Casanova has amassed a huge amount of contextualised data that throws light onto the mores, beliefs, customs and behaviour of eighteenth-century Europe without any overt attempt to impose upon that material, as Rousseau did with his own memoirs, a speculative philosophy or system. The fact that *History of My Life* draws on novelistic conventions, picaresque and libertine, did not delegitimise its scientific value in the eyes of contemporary experimental philosophers. The memoirs can be regarded as a self-consciously observational project, whatever inevitable authorial biases it may contain. Perhaps it is for this reason that for two centuries *History of My Life* has stood as a confounding challenge to those who have attempted to make sense of it through the lens of a particular moral system, either their own or ones presumed to be universal and absolute.

Notes

My primary resource for Casanova has been Willard R. Trask's authoritative English translation of Casanova's memoirs which is now over fifty years old. I have supplemented it with the recent Bouquins French edition (2013–2018). Using Bouquins, I have produced my own translations of material I have taken from the memoirs. I have toned down the formality of Trask a little but not too much. To help guard against the dangers of presentism it is useful to maintain something of the more formal register typical of educated elites of the past. In his preface, Casanova is explicit that he wrote for a 'well-bred audience'.

For the most part the variations between my translations relative to Trask's are minor and make little difference to the informational content. But this is not always the case. An example would be Casanova's homosexual encounter with Ismail. In the French we have: '*je n'ai pas trouvée de mon goût ... je n'étais pas amateur de la chose.*' (*HV* 1:377) In Trask: 'it was not to my taste … I was not of that persuasion.' (*HL* 2:83) And in mine: 'I didn't find it to my taste … I wasn't a fan of it.' Trask's use of the word 'persuasion' could signify homosexuality in the modern sense of being an identity whereas across most of Europe, for most the eighteenth century, it was seen as a behaviour. Trask's translation here could complicate our understanding of Casanova's perception of homosexuality. Likewise with women. Casanova thought highly of women who were intelligent and well-read yet in Trask here we have him complaining that 'In a woman learning is out of place' from the French '*Dans une femme la science est déplacée.*' (*HL* 3:50, *HV* 1:631) In reality, for Casanova it seems that the issue was not with women who were educated but with women who engaged in academic study, hence my translation, 'In a woman scholarship is out of place.' In his 1797 Preface, Casanova describes God as the '*maître de toutes les formes*'. (*HV* 1:4) In Trask: 'creator and lord of all forms.' (*HL* 1:25) Trask's inclusion of 'creator' is seriously misleading. Casanova believed that matter was co-eternal with God. God may have shaped that matter but he did not create it. Hence my translation, 'master of all forms'.

I have used short abbreviations to indicate where the material can be found in both the Trask and Bouquins editions. For Trask I have used *HL* (*History of*

My Life) and for Bouquins *HV* (*Histoire de Ma Vie*). In the notes, references such as the above would look like: 'I didn't find it to my taste': *HL* 2:83 / *HV* 1:377, where the first number is the edition volume and the second number is the page reference.

Short title abbreviation

HL Casanova, Giacomo, *History of My Life*, trans. W.R. Trask (Johns Hopkins, 1997)

HV Casanova, Giacomo, Jean-Christophe Igalens, and Érik Leborgne. *Histoire de ma vie*. Vols. 1–3. (Bouquins, 2013–2018).

Introduction

'we talk, and we become good friends': *HL* 7:181 / *HV* 2:725

1. 'People became more reflective': Dupré, *The Enlightenment and the Intellectual Foundations of Modern Culture*, 9
2. 'The members of the English Parliament': Voltaire, *Letters on England*, 44
3. 'modern pagans': Gay, *The Enlightenment: An Interpretation,* 8
4. 'classicism was a bridge': Gay, *The Enlightenment: An Interpretation,* 58

1. Enlightenment Roots

'The next day at nine o'clock': *HL* 3:47 / *HV* 2:628

The moral mind

1. 'The material cause': 'Aristotle on causality', online Stanford Enyclopedia of Philosophy
2. 'great abuse of words': Locke, *An Essay Concerning Human Understanding*, 442
3. 'endless train of syllogisms': Ibid, 531
4. 'maxims and axioms': Ibid, 523
5. 'To avoid the attentions of the censor … This was a strategy used by La Mettrie': Wolfe, 'A happiness fit for organic bodies: La Mettrie's medical Epicureanism', 69

Religion

6. 'Moral and legal rules': McCall, 'The New Protestant Bargain', Kindle locations 3770–3772
7. 'The heart has its reasons of which reason does not know': Pascal, *Thoughts,* 99
8. 'has in all times overwhelmed mankind': Holbach, *The System of Nature*, 11

Natural philosophy

9. 'I would address one general admonition': Bacon, *The New Organon: and related writings*, 15
10. 'would not only be desirable': Descartes, René, *Discourse on Method,* 40

2. Horace: 65–8 BCE

'Horace, whom I know by heart': *HL* 6:225 / *HV* 2:486

Popularity

1. 'each quoting': *HL* 10:165 / *HV* 3:390
2. 'From 1660 to 1790 there were 120 English translations': Ohsumi, *Pope and Horace*, 85
3. 'in the first half of the eighteenth century': Money, 'The reception of Horace in the seventeenth and eighteenth centuries', *The Cambridge Companion to Horace,* Harrison, Stephen (ed.), 321
4. 'no one is born without vices': Buckley, *The Works of Horace*, 151 (*Satires 1.3)*
5. 'I feel no shame': Horace, *Satires and Epistles*, 82
6. 'the sentiments of sociability': Rousseau, *The Social Contract,* in *Ideal Empires and Republics*, Charles M. Andrews (ed.), 124.
7. 'He who judges': Ibid, 114.
8. 'a moderate and gentle tone': Melton, *The Rise of the Public in Enlightenment Europe*, 96
9. 'True happiness': cited by Brian Cowan in 'Joseph Addison', *The Digital Encyclopedia of British Sociability in the Long Eighteenth Century*, accessed on 12/16/2022.

Life

10. 'Captive Greece took captive': Buckley, *The Works of Horace*, 284. (*Epistles 2.1*)
11. 'And yet if my disposition': Ibid, 167. (*Satires 1.6*)
12. 'precipitate flight': Ibid, 46. (*Odes 2.7*)
13. 'poverty urged me on': Ibid, 46. (*Epistles 2.2*)
14. 'When you have a mind to laugh': Ibid, 237. (*Epistles 1.4*)
15. 'Horace's solutions to imperial suggestion': Lowrie, 'Horace and Augustus', *The Cambridge Companion to Horace*, Harrison, Stephen (ed.), 87

Works

16. 'when the fighting got hot': Archilochus, *7 Greeks*, trans. Guy Davenport, 50.
17. 'grown rank with lengthened age': Buckley, *The works of Horace*, 123. (*Epodes 8*)
18. 'The vessel that carries': Buckley, *The works of Horace*, 124–125. (*Epodes 10*)
19. 'Just as little children believe': Evans, *The Satires of Juvenal, Persius, Sulpicia and Lucilius*, 336.
20. 'Albinus': Evans, *The Satires of Juvenal, Persius, Sulpicia and Lucilius*, 357.
21. 'When he sees me': Evans, *The Satires of Juvenal, Persius, Sulpicia and Lucilius*, 357.
22. 'Meanwhile he kept prating': Buckley, *The works of Horace*, 174–175.
23. 'Write to me': Buckley, *The works of Horace*, 256–257. (*Epistles* 1.15)
24. 'He invites an advocate friend': Reference to *Epistles* 1.5
25. 'To admire nothing': Buckley, *The works of Horace*, 239. (*Epistles* 1.6)

26. 'In a letter to Fuscus': Reference to *Epistles* 1.10
27. 'To quarrel over your cups': Buckley, *The works of Horace*, 144–145. (*Satires* 2.1)

Philosophy

28. 'It is worth your while': Buckley, *The works of Horace*, 28. (*Odes* 1.27)
29. 'When your passions are inflamed': Buckley, *The works of Horace*, 147. (*Satires* 2.1)
30. 'monstrous coupling': Casanova, *Della Filosofia e de' Filosofi*, trans. author, 3

Casanova

31. 'scoundrel': *HL* 1:107 / *HV* 1:88
32. '*Philocalies on the Foolishness of Mortals*': Casanova
33. 'the place for exchange among unequal individuals:' Barchiesi, '*Carmina: Odes* and *Carmen Saeculare*', *The Cambridge Companion to Horace*, Harrison, Stephen (ed.), 159
34. 'Those who don't talk about their needs': *HL* 10:166 / *HV* 3:391
35. 'rule your passion': Buckley, *The works of Horace*, 147. (*Epistles* 1.2)
36. 'Harvest the day': West, *Horace: The Complete Odes and Epodes*, 34
37. 'pleasure … is always pure; pain is always tempered': *HL* 2:37 / *HV* 1:329
38. 'Do you see, my dear reader': *HL* 2:37 / *HV* 1:330
39. 'How an immaterial substance': *HL* 1:29 / *HV* 1:8
40. 'immaterial': Casanova, fragment, Marr 16 K 57, University of Liège Library
41. 'the material pains': *HL* 4:256–257 / *HV* 1:1233
42. 'Any man called upon to judge': *HL* 4:256 / *HV* 1:1233
43. 'Unable to study either men or nature,': Casanova, *Della filosofia e de' filosofi*, trans. author, 4
44. 'Those whom we instruct': *HL* 1:92 / *HV* 1:74
45. 'A true collection': Casanova, *Della filosofia e de' filosofi*, trans. author, 10
46. 'The people will be happy': Ibid, 11

3. Ludovico Ariosto: 1474 –1533

'Not knowing what method': *HL* 4:285/ *HV* 1:1259–260

1. 'Ariosto; and I can't say that I love him': *HL* 6:226 / *HV* 2:486
2. 'the masterpiece of the human mind': *HL* 8:249/ *HV* 2:1062

The Frenzy of Orlando

3. All *Orlando Furioso* translations are taken from the William Stuart Rose translation.
4. 'elevated a popular vernacular genre': Gregory, *From Many Gods to One*, 105
5. 'It [*The Frenzy of Orlando*] is at once the Iliad': Voltaire. The Works of Voltaire: a contemporary version, vol. 4, 257–258

6. 'After a love-philtre had turned him mad': cited in Greenblatt, *The Swerve: how the Renaissance began*, 53
7. 'It is religion breeds wickedness': Lucretius, *The Nature of Things*, 5 (1:83–844)
8. 'O what things may he do!': Ariosto, *Orlando Furioso, Part Two*, 418 (38:33)

The Frenzy of Orlando and Casanova

9. 'Between the end of October': *HL* 4:285 / *HV* 1:1260
10. 'Casanova had been smitten': *HL* 6:228 / *HV* 2:490
11. 'He claimed to read it': Ibid
12. The words 'honour', 'dishonour', 'honourable': For convenience this estimate is based on a count using the Gutenberg digital Arthur Machan translation of Casanova's memoirs, which itself is derived from the very unreliable LaForgue edition. While this version is unsatisfactory in many ways, it is unlikely that it will have significantly misrepresented the prevalence of 'honour' etc in *History of My Life*.
13. 'I replied, embracing him': *HL* 8:148–149 / *HV* 2:963
14. 'great paroxysm': *HL* 3:37 / *HV* 1:619
15. 'the extent of my happiness too much for my faculties': *HL* 3:39 / *HV* 1:620
16. 'I want to be your only lover': *HL* 3:36 / *HV* 1:617
17. 'it is a great pleasure to do whatever the object of one's love commands': *HL* 3:51 / *HV* 1:631
18. 'Why,' he [a German magistrate] asked': *HL* 8:38–39/ *HV* 2:872
19. 'irrepressible laughter…his delight in the absurd': Reynolds, *Orlando Furioso, Part Two*, 20
20. 'youthful madness': *HL* 1:27 / *HV* 1:6
21. 'I found myself all the more piqued': *HL* 2:103 / *HV* 1:397
22. 'You shall be my wife': *HL* 5:53 / *HV* 2:39
23. 'I was in love with Mademoiselle de la M-re': *HL* 5:71 / *HV* 2:56
24. 'We complain of women': *HL* 5:71 / *HV* 2:56

4. Pierre Gassendi: 1592–1655

'The doctrine of the Stoics': *HL* 1:25 / *HV* 1:3

1. 'the best philosopher I have yet met': cited in Lolordo, *Pierre Gassendi and the birth of early modern philosophy*, 11
2. 'I did this not to assert the motion': Ibid, 27–28
3. 'despite the fact that he held views': Ibid, 19
4. 'those who maintain that the soul': Daniel Klein, *The Art of Happiness,* 104
5. John R. Milton. 'Locke and Gassendi: a reappraisal'.
6. 'In general Gassendi's "Neo-Epicurean' system': Paganini, 'Early modern Epicureanism', in *Oxford Handbook Of Epicurus and Epicureanism*, Philip Mitsis (ed.), 861–862
7. Implications of Neo-Epicureanism: Paganini, Ibid, 853–902.

5. Libertinism

'The mythic character': Abramovici, *Encyclopedia of the Enlightenment*, Vol. 1, 775
'In Venice there was not a greater libertine than myself'.: *HL* 4:197 / *HV* 1:1173

God's anarchist

1. 'to turn heaven and Earth upside down': cited in Thysell, *The Pleasure of Discernment*, 28
2. 'It can be questioned for example': Veen, *Ioannis Calvini Scripta didactica et polemica, Vol. 1,* 10
3. 'Free from all forms of power': Cavaillé, '*Libertine* and *Libertinism*', 29

The eighteenth century

4. 'Cultivating the pleasures of my senses': *HL* 1:31 / *HV* 1:12
5. 'English, French and Dutch usages': Turner, James, 'The Properties of Libertinism', 78
6. 'libertine mind': Cryle, *Libertine Enlightenment,* 77
7. 'not so much a concept': Abramovici, *Encyclopedia of the Enlightenment*, Vol. 1, 773
8. 'Who is this girl': *HL* 3:31/ *HV* 1:613

Casanova

9. 'Libertine, braggart, habitual liar': *HL* 12:193 / *HV* 3:1083
10. 'I began to live truly independent': *HL* 2:201 / *HV* 1:488
11. Number of Casanova's partners: Kelly, *Casanova: Actor, Spy, Lover, Priest*, 124–125
12. 'That was when the great orgy began': *HL* 7:245/7 / *HV* 2:787/8
13. 'Despite this, I went to bed very happy': *HL* 7:247 / *HV* 2:788
14. 'As far as women are concerned': *HL* 1:32–33 / *HV* 1:13
15. 'I have always loved strong savoury dishes': *HL* 1:32 / *HV* 1:12–13
16. *The History of My Life*: Kelly, *Casanova: Actor, Spy, Lover, Priest*, 296
17. 'game, sturgeon, truffles, oysters and perfect wines': *HL* 4:47 / *HV* 1:1035
18. 'We suffer hunger': *HL* 4:34 / *HV* 1:1022
19. 'Happy are those': *HL* 1:33 / *HV* 1:13
20. 'Casanova sought an accommodation with virtue': Cryle, *Libertine Enlightenment,* 59

6. Voltaire: 1694–1778

'"This," I said to him, "is the happiest moment of my life"': *HL* 6:223 / *HV* 2:483

1. 'This deist reader of Locke': Pearson, Voltaire Almighty: a life in pursuit of freedom, 73

2. 'What! Aren't the French fond of life?': Voltaire, Letters on England, 56
3. 'When one considers that Newton': Voltaire, The Works of Voltaire: a contemporary version, 174
4. 'At Cirey we cultivated all the arts': Voltaire. *Memoirs of the Life of Voltaire*, 8
5. 'Some fanatic in the crowd': Voltaire, Toleration and other essays, 4

Newton

6. 'Fontenelle in effect fostered the perception': Shank, *The Newton Wars and the Beginning of the French Enlightenment*, 69
7. 'infusing the much older tradition': Ibid., 485
8. 'I don't think we really dare compare': Voltaire, Letters on England, 74
9. 'I was praised by a king, from the crown of my head': Voltaire. *Memoirs of the Life of Voltaire*, 45
10. 'For Voltaire, Maupertuis' success': Shank, *The Newton Wars and the Beginning of the French Enlightenment*, 425

Casanova

11. 'With an imagination comparable': Marrone, *Encyclopedia of Italian Literary Studies*, 400
12. 'one of the most engaging': Ibid., 400
13. 'a refined observer of political culture': Cerman, *Casanova: Enlightenment philosopher*, 120
14. 'While Damiens was being tortured': *HL* 5:57 / *HV* 2:43
15. '"My dear Candide!"': Voltaire. *Candide, or Optimism*, 11
16. 'everyone wanted to give me letters': *HL* 6:210 / *HV* 2:470
17. '"This," I said to him': *HL* 6:223 / *HV* 2:483
18. 'He maintained a residence': *HL* 6:235 / *HV* 2:497
19. 'He [Voltaire] opened a door"': *HL* 6:234 / *HV* 2:497
20. 'A poor compliment': *HL* 6:224 / *HV* 2:483
21. '[Voltaire] "Martelli proves"': *HL* 6: 243 / *HV* 2:507
22. 'I repent of it today': *HL* 6:246 / *HV* 2:512

7. Denis Diderot: 1713–1784

'There is no man in the world': *HL* 3:116 / *HV* 1:696

1. 'the most creative and noteworthy thinker': Curran, *Diderot and the Art of Thinking Freely,* 15
2. Comparison to d'Alembert and Diderot: Cerman, *Casanova: Enlightenment philosopher*, 28
3. 'And its [mankind's] hands': Diderot, *Les éleuthéromanes: avec un commentaire historique,* 96

4. 'vermin which gnaw': Diderot, *Lettres à Sophie Volland*, Vol. 2, 58–59, trans. author
5. 'I believe that a Jansenist': Diderot, *Lettres à Sophie Volland*, Vol. 1, 230, trans. author
6. 'wonders of nature': Diderot, An Essay on Blindness in a Letter to a Person of Distinction, 40
7. 'monsters have successively destroyed': Ibid., 42
8. 'And anyone lecturing to the Academy': Diderot, *Rameau's Nephew and D'Alembert's Dream,* 153
9. 'Imagine a spider': Ibid., 182
10. 'regular or irregular formation': Ibid., 190
11. 'Take another thread away': Ibid., 190
12. 'It [consciousness] can only be': Ibid., 210
13. 'With this argument': Dupré, *The Enlightenment and the Intellectual Foundations of Modern Culture*, 31
14. 'You poor philosophers': Ibid., 180–181
15. 'Every abstraction is merely a symbol': Ibid., 221–222
16. 'My history': *HL* 1:29 / *HV* 1:8
17. 'They were made without regard': Diderot, *Rameau's Nephew and D'Alembert's Dream*, 225
18. 'chastity and absolute continence': Ibid., 227
19. 'To Diderot, erotic desire': Blom, *Wicked Company: freethinkers and friendship in pre-revolutionary Paris,* 189
20. 'Our steps cease': Diderot, *Sur la peinture*, trans. author, 39
21. 'Nature, or the art that copies it': Ibid., trans. author, 67

The Encyclopedia

22. 'This work will surely': Diderot, *Lettres à Sophie Volland*, Vol. 2, trans. author, 8–9
23. 'Encyclopedia': Diderot, *Encyclopedia of Diderot & d'Alembert, collaborative translation project,* Vol. 5, 635
24. 'Passing on life's torch': Lucretius, *The Nature of Things*, 38 (2: 79)
25. 'The Eleatic school'. Diderot, *Encyclopedia of Diderot & d'Alembert, collaborative translation project,* Vol. 5, 779
26. 'Nobility': Jaucourt, *Encyclopedia of Diderot & d'Alembert, collaborative translation project,* Vol. 11, 167
27. 'Ecclesiastic intolerance': Diderot, Ibid., vol. 8, 843

8. Jean-Jacques Rousseau: 1712–1778

'At that time, Madame d'Urfé': *HL* 5:223 / *HV* 2:217

1. 'Notwithstanding Casanova's claims': Marco Leeflang & Tom Vitelli. 'C. sur C'., *Casanoviana 1,* (2018), 35.

2. 'Ideas take shape in my head': Rousseau, *The Confessions*, 113
3. 'It is as if my heart and my brain': Ibid.
4. 'a store of ideas': Ibid., 226
5. 'I have loved with too much sincerity': Ibid., 80
6. 'intimate friendship is precious': cited in Damrosch, *Jean-Jacques Rousseau: restless genius*, 288
7. 'I acquired by this method': Rousseau, *The Confessions*, 20
8. 'that created in me that proud and intractable spirit': Ibid.
9. 'My master's tyranny … drove me to vices': Ibid., 40–41
10. 'not as impious': Rousseau, The Social Contract, or Principles of Political Right, 237
11. 'a virtual parody of a parasitic aristocrat': Damrosch, *Jean-Jacques Rousseau: restless genius*, 168
12. 'I got the captain of a merchant vessel': Rousseau, *The Confessions*, 284
13. 'I should have to flatter or be silent': Ibid., 354
14. 'Highlighting the importance of Plato': Williams, *Rousseau's Platonic Enlightenment,* 62
15. 'as soon as I had a name, I ceased to have friends': *The Confessions*, 338
16. 'shall be forced to be free': Rousseau, *The Social Contract, or Principles of Political Right*, 31
17. 'woman is made specially to please man': Rousseau, *Emile, or on Education*, 358
18. 'I will tell you plainly': cited in Blom, *Wicked Company: freethinkers and friendship in pre-revolutionary Paris,* 233
19. 'springs forth so to speak': Rousseau, *The Social Contract, or Principles of Political Right*, 71
20. 'we are approaching a state of crisis': Rousseau, *Emile, or on Education*, 194

9. Threads of Recollection

'I have done many foolish things in my life': *HL* 8:24 / *HV* 2:859–860

The Confessions

1. 'Oh! that I might repose on Thee!': Augustine, *The Confessions of St Augustine*, 3
2. 'We confess with pain': Voltaire, *Sentiment des citoyen,* trans. author
3. 'Let the last trumpet sound': Rousseau, *The Confessions*, 17
4. 'No royal child': Ibid., 21
5. 'who managed in a very short time': Ibid., 39
6. 'falsehood, idleness, and theft': Ibid., 40
7. 'I saw nothing but dirty, stinking, little streets': Rousseau, *The Confessions*, 155
8. 'It is in the country that one learns to love and serve humanity': Ibid, 427
9. 'I know that, whatever you do': Ibid, 442
10. 'on the whole the best of men': Rousseau, *The Confessions*, 479
11. 'He would acknowledge his sins': Damrosch, *Jean-Jacques Rousseau: restless genius*, 435

12. 'If I were one of those low-born men': *The Confessions*, 332
13. 'Never was deliberate wickedness': Ibid., 88
14. 'But all they did was to frighten me': Ibid., 89
15. 'there are moments of a kind of delirium': Ibid., 46
16. 'the follies which the memory': Ibid., 108
17. 'free and open nature': Ibid., 458
18. 'too loving and tender heart': Ibid., 460
19. 'My lack of success with women': Ibid., 80
20. 'Grim fate': Damrosch, *Jean-Jacques Rousseau: restless genius*, 166
21. 'I must remain incessantly beneath his [the reader's] gaze': Rousseau, *The Confessions*, 65
22. 'Intelligent reader, consider and decide': Ibid., 519
23. 'Anyone reading this': Ibid., 136
24. 'a passion perhaps stronger': Ibid., 446
25. 'Here is one more of these confessions': Ibid., 595
26. 'I have told the truth': Ibid., 605
27. 'that fatal moment': Ibid., 247
28. 'In the midst of this temporary prosperity': Ibid., 489
29. 'Here begins the work of darkness': Ibid., 544

The Confessions and History of My Life

30. 'JJ Rousseau, famous relapser': Casanova, *Histoire de ma Fuite des Prisons de la République de Venise*, trans. author, 7
31. 'because he only made it brilliant': *HL* 6:206 / *HV* 2:467
32. 'Inspired by this sensualist conception': Cerman, *Casanova: Enlightenment philosopher*, 42
33. 'my mind and my matter': *HL* 10:19 / *HV* 3:229
34. 'I shall come forward': Rousseau, *The Confessions*, 17
35. 'I imagine myself giving an account': *HL* 1:29 / *HV* 1:8
36. 'I set down my thoughts on': *HL* 1:30 / *HV* 1:10
37. 'I begin by declaring': *HL* 1:25 / *HV* 1:3
38. 'I hope, dear reader': *HL* 1:27 / *HV* 1:6
39. 'I declare that I have written nothing': Casanova, *Histoire de ma Fuite des Prisons de la République de Venise*, trans. author, 11
40. 'I prefer a judgement based on the truth': Ibid., trans. author, 12
41. 'They invented descriptions of battles': Cerman, 'Observtions on moral philosophy,' in Cerman, *Casanova: Enlightenment philosopher*, 43
42. 'No material creature is active by itself': Rousseau, *Emile,* 280
43. 'Casanova's autobiography is unique': Kavanagh, *Esthetics of the Moment: Literature and Art in the French Enlightenment*, 102
44. 'In the nine to ten days': *HL* 2:39 / *HV* 1:332
45. 'preparing afar off': Rousseau, *The Confessions*, 489
46. Trocchio, 'The philosophy of the adventurer' in Cerman, *Casanova: Enlightenment philosopher*, 49–91

47. 'a determined Epicurean': *HL* 11:158 / *HV* 3:720
48. 'They who believe that a woman': *HL* 3:49–50
49. 'Casanova has distanced himself': Trocchi, 'The philosophy of the adventurer,' in Cerman, *Casanova: Enlightenment philosopher*, 67
50. 'To crown all, there arrived from the Val d'Aosta': Rousseau, *The Confessions*, 178
51. 'Madame Quinson': *HL* 3:174 / *HV* 1:812
52. 'I have resolved on an enterprise': Rousseau, *The Confessions*, 17

10. A Philosopher and a Christian

'Man is free': *HL* 1: 26 / *HV* 1:4

'Casanova was intensively preoccupied': Cerman, *Casanova: Enlightenment philosopher*, 2

1. 'this diversity of forms': Michael B. Gill, 'Lord Shaftesbury [Anthony Ashley Cooper, 3rd Earl of Shaftesbury]', *The Stanford Encyclopedia of Philosophy* (Fall 2021 Edition), Edward N. Zalta (ed.), https://plato.stanford.edu/archives/fall2021/entries/shaftesbury/
2. 'A man deep in knowledge': Johnson, Samuel. https://johnsonsdictionaryonline.com/
3. 'He claims to have met Rousseau': Cerman, *Casanova: Enlightenment Philosopher*, 25

Philosophical Pursuit

4. 'Ivo Cerman has identified': '8 "Je viens pour vous convertir": Casanova's dialogues on philosophy and religion'. *Casanova: Enlightenment philosopher*, 201–224
5. [Mademoiselle Vesian]: *HL* 3: 194–195 / *HV* 1:848, 850
6. 'morality is the metaphysics of physics': *HL* 3: 195 / *HV* 1:850
7. 'our soul can only be happy': *HL* 3: 196 / *HV* 1:852
8. 'M Tronchin asked her': *HL* 8:104–105 / *HV* 2:925–926
9. 'in one dialogue he pits a Jesuit theologian against a cook': *Casanova: Enlightenment Philosopher*, 221
10. 'Christoph Meiners and Michael Hißmann': Falk Wunderlich, 'Materialism at the University of Göttingen', *Reassessing the Radical Enlightenment*, Steffan Ducheyne (ed.), 223–239
11. 'is only vegetative': Diderot, *Encyclopédie, ou dictionnaire raisonné des sciences, des arts et des métiers,* vol. 1, 332
12. 'a particle of the Creator's divinity': *HL* 1: 26 / *HV* 1:4
13. 'Defects of temperament': *HL* 1: 31 / *HV* 1:11
14. 'A man of intelligence': Casanova, *Soliloquy of a Thinker*, 15
15. 'the goal of all good education': Ibid., 13–14
16. Casanova's Socratic dialogues: Cerman, *Casanova: Enlightenment Philosopher*, Table of Socratic social dialogues, 223

17. 'Casanova's most extensive overtly philosophical text': Rother, 'Italian enlightenment debates on religion and church. Casanova's philosophy and its background,' in *Casanova: Enlightenment Philosopher*, Ivo Cerman (ed.), 95–117
18. 'Casanova blames the indecent life of the cardinals in Rome': Ibid., 117
19. 'I can say that I only began to love God': *HL* 4:56 / *HV* 1:1042
20. 'superstition is necessary': *HL* 6: 244 / *HV* 2:508
21. 'The question of suicide': Bernadini & Lucci, 'Casanova on Suicide,' in *Casanova: Enlightenment Philosopher*, Ivo Cerman (ed.), 135–155
22. 'What is sure': Ibid., 153
23. 'if, after a true or faulty reckoning': *HL* 1:33/ *HV* 1:13
24. 'I am far from consoling myself': *HL* 1: 35 / *HV* 1:16

Casanova the Eclectic

25. 'ingenious and chimerical': Casanova, *Della filosof ia e de' filosofi*, trans. author, 4
26. 'the eternal existence of matter': Casanova, *Essay on Created or Uncreated Matter*, trans. author, 1
27. 'if He has found: Casanova, *On the Existence of God and Co-eternal Matter*, trans. author, 2
28. 'but God': *Freedom of Will*, trans. author, 2
29. 'The greatest philosophers': Casanova, *Essay on Matter*, trans. author, 6
30. 'With regards to my future': *HL* 1:29 / *HV* 1:8
31. 'The happiest of men': *HL* 4:35 / *HV* 1:1023
32. 'the strength of my senses': *HL* 1:32 / *HV* 1:12
33. 'Feelings of love must give way': *HL* 5:192 / *HV* 2:187
34. 'a merging of the Epicurean's': Kavanagh, *Enlightened Pleasures*, 4

A philosophical framework

35. 'great principle of all principles': *HL* 1:33 / *HV* 1:15
36. 'master of all forms': *HL* 1:25 / *HV* 1:4
37. He specifically rejects': *HL* 1:33–34 / *HV* 1:14
38. 'the original Hebrew text': Cerman, *Casanova: Enlightenment Philosopher*, 38
39. 'matter, never perishing': Rava, *Lettere di donne à Giacomo Casanova*, 303
40. 'master of all forms': *HL* 1:25 / *HV* 1:4
41. 'But whether this is sufficient': Rother, 'Italian enlightenment debates …' in *Casanova: Enlightenment Philosopher*, Ivo Cerman (ed.), 116
42. 'If we don't doubt it': *HL* 1:33 / *HV* 1:14
43. 'I have always counted on His providence': *HL* 1:25 / *HV* 1:4
44. 'imprinted by God in your soul': Casanova, cited by Ivo Cerman in *Casanova: Enlightenment Philosopher*, 212
45. 'divine moral principles': *HL* 1:27 / *HV* 1:5
46. 'Every aphorism': Casanova, Giacomo, *Della spiritualità dell'anima mia*, 1,
47. 'Life in general is nothing but the soul of the universe': *HV* 1:1322, trans. author, 1791 Preface

48. 'the globe on the surface': Casanova, *Lana Caprina*, trans. author, Kindle location 700
49. 'For Casanova, belief in a material soul': Casanova, *Reflections on God and Matter*, trans. author, 1
50. 'that a desire for reward': *HL* 1:34 / *HV* 1:15
51. 'But always do good': *HV* 1:1326, trans. author, 1791 preface
52. 'Everything unfortunate': *HL* 6:73 / *HV* 2:335
53. 'I can never have done anything': *HV* 1319, trans. author, 1791 preface
54. Casanova's criticism of allegorical interpretations of the bible: Casanova, *Essay on Matter*, 6
55. 'Happy are those': *HL* 1:33 / *HV* 1:13
56. 'He engraved natural religion on our hearts': *HV* 1:1324, trans. author, 1791 preface
57. 'God can only require of his creatures': *HL* 1:33 / *HV* 1:13
58. 'man can neither adore': *HV* 1:1321, trans. author, 1791 preface
59. 'The human race hates the wicked': *HV* 1:1324, Ibid
60. 'in this world, to be happy you must be loved': *HL* 5:148 / *HV* 2:141
61. 'being entirely submissive': *HV* 1:1324, trans. author, 1791 preface
62. 'The pious pastor must preach': Casanova, *Essay on Matter*, trans. author, 4
63. 'He [God] will show us': Ibid
64. 'the horrible man is the intolerant': *HV* 1:1329, trans. author, 1791 preface
65. 'For Casanova, self-preservation involved three primary needs': *HL* 4:33–34 / *HV* 1:1021–1022

11. An Experimental Moral Philosopher

[Casanova] 'I read as much as I can: *HL* 6:225 / *HV* 2:485–486

1. 'If the cries of this fish': cited in Hauc, 'Casanova et la souffrance animale', *Casanoviana 4*, (2021) trans. author, 9
2. 'I had read and learned from the great book of experience': *HL* 4:274 / *HV* 1:1250
3. 'woe to all those who love the truth': *HL* 7:186 / *HV* 2:730
4. 'the wise man who wants to learn': *HL* 6:201 / *HV* 2:461
5. 'This was a movement': Anstey, *Experimental Philosophy and the Origins of Empiricism*. Vol. 145, 2
6. The historiography of experimental philosophy is relatively recent. The description of the movement as outlined in this chapter will largely draw on works written or edited by Peter Anstey & Alberto Vanzo

Experimental philosophy

7. 'many of Aristotle's principles': Anstey, *Experimental Philosophy and the Origins of Empiricism*. Vol. 145, 22

8. 'Indeed, it is argued': Anstey, *Experimental Philosophy and the Origins of Empiricism*
9. 'This new emphasis on observation': Levitin, 'Early Modern Experimental Philosophy: A Non-Anglocentric Overview', *Experiment, Speculation and Religion in Early Modern Philosophy*, Peter R. Anstey & Alberto Vanzo (eds.), 237
10. 'The new experimental philosophers': Anstey, 'Early modern experimental philosophy', 3
11. 'Newton describes two permissible roles': Walsh, 'Newton's Scaffolding: The Instrumental Roles of His Optical Hypotheses', *Experiment, Speculation and Religion in Early Modern Philosophy*, Peter R. Anstey & Alberto Vanzo (eds.), 126
12. 'Hobbes, who privileged deductive reasoning': Sorell, 'Appeals to Experience in Hobbes' Science of Politics', *Experiment, Speculation and Religion in Early Modern Philosophy*, Peter R. Anstey & Alberto Vanzo (eds.), 81–100
13. 'a … true history': Locke, *An Essay Concerning Human Understanding*, 158
14. 'we have seen the experimental physics': Casanova, *Philocalia*, 25
15. 'There is a suggestion': Locke, *Essay concerning Human Understanding*, xi
16. 'In his denial of the possibility': Ibid, 74–91
17. 'preserve and cherish': Ibid, 81
18. 'I am bold to think': Locke, *An Essay Concerning Human Understanding*, 459
19. 'from self-evident propositions': Ibid, 487
20. 'moral knowledge': Ibid, 501
21. 'I doubt not': Ibid, 568
22. 'Reason is natural revelation:' Ibid, 616

Casanova

23. 'The goal was to set up': Marcon, 'The Physics Cabinet of the University of Padua. At the crossroads between Veneto and Europe', 160
24. 'experimental': *HL* 1:147 / *HV* 1:128
25. 'After reading it': *HL* 5:264 / *HV* 2:259
26. 'Reason does not recognise': Casanova, *Philocalia*, trans. author, 42
27. 'Our reason begins with doubt': Ibid, 43
28. 'to which his secret inclination is repugnant': Ibid, 6
29. 'a cabinet of natural history': Ibid, 9
30. 'the greater part of the unfortunate': Ibid, 1
31. 'Everything I have written': Ibid, 29
32. 'who treat the body like a very simple machine': Ibid, 30
33. 'imitates the system of knowledge': Denieul, 'Essai de critique sur les sciences …', trans. author, 123
34. 'Denieul points out': Ibid, 129
35. 'What must one do': Casanova, *L'essai de critique sur les sciences, sur les moeurs et sur les arts*, cited in Denieul, 'L'essai de critique sur les sciences, sur les moeurs et sur les arts de Casanova', trans. author, 132

36. 'What distinguishes Casanova': Forycki, 'Casanova and his considerations on the partition of Poland', in *Casanova: Enlightenment Philosopher*, Ivo Cerman, Susan Reynolds & Diego Lucci (eds.), 130
37. 'My story is a school of morality': *HV* 1:1326, trans. author, 1791 Preface
38. 'I open my trunk': *HL* 11:134 / *HV* 3:694
39. 'I was conducting an experiment on myself': *HL* 2:213 / *HV* 1:499
40. 'I had just performed an experiment on myself': *HL* 4:149 / *HV* 1:1128

Bibliography

Specialist texts and primary sources

Addison, Joseph & others. *The Spectator*, Vol. I. J.M. Dent & Co, 1897.

Aleksić, Branko. 'Casanova, à l'école buissonnière d'Épicure'. In *Dix-huitième Siècle*, 35, no.1 (2003): 241–252.

Aleksić, Branko. 'Casanova et D'Alembert'. *Recherches sur Diderot et sur l'Encyclopédie,* 42 (2007): 83–94.

Aleksić, Branko. 'Effets des Passions (Anon, 1776): la source de "Delle Passioni, Traduzione di Giacomo Casanova"'. *Topique* 1 (2012): 151–165.

Allen, Douglas W. & Clyde G. Reed. 'The duel of honor: screening for unobservable social capital'. *American Law and Economics Review* 8, no. 1 (2006): 81–115.

Andrews, Charles M. *Ideal Empires and Republics*. 1901.

Anstey, Peter R. 'D'Alembert, the "Preliminary Discourse" and experimental philosophy'. *Intellectual History Review* 24, no. 4 (2014): 495–516.

Anstey, Peter R. & Alberto Vanzo. 'Early modern experimental philosophy'. *A Companion to Experimental Philosophy* (2016): 87–102.

Anstey, Peter R. & Alberto Vanzo. *Experimental Philosophy and the Origins of Empiricism*. Vol. 145. Cambridge University Press, 2023.

Anstey, Peter R. & Alberto Vanzo (eds.). *Experiment, speculation and religion in early modern philosophy*. Routledge, 2019.

Antony, Robert, Stuart Carroll & Caroline Dodds Pennock (eds.). *The Cambridge World History of Violence: Volume 3, AD 1500–AD 1800.* Cambridge University Press, 2020.

Augustine. *The Confessions of St Augustine*, trans. E.B. Pusey. J.M. Dent & sons, 1939.

Bacon, Francis, *The New Organon: and related writings*. Liberal Arts Press, 1960.

Bateman, J. Chimène. 'Amazonian Knots: Gender, Genre & Ariosto's Women Warriors'. *MLN* 122, no. 1 (2007): 1–23.

Beales, Derek. *Prosperity and Plunder: European Catholic monasteries in the Age of Revolution, 1650–1815.* Cambridge University Press, 2003.

Bellamy, Elizabeth J. 'Alcina's Revenge: Reassessing Irony and Allegory in *Orlando Furioso*'. *Annali d'italianistica 12* (1994): 61–74.

Bernardini, Paolo & Diego Lucci (eds.). 'Politica e filosofia in Giacomo Casanova. Quattro inediti'. First published in *Annali dell'Università di Ferrara. Sezione di Storia 2* (2005), 251–270.

Bernis, François-Joachim de Pierre de. *Memoirs and Letters of Cardinal de Bernis*, trans. Katherine Prescott Wormeley. Hardy, Pratt & Co, 1902.

Boros, Gábor & Herman De Dijn. *The concept of love in 17th and 18th Century Philosophy*. Martin Moors (ed.). Leuven: Leuven University Press, 2007.

Bregoli, Francesca & Federica Francesconi. 'Tradition and transformation in eighteenth-century Europe: Jewish integration in comparative perspective'. *Jewish History* Vol. 24, no. 3–4 (2010): 235–246.

Brown, Alison. 'Lucretius and the Epicureans in the Social and Political Context of Renaissance Florence'. *I Tatti Studies in the Italian Renaissance* 9 (2001): 11–62.

Brown, John Russell (ed.). *The Oxford Illustrated History of Theatre*. Oxford University Press, 1995.

Buck, Mitchell. *The Life of Casanova from 1774–1798: a supplement to the memoirs*. Nicholas Brown, 1924.

Buckley, Theodore Alois (ed.) *The works of Horace*, trans. C. Smart. H.G. Bohn, 1856.

Byars, Jana. *Informal Marriages in Early Modern Venice*. Routledge, 2019.

Capaci, Bruno and Gianluca Simeoni: Giacomo Casanova: una biografia intellettuale e romanzesca, Napoli: Liguori, 2009. Kindle Edition.

Casanova, Giacomo. *Confutazione della* 'Storia del Governo Veneto' *d'Amelot de la Houssaie*. Divisa in tre parti (I parte), Amsterdam, presso Pietro Mortier, 1769.

Casanova, Giacomo. *Della filosofia e de' filosofi*. Marr 1-1, University of Liège Library, (1780?).

Casanova, Giacomo. *Della spiritualità dell'anima mia*. Marr 31-36, University of Liège Library, (1796?).

Casanova, Giacomo. *Essay on Created or Uncreated Matter*. Marr 18-8, University of Liège Library, (1795?).

Casanova, Giacomo. *Essay on Matter*. Marr 6-1, University of Liège Library, (1789–1790?).

Casanova, Giacomo. *Freedom of Will*, Marr 9-7, University of Liège Library, (1769?).

Casanova, Giacomo. *Histoire de ma fuite des Prisons de la République de Venise*. Éditions Allia, 2018.

Casanova, Giacomo, Jean-Christophe Igalens & Érik Leborgne. *Histoire de ma vie*. Vols. 1–3. Bouquins, 2013–2018.

Casanova, Giacomo. *History of My Life*, trans. W.R. Trask. Vols. 1–12. Johns Hopkins University Press, 1997.

Casanova, Giacomo. *Casanova's "Icosameron", Or, The Story of Edward and Elizabeth: Who Spent Eighty-one Years in the Land of the Megamicres, Original Inhabitants of Protocosmos in the Interior of Our Globe*, trans. and abridged by Rachel Zurer, Jenna Press, 1986.

Casanova, Giacomo. *Lana Caprina.* I edizione eBook: giugno 2014.

Casanova, Giacomo. *On the Existence of God and Co-eternal Matter*. Marr 18-7, University of Liège Library, (1795?).

Casanova, Giacomo. *Philocalies sur les Sottieses des Mortels*, Marr 22-1, University of Liège Library, (1784).

Casanova, Giacomo. *Reflections on God and Matter* Marr 31-26, University of Liège Library.

Casanova, Giacomo. *Soliloque d'un penseur*. Vol. 1. Editions Allia, 1998.

Casanova, Giacomo. *The Duel*, trans. J.G. Nichols. Hesperus Press, 2003.

Cavaillé, Jean-Pierre. 'Libertine and libertinism: polemic uses of the terms in sixteenth- and seventeenth-century English & Scottish literature'. *Journal for Early Modern Cultural Studies* 12, no. 2 (2012): 12–36.

Cavallo, Jo Ann. 'Orlando Furioso'. *The Literary Encyclopedia*. 30 December 2014.

Cerman, Ivo, Susan Helen Reynolds & Diego Lucci (eds.). *Casanova: Enlightenment philosopher*. Voltaire Foundation, 2016.

Childs, James Rives. *Casanova: a biography based on new documents.* George Allen & Unwin Ltd, 1961.

Childs, James Rives. *Casanova: a new perspective.* Paragon House, 1988.

Childs, James Rives. *Casanoviana: an annotated world bibliography of Jacques Casanova de Seingalt and of works concerning him*. C.M. Nebehay, 1956.

Clay, Lauren. 'Provincial actors, the Comédie-Française, and the business of performing in eighteenth-century France'. *Eighteenth-century studies* (2005): 651–679.

Clementsson, Bonnie. *Incest in Sweden, 1680–1940: A history of forbidden relations*. Lund University Press, 2020.

Coleman, James K. 'Translating Impiety: Girolama Frachetta and the first vernacular commentary on Lucretius'. *Quaderni d'italianistica* 35, no. 1 (2014).

Collins, Nancy W. *The problem of the Enlightenment salon: European history or post-revolutionary politics 1755–1850*. University of London, University College London (United Kingdom), 2006.

Cowan, Alexander. *Marriage, Manners and Mobility in Early Modern Venice.* Ashgate, 2007.

Cryle, Peter & Lisa O'Connell (eds.). *Libertine Enlightenment: sex, liberty and licence in the eighteenth century.* Palgrave, 2003.

Davenport, Guy. *7 Greeks*. New Directions Paperbook 799, 1995.

Davis, Gregson (ed.). *A Companion to Horace.* Wiley-Blackwell, 2010.

Delon, Michel (ed.). *Encyclopedia of the Enlightenment.* Fitzroy Dearborn, 2001.

Denbo, Seth J. 'Speaking relatively: a history of incest and the family in eighteenth-century England'. Thesis submitted for the degree of Doctor of Philosophy at University of Warwick, 2001.

Denieul, Séverine. 'Essai de critique sur les sciences, sur les mœurs et sur les arts de Casanova: un dictionnaire raisonné de la sottise?' In *Casanova à tort et à travers*, 123–142. Classiques Garnier, 2014.

Denieul, Séverine. 'Casanova lecteur et critique de Voltaire'. In *Voltaire philosophe: regards croisés*. Textes réunis par Sébastien Charles et Stéphane Pujol. Publications de la Société Voltaire (2017): 125–139.

Descartes, René & Laurence Julien Lafleur. *Discourse on Method: Translated, with an Introduction, by Laurence J. Lafleur*. Bobbs-Merrill, 1956.

Diderot, Denis. *An Essay on Blindness in a Letter to a Person of Distinction*, trans. unknown. Richard Dymot, 1895.

Diderot, Denis & Jean-Baptiste le Rond d'Alembert. *Encyclopédie, ou dictionnaire raisonné des sciences, des arts et des métiers*. Collaborative Digital Edition of the Encyclopedia (1751–1772).

Diderot, Denis. *Les éleuthéromanes: avec un commentaire historique.* Paris: [s.n.] 1884.

Diderot, Denis. *Lettres à Sophie Volland: textes publiés d'après les manuscrits originaux avec une introd., des variantes et des notes*. Gallimard, 1950.

Diderot, Denis. *Sur la peinture*. Moritz Diesterweg, 1909.

Ducheyne, Steffen (ed.). *Reassessing the radical enlightenment*. Taylor & Francis, 2017.

Dupré, Louis. *The Enlightenment and the Intellectual Foundations of Modern Culture*. Yale University Press, 2004.

Emery, Ted. 'Queer Casanova: Subversive Sexuality and the (Dis) embodied Subject in History of My Life'. *Italian Culture* 24, no. 1 (2007): 23–44.

Evans, Lewis. *The Satires of Juvenal, Persius, Sulpicia and Lucilius*. H.G. Bohn, 1861.

Faubert, Michelle. 'Romantic Suicide, Contagion & Rousseau's Julie'. In *Romanticism, Rousseau, Switzerland*, 38–53. Palgrave Macmillan, London, 2015.

Fee, Jerome. 'Maupertuis and the principle of least action'. *American Scientist* 30, no. 2 (1942): 149–158.

Field, Clive D. 'The social composition of English Methodism to 1830: a membership analysis'. *Bulletin of the John Rylands Library* 76, no. 1 (1994): 153–178.

Force, Pierre. 'Helvétius as an Epicurean political theorist'. *Epicurus in the Enlightenment* 12, Neven Leddy & Avi S. Lifschitz (eds.), (2009): 105–118.

Frederick II. *Memoirs of the House of Brandenburg,* trans. unknown. J Nourse, 1758.

Gaisser, Julia Haig. 'Poggio and Other Book Hunters'. Ricci, Roberta. *Poggio Bracciolini and the Re (dis)covery of Antiquity: Textual and Material Traditions: Proceedings of the Symposium Held at Bryn Mawr College on April 8–9, 2016.* Firenze University Press, 2020.

Gawthrop, Richard & Gerald Strauss. 'Protestantism and literacy in early modern Germany'. *Past & Present* 104 (1984): 31–55.

Gay, Peter. *The Enlightenment: An Interpretation.* Alfred A Knopf, 1966.

Gliozzo, Charles A. 'The Philosophes and Religion: Intellectual Origins of the Dechristianization Movement in the French Revolution'. *Church History* 40, no. 3 (1971): 273–283.

Goodman, Dena. *Marriage Calculations in the Eighteenth Century: Deconstructing the Love vs. Duty Binary*. Ann Arbor, MI: Michigan Publishing, University of Michigan Library, 2005.

Gorrie, Richard. *Gentle Riots? Theatre Riots in London, 1730–1780*. Thesis submitted for the degree of Doctor of Philosophy, University of Guelph, 2000.

Goulemot, Jean-Marie & Arthur Greenspan. 'Toward a definition of libertine fiction and pornographic novels'. *Yale French Studies*, no. 94 (1998): 133–145.

Greenstone, Gerry. 'The history of bloodletting'. *BC Medical Journal* 52, no. 1 (2010): 12–14.

Greer, Margaret R. 'Playing the palace: space, place and performance in early modern Spain'. *A History of Theatre in Spain*: 79–102. Cambridge University Press, 2012.

Greig, Hannah. 'Faction and Fashion: the politics of court dress in eighteenth-century England' in I. Paresys & N Coquery (eds.), Se Vêtir à la Cour en Europe (1400–1815). IRHiS, 2011.

Gregory, Mary. *Diderot and the Metamorphosis of Species*. Routledge, 2006.

Gregory, Tobias. *From Many Gods to One: Divine Action in Renaissance Epic*. Chicago University Press, 2009.

Gregory, Tullio. "Libertinisme érudit' in seventeenth-century France and Italy: The critique of ethics and religion'. *British journal for the history of philosophy* Vol. 6, no. 3 (1998): 323–349.

Grendler, Paul F. *Humanism, Universities, and Jesuit Education in Late Renaissance Italy*. Vol. 4. Brill, 2022.

Habermas, Jurgen. *The Structural Transformation of the Public Sphere*, trans. Thomas Burger. MIT Press, 1991.

Harrison, Stephen (ed.). *The Cambridge Companion to Horace*. Cambridge University Press, 2007.

Harvey, Karen. 'The century of sex? Gender, bodies, and sexuality in the long eighteenth century'. *The Historical Journal* 45, no. 4 (2002): 899–916.

Hitchcock, Tim. 'Sex and gender: Redefining sex in eighteenth-century England'. In *History Workshop Journal*, Vol. 41, no. 1, 72–90. Oxford University Press, 1996.

Hitchcock, Tim. 'The Reformulation of Sexual Knowledge in Eighteenth-Century England'. *Signs: Journal of Women in Culture and Society* 37, no. 4 (2012): 823–832.

Holbach, Paul Henri Thiry. *The System of Nature*, trans. W. Hodgson. W. Hodgson, 1795.

Hume, Robert D. 'The value of money in eighteenth-century England: incomes, prices, buying power—and some problems in cultural economics'. *Huntington Library Quarterly* 77, no. 4 (2014): 373–416.

Huzzey, Richard. 'Contesting Interests: Rethinking Pressure, Parliament, Nation, and Empire'. *Parliamentary History* 37 (2018): 1–17.

Huzzey, Richard & Henry Miller. 'Petitions, Parliament and Political Culture: Petitioning the House of Commons, 1780–1918'. *Past & Present* 248, no. 1 (2020): 123–164.

Iordanou, Ioanna. *Venice's Secret Service: Organising Intelligence in the Renaissance*. Oxford University Press, 2019.

Jacob, Margaret. 'The Nature of Early Eighteenth-Century Religious Radicalism'. *Republics of Letters: A Journal for the Study of Knowledge, Politics, and the Arts* 1, no. 1 (2009): 1–11.

Jalobeanu, Dana & Charles T. Wolfe, eds. *Encyclopedia of Early Modern Philosophy and the Sciences*. Cham: Springer International Publishing, 2022.

Johnson, James H. 'Deceit and Sincerity in Early Modern Venice'. *Eighteenth-Century Studies* 38, no. 3 (2005): 399–415.

Johnson, Marguerite. 'Witches in time and space: "Satire" 1.8, "Epode" 5 and landscapes of fear'. *Hermathena* 192 (2012): 5–44.

Johnson, Monte Ransome. 'Was Gassendi an Epicurean?' *History of Philosophy Quarterly* 20, no. 4 (2003): 339–60.

Kant, Immanuel. *Lectures on Ethics*, trans. Infield Louis. Methuen & Co, 1930.

Kavanagh, Thomas M. *Enlightened Pleasures: Eighteenth-Century France and the New Epicureanism.* Yale University Press, 2010.

Kavanagh, Thomas M. *Esthetics of the Moment: Literature and Art in the French Enlightenment.* Pennsylvania University Press, 1996.

Kelly, George Armstrong. 'The Point of Honour'. *Historical Reflections/Réflexions Historiques* (1986): 103–125.

Kennedy, William J. 'Ariosto's ironic Allegory'. *MLN* 88, no. 1 (1973): 44–67.

Kerhervé, Alain & Valérie Capdeville. *British Sociability in the Long Eighteenth Century. Challenging the Anglo-French Connection.* Boydell Press, 2019.

Kesselring, Krista J. 'No greater provocation? Adultery and the mitigation of murder in English law'. *Law and History Review* 34, no. 1 (2016): 199–225.

Klein, Daniel. *The Art of Happiness,* trans. George K. Strodach. Penguin, 2012.

Kruckeberg, Robert D. 'The wheel of fortune in eighteenth-century France: The lottery, consumption, and politics'. Thesis submitted for the degree of Doctor of Philosophy at University of Michigan, 2009.

Lahouati, Gérard. 'Être ou ne pas être matérialiste?' *Avec Casanova. Penser, songer et rire*, Classiques Garnier, 2020 157–167.

Leneman, Leah. 'Wives and mistresses in eighteenth-century Scotland', *Women's History Review*, (1999), 8:4, 671–692.

Levack, Brian P. 'The Prosecution of Sexual Crimes in Early Eighteenth-Century Scotland'. *Scottish Historical Review* 89, no. 2 (2010): 172–193.

Levi, Peter. *Horace: a life*. Gerald Duckworth & Co, 1997.

Ligne, Charles Joseph. *The Prince de Ligne: his memoirs, letters, and miscellaneous papers*, trans. Katherine Prescott Wormeley. Hardy, Pratt & Co 1899.

Lindert, Peter H. & Jeffrey G. Williamson. "English Workers' Living Standards during the Industrial Revolution: A New Look." *The Economic History Review* 36, no. 1 (1983): 1–25.

Locke, John. *An Essay Concerning Human Understanding*. Penguin, 1997.

Lolordo, Antonia. *Pierre Gassendi and the birth of early modern philosophy.* Cambridge University Press, 2006

London Gazette. Authority, Est 1665.

Marcon, Fanny, Giulio Peruzzi & Sofia Talas. 'The Physics Cabinet of the University of Padua. At the crossroads between Veneto and Europe'. *Opuscula Musealia* 26, no. Vol. 26 (2019): 157–172.

Marrone, Gaetana, Paolo Puppa & Luca Somigli. Encyclopedia of Italian Literary Studies. Routledge, 2007

McCall, Brian. 'The New Protestant Bargain: the influence of Protestant theology on contract and property law'. In C. Rao (ed.), *Luther and His Progeny: 500 Years of Protestantism and Its Consequences for Church, State, and Society*. Angelico Press (2017), Kindle Edition.

McDonald, Christie V. 'The Utopia of the Text: Diderot's "Encyclopédie"'. *The Eighteenth Century* 21, no. 2 (1980): 128–144.

McPherson, Heather. 'Theatrical riots and cultural politics in eighteenth-century London'. *The Eighteenth Century* 43, no. 3 (2002): 236–252.

Milanovic, Branko. 'Level of income and income distribution in mid-18th century France, according to Francois Quesnay'. *World Bank Policy Research Working Paper* 10545 (2010).

Milton, John R. 'Locke and Gassendi: a reappraisal'. In MA Stewart (ed.), *English Philosophy in the Age of Locke*. Oxford University Press. (2000): 87–109.

Mitsis, Phillip (ed.). *Oxford Handbook of Epicurus and Epicureanism*. Oxford University Press, 2020.

Morabia, Alfredo. 'Pierre-Charles-Alexandre Louis and the evaluation of bloodletting'. *Journal of the Royal Society of medicine 99,* no.3 (2006): 158–160.

Muravyeva, Marianna. '"A king in his own household": domestic discipline and family violence in early modern Europe reconsidered'. *The History of the Family* 18, no. 3 (2013): 227–237.

O'Connell, Lisa. 'The Libertine, the Rake, and the Dandy: Personae, Styles, and Affects'. *Cambridge History of Gay and Lesbian Literature,* edited by E.L. McCallum & Mikko Tuhkanen, Cambridge University Press (2014): 218–238.

Ohsumi, Megumi. *Pope and Horace: Imitation and Independence.* Doctoral dissertation. Université de Neuchâtel, 2013.

O'Rourke, James. *Sex, Lies and Autobiography: The Ethics of Confession.* Virginia University Press, 2006.

Ottenheimer, Martin. *Forbidden relatives: The American myth of cousin marriage*. University of Illinois Press, 1996.

Pascal, Blaise. *Thoughts*, trans. W.F. Trotter. P.F. Collier, 1910.

Peltonen, Markku. 'Francis Bacon, the Earl of Northampton, and the Jacobean anti-duelling campaign'. *The Historical Journal* 44, no. 1 (2001): 1–28.

Pizzamiglio, Gilberto (ed.). *Giacomo Casanova: tra Venezia e l'Europa.* Firenze: Leo S. Olschki, 2001.

Quint, David. 'Duelling and Civility in Sixteenth Century Italy'. *I Tatti Studies in the Italian Renaissance* 7 (1997): 231–278.

Quint, David. 'The Figure of Atlante: Ariosto and Boiardo's Poem'. *MLN* (1979): 77–91.

Ravà, Aldo. *Lettere di donne à Giacomo Casanova*. Milano: Fratelli Treves, 1912.

Reyfman, Irina. 'The emergence of the duel in Russia: corporal punishment and the honour code'. *The Russian Review*, 54, no. 1 (1995): 26–43.

Robertson, Ritchie. *Mock-epic poetry from Pope to Heine*. Oxford University Press, 2009.

Rosenberg, Daniel. 'An Eighteenth-Century Time Machine: The "Encyclopédia" of Denis Diderot'. *Historical Reflections/Réflexions Historiques* (1999): 227–250.

Roth, Ben. 'Confessions, excuses, and the storytelling self: rereading Rousseau with Paul de Man'. In *Rethinking European politics and history: IWM Junior visiting fellows' conferences*, Vol. 32. 2012.

Rousseau, Jean-Jacques. *Eloisa, or a series of original letters*, Vol. 2 trans. William Kenrick. Samuel Longcope, 1796.

Rousseau, Jean-Jacques. *Politics and the Arts: Letter to M. D'Alembert on the theatre*, trans. Allan Bloom. Cornell University Press, 1959.

Roustang, François. *The Quadrille of Gender: Casanova's Memoirs*, trans. Anne C. Vila. Stanford University Press, 1988.

Rudé, George E. 'Prices, wages and popular movements in Paris during the French Revolution'. *The Economic History Review* 6, no. 3 (1954): 246–267.

Sarasohn, Lisa T. 'Motion and morality: Pierre Gassendi, Thomas Hobbes and the mechanical worldview'. *Journal of the History of Ideas,* Vol. 53 no. 3 (1985): 363–379.

Shammas, Carole. 'Food expenditures and economic well-being in early modern England'. *The Journal of Economic History*, 43, no. 1 (1983): 89–100.

Scherr, Arthur. 'Jews in Voltaire's "Candide"'. *Romance Notes* 46, no. 3 (2006): 297–308.

Schutte, Anne Jacobson. 'Society and the sexes in the Venetian Republic'. In *A Companion to Venetian History, 1400–1797*, 353–377. Brill 2013.

Schutte, Anne Jacobson. 'Between Venice and Rome: the dilemma of involuntary nuns'. *The Sixteenth century journal* (2010): 415–439.

Sciascia, Leonardo. 'L'utopia di Casanova'. *Belfagor* 34, no. 5 (1979): 505–11.

Sha, Richard. 'Medicalizing the Romantic Libido: Sexual Pleasure, Luxury, and the Public Sphere'. *Romanticism on the Net 31* (2003).

Shoemaker, Robert B. *Gender in English Society, 1650–1850.* Longman, 1998.

Shoemaker, Robert B. 'The taming of the duel: masculinity, honour and ritual violence in London, 1660–1800'. *The Historical Journal* 45, no. 3 (2002): 525–545.

Simonton, Deborah (ed.). *The Routledge history of women in Europe since 1700.* Routledge, 2006.

Singh, Christine M. 'The Lettre sur les aveugles: Its Debt to Lucretius'. *Studies in Eighteenth-Century French Literature Presented to Robert Niklaus* (1975): 233–242.

Skipp, Jenny. 'Masculinity and Social Stratification in Eighteenth-Century Erotic Literature, 1700–1821'. *Journal for Eighteenth-Century Studies* 29, no. 2.

Spencer, Jane. '"The link which unites man with brutes": Enlightenment Feminism, Women and Animals'. *Intellectual History Review* 22, no. 3 (2012): 427–444.

Stefanovska, Malina. *Casanova in the Enlightenment: From the Margins to the Centre*. Vol. 30. Toronto University Press, 2021.

Symons, Arthur. 'Casanova at Dux: An Unpublished Chapter of History'. *The North American Review* Vol. 175, no. 550 (1902): 329–346.

Tague, Ingrid H. 'Love, honor, and obedience: Fashionable women and the discourse of marriage in the early eighteenth century'. *Journal of British Studies* 40, no. 1 (2001): 76–106.

Thomas, Chantal. 'Casanova and the Revolution', trans Nicole Santilli. *Public* (1994).

Thysell, Carol. *The Pleasure of Discernment: Marguerite de Navarre as Theologian*. Oxford University Press, 2000.

Traer, James F. *Marriage and the Family in Eighteenth-Century France*. Cornell University Press, 1980.

Trampus, Antonio (ed.). (2018–2021). *Casanoviana*.

Trumbach, Randolph. 'The transformation of sodomy from the renaissance to the modern world and its general sexual consequences'. *Signs: Journal of Women in Culture and Society* 37, no. 4 (2012): 832–848.

Turner, James G. 'The Properties of Libertinism'. In *'Tis Nature's Fault: Unauthorized Sexuality during the Enlightenment*. Cambridge University Press 1988.

Veen, Mirjam van (ed.). *Ioannis Calvini Scripta didactica et polemica, Volume 1*. Librairie Droz, 2005.

Vinovrški, Nicola. 'Casanova: A Case Study of Celebrity in 18th Century Europe'. *Historical Social Research/ Historische Sozialforschung. Supplement*, no. 32 (2019): 99–120.

Vinovrški, Nicola. 'Casanova's Celebrity: A Case Study of Well-knownness in 18th Century Europe'. Thesis submitted for the degree of Doctor of Philosophy at the University of Queensland (2015).

Voltaire, *Sentiment des citoyens*. In *Oeuvres completes de Voltaire*, Louis Moland (ed.), Vol. 25. Garnier Frères, 1877–1885.

Voltaire. *Memoirs of the Life of Voltaire,* trans unknown. G Robinson, 1784.

Voltaire. *A Philosophical Dictionary, Vol. 2*. W Dugdale, 1843.

Voltaire. *Toleration and other essays*, trans. Joseph McCabe. G.P. Putnam's Sons, 1912.

Voltaire. *The Works of Voltaire: a contemporary version*, trans. William F. Fleming. E.R. Dumont, 1901.

Walker, Jonathan. 'Gambling and Venetian noblemen'. *Past & Present* 162, no. 1 (1999): 28–69.

Walpole, Horace. *Memoirs of the Reign of King George III*. Yale University Press, 2000.

Weidinger, H E. 'The "Dux Drafts". Casanova's Contribution to Da Ponte's and Mozart's Don Giovanni'. *Maske und Kothurn* 52, no. 4 (2006): 95–130.

Wilkes, John. *The North Briton: revised and corrected*, Vol. 1 (1766).

Williams, David Lay. *Rousseau's Platonic Enlightenment*. Penn State University Press, 2007.

Wolfe, Charles T. 'A happiness fit for organic bodies: La Mettrie's medical Epicureanism'. in *Epicurus in the Enlightenment* 12, Neven Leddy & Avi S. Lifschitz (eds.), (2009), 69–83.

Wright, D.G. 'Rousseau's Confessions: The Tragedy of Teleology'. *Journal of Social and Political Thought*, Vol. 1 no. 4 (2003).

Yack, Bernard. 'Popular Sovereignty and Nationalism'. *Political Theory* 29, no. 4 (2001): 517–36.

Yona, Sergio. *Epicurean Ethics in Horace: The Psychology of Satire*. Oxford University Press, 2018.

Zweig, Paul. *The Adventurer.* Akadine Press, 1999.

Texts for the general reader

Andrieux, Maurice. *Daily Life in Venice at the Time of Casanova,* trans. Mary Fitton. Praeger, 1972.

Ariosto, Ludovico. *Orlando Furioso, Part One*, trans. Barbara Reynolds. Penguin, 1973.

Ariosto, Ludovico. *Orlando Furioso, Part Two*, trans. Barbara Reynolds. Penguin, 1977.

Ariosto, Ludovico. *Orlando Furioso*, trans. William Stuart Rose. Stewart A. Baker & A. Bartlett Giamatti (eds.). Bobbs-Merrill, 1968.

Bergreen, Laurence. *Casanova: the world of a seductive genius*. Simon & Schuster, 2016.

Blanning, Tim. *Frederick the Great: King of Prussia*. Allen Lane, 2015.

Blanning, Tim. *The Pursuit of Glory.* Penguin, 2008.

Blom, Philip. *Wicked Company: freethinkers and friendship in pre-revolutionary Paris.* Phoenix, 2011.

Bloom, Allan & Adam Kirsch. *The republic of Plato*, trans. Allan Bloom. Basic books, 2016.

Casanova, Giacomo. *The Story of My Life* (abridged), trans. S. Hawkes & S. Sartarelli. Penguin 2001.

Cash, Arthur H. *John Wilkes: the scandalous father of civil liberty.* Yale University Press, 2006.

Curran, Andrew S. *Diderot and the Art of Thinking Freely.* Other Press, 2020.

Damrosch, Leo. *Adventurer: the life and times of Giacomo Casanova.* Yale University Press, 2022.

Damrosch, Leo. *Jean-Jacques Rousseau: restless genius.* Mariner Books, 2007.

Davie, John. *Horace: Satires and Epistles*. Oxford University Press, 2011.

Diderot, Denis. *Rameau's Nephew and D'Alembert's Dream,* trans. L.W. Tancock. Penguin, 1976.

Flem, Lydia. *Casanova: the man who really loved women*, trans. Catherine Temerson. Farrar, Straus & Giroux, 1997.

Goldoni, Carlo. *The Comic Theatre,* trans. J.W. Miller. Nebraska University Press, 1969.

Greenblatt, Stephen. *The Swerve: how the Renaissance began.* Vintage, 2012.

Holme, Timothy. *A Servant of Many Masters: The Life and Times of Carlo Goldoni.* London: Jupiter, 1976.

Hunt, Margaret. *Women in Eighteenth-Century Europe.* Routledge, 2014.

Ilchman, Frederick, Thomas Michie, C.D. Dickerson III & Esther Bell (eds.). *Casanova: the seduction of Europe*. MFA, 2017.

Johnson, James H. *Venice Incognito: masks in the serene republic*. California University Press, 2011.

Kelly, Ian. *Casanova: actor, spy, lover, priest.* Hodder & Stoughton, 2008.

Lilti, Antoine. *The World of the Salons: sociability and worldliness in eighteenth-century Paris,* trans. Lydia G. Cochrane. Oxford University Press, 2020.

Lovett, Lisetta. *Casanova's Guide to Medicine: 18th-century medical practice*. Pen & Sword History, 2021.

Lucretius. *The Nature of Things*, trans. A.E. Stallings. Penguin, 2007.

Masters, John. *Casanova.* Michael Joseph, 1969.

Melton, James Van Horn. *The Rise of the Public in Enlightenment Europe*. Cambridge University Press, 2001.

Norwich, John Julius. *A History of Venice*. Vintage Books, 1989.

Parker, Derek. *Casanova*. Sutton, 2003.

Pearson, Roger. *Voltaire Almighty: a life in pursuit of freedom*. Bloomsbury, 2006.

Robilant, Andre di. *A Venetian Affair*. Harper Perennial, 2005.

Rousseau, Jean-Jacques. *The Confessions*, trans. J.M. Cohen. Penguin, 1977.

Rousseau, Jean-Jacques. *Emile or on Education*, trans. Allan Bloom. Basic Books, 1979.

Rousseau, Jean-Jacques. *The Social Contract, or Principles of Political Right*, trans. C.M. Sherover. Meridian Books, 1974.

Sollers, Philippe. *Casanova the Irresistible*, trans. Armine Kotin Mortimer. Illinois University Press, 2016.

Shank, J.B. *The Newton Wars and the Beginning of the French Enlightenment*. Chicago University Press, 2008.

Summers, Judith. *Casanova's Women.* Bloomsbury, 2007.

Szabo, Franz A.J. *The Seven Years War in Europe (1756–1763).* Routledge, 2013.

Voltaire. *Candide, or Optimism*. Penguin, 2005.

Voltaire. *Letters on England*, trans. Leonard Tancock. Penguin, 2005.

West, David. *Horace: The Complete Odes and Epodes*. Oxford University Press, 2008.

Williams, Abigail. *The Social Life of Books*. Yale University Press, 2017.

Woloch, Isser & Gregory S. Brown. *Eighteenth-Century Europe: tradition and progress, (1715–1789).* W.W. Norton & Co, 2012.

Useful online resources

ARTFL Project: https://artfl-project.uchicago.edu/
Digital Encyclopedia of British Sociability in the Long Eighteenth Century: www.digitens.org/en
Édition Numérique Collaborative et Critique de l'Encyclopédie: http://enccre.academie-sciences.fr/encyclopedie/
Encyclopedia of Diderot & d'Alembert, collaborative translation project: https://quod.lib.umich.edu/d/did/
Internet Archive: https://archive.org/
Internet Encyclopedia of Philosophy: https://iep.utm.edu/
Johnson's Dictionary Online: https://johnsonsdictionaryonline.com/
JSTOR: www.jstor.org/
OpenEdition Books: https://books.openedition.org/
OpenEdition Journals: https://journals.openedition.org/
Project Gutenberg: www.gutenberg.org/
Répertoire des oeuvres de Giacomo Casanova conservées au chateau de Dux: https://app.lib.uliege.be/casanova/
Stanford Encyclopedia of Philosophy: https://plato.stanford.edu/

Index